THE ORDER OF CHRISTIAN INITIATION OF ADULTS

THE ROMAN RITUAL

RENEWED BY DECREE OF
THE MOST HOLY SECOND ECUMENICAL COUNCIL OF THE VATICAN
AND PROMULGATED BY AUTHORITY OF POPE PAUL VI

THE ORDER OF CHRISTIAN INITIATION OF ADULTS

ENGLISH TRANSLATION ACCORDING TO THE TYPICAL EDITION

For Use in the Dioceses of the United States of America

Approved by the
United States Conference of Catholic Bishops
and Confirmed by the Apostolic See

2024

Concordat cum originali:
✠ Steven J. Lopes
Chairman, USCCB Committee on Divine Worship
after review by Rev. Dustin P. Dought
Executive Director, USCCB Secretariat of Divine Worship

Imprimatur:
✠ Most Rev. Patrick M. Neary, C.S.C., Bishop of St. Cloud, September 13, 2024

Cover design by Monica Bokinskie.

Cover art by Br. Martin Erspamer, OSB, a monk of Saint Meinrad Archabbey, Indiana. Used with permission.

Library of Congress Control Number: 2024940793

ISBN 978-0-8146-8954-7

CONTENTS

FOREWORD TO THE REVISED EDITION

By his Death and Resurrection, Christ has opened for us a wellspring of holiness and grace. This gift is made available to us in an especially powerful way in the Church's Sacraments. The Sacraments of Initiation are those through which Christians receive birth, growth, and nourishment. Whether celebrated at Easter or at some other time of the year, these Sacraments provide the Church with new birth in Christ through water and the Holy Spirit.

Following the mandate of the Second Vatican Council to reform the rites of baptizing adults into the Catholic Church, the Latin typical edition of the *Ordo initiationis christianæ adultorum* was issued in 1972, and its first interim English translation was used in the United States from 1974 to 1988. The experiences learned in that time prompted the International Commission on English in the Liturgy (ICEL) to prepare a more thorough edition in 1985: the entire text was translated afresh, its contents were reorganized into a more pastorally useful order, texts from other liturgical books were introduced and cross-referenced, and one "Combined Rite" of the Easter Vigil celebration of both the Sacraments of Initiation and the Rite of Reception was added. To further enhance ICEL's excellent work, the ritual and textual adaptations approved by the bishops of the United States were incorporated, and ten additional rites were added for use in this country.

Over these last 30 years, the People of God have been well served by the *Rite of Christian Initiation of Adults*, which was implemented by the bishops of the United States in 1988. The rituals have helped countless men, women, and children come to know Jesus Christ in his Church as they progressed through the steps leading to Initiation. We are grateful for this increase and renewal, and are indebted to the numerous men and women who have dedicated themselves to assisting their pastors with this process.

This new English translation, the *Order of Christian Initiation of Adults*, has been prepared in light of the principles of translation articulated in the Instruction *Liturgiam authenticam*. Approved by the bishops in 2021 and confirmed by the Holy See in 2024, this edition maintains the arrangement of the former English translation. The numbering is identical to the previous edition, and the U.S. adaptations previously approved have been retained. However, the translation has been updated and is consistent with the third edition of the *Roman Missal* and the current English translations of the *Order of Baptism of Children* and the *Order of Confirmation*.

A few modifications have also been introduced, aimed at supporting the pastoral use of the book. For example, the 1988 English translation, like the Latin edition, uses the term "candidate" in a broad sense to refer to any person preparing to undergo a step in the process or to receive a Sacrament. To correspond better with common pastoral practice in this country, this edition now reserves that term for use only in reference to an already baptized person who is preparing to receive the other Sacraments of Initiation. In other instances, the term has been replaced with a suitable alternative, such as "inquirer" or "catechumen."

In addition, the Combined Rite for use at the Easter Vigil (Appendix I, 4) now includes examples of instructions for the celebrant's use at nos. 567, 584, and 588. These admonitions help maintain the distinctions, often important from an ecumenical perspective, between the various categories of people who might be receiving the Sacraments: unbaptized adults, children and infants; validly baptized Christians being received into full communion; and validly baptized Catholics seeking Confirmation and Holy Communion. This new version of the Combined Rite also introduces material from the *Order of Baptism of Children*, which facilitates the Baptism of infants at the Easter Vigil, since both the *Order of Baptism of Children* and the *Roman Missal* make provision for this form of celebration.

Finally, the *National Statutes for the Christian Initiation of Adults*, the norms which regulate the discipline of Christian Initiation as well as the duties and prerogatives of catechumens, have also been revised to better reflect the experience of the Church in the United States. These statutes, which abrogate the National Statutes of 1988, are fewer in number and include only those statutes which are truly legislative, complementary to the universal law, and unique to the United States. They do not reiterate norms already contained in the ritual text or the universal law.

It is the hope of the United States Conference of Catholic Bishops that this new translation will be an occasion for each of us to live more deeply the promises of our own Baptism and to dedicate ourselves more intensely to the increase of God's holy People.

✠ STEVEN J. LOPES
Bishop of the Ordinariate of the Chair of Saint Peter
Chairman, Committee on Divine Worship
United States Conference of Catholic Bishops

May 19, 2024
Pentecost Sunday

SACRED CONGREGATION FOR DIVINE WORSHIP

Prot. n. 15/72

DECREE

The Second Vatican Ecumenical Council ordered the revision of the *Ordo Baptismi adultorum,* decreeing that the catechumenate for adults, divided into several steps, should be restored, so that the time of the catechumenate, intended for suitable instruction, could be sanctified by sacred rites to be celebrated at successive intervals of time. Moreover, the same Council likewise decreed that both the more solemn and the simpler rites of baptizing adults should be revised with close attention to the restoration of the catechumenate.

In compliance with these decrees, the Sacred Congregation for Divine Worship has created a new *Ordo initiationis christianæ adultorum,* which, having been approved by the Supreme Pontiff PAUL VI, it has commanded to be published, and it declares that its edition, which is now brought forth, is the typical edition, so that it may replace the *Ordo Baptismi adultorum* presently set forth in the *Rituale Romanum.* It likewise has decreed that this new *Ordo* may be used in Latin immediately, and in the vernacular from the day indicated by a Conference of Bishops after the translation has been prepared and the Apostolic See has confirmed it.

All things to the contrary notwithstanding.

From the offices of the Sacred Congregation for Divine Worship, January 6, 1972, Solemnity of the Epiphany of the Lord.

ARTURO Card. TABERA
Prefect

A. BUGNINI
Secretary

DICASTERIUM DE CULTU DIVINO ET DISCIPLINA SACRAMENTORUM

Prot. n. 234/22

CIVITATUM FŒDERATARUM AMERICÆ SEPTENTRIONALIS

Instante Excellentissimo Domino Iosepho Horatio Gomez, Archiepiscopo Angelorum in California, tunc Conferentiæ Episcoporum Civitatum Fœderatarum Americæ Septentrionalis Præside, litteris die 4 mensis aprilis 2022 datis, vigore facultatum huic Dicasterio a Summo Pontifice Francisco tributarum, textum translationis in linguam *anglicam* partis Ritualis Romani cui titulus est *Ordo initiationis christianæ adultorum*, ab eadem Conferentia Episcoporum ad normam iuris die 17 mensis novembris 2021 approbatum, prout in adiecto exstat exemplari, legitimis aptationibus recognitis, perlibenter probamus et confirmamus.

In textu imprimendo inseratur ex integro hoc Decretum. Eiusdem insuper textus impressi duo exemplaria ad hoc Dicasterium transmittantur.

Contrariis quibuslibet minime obstantibus.

Ex ædibus Dicasterii de Cultu Divino et Disciplina Sacramentorum, die 14 mensis februarii 2024, in feria quarta Cinerum.

Arturus Card. Roche
Præfectus

✠ Victorius Franciscus Viola, O.F.M.
Archiepiscopus a Secretis

UNITED STATES CONFERENCE OF CATHOLIC BISHOPS

DECREE OF PROMULGATION

In accord with the norms established by the Holy See, this edition of the *Order of Christian Initiation of Adults* is declared to be the definitive approved English translation of the *Ordo initiationis christianæ adultorum, editio typica* (1972), and is hereby promulgated by authority of the United States Conference of Catholic Bishops.

The *Order of Christian Initiation of Adults* was canonically approved for use by the United States Conference of Catholic Bishops on November 17, 2021, and was subsequently confirmed by the Apostolic See by decree of the Dicastery for Divine Worship and the Discipline of the Sacraments on February 14, 2024 (Prot. n. 234/22).

This rite may be used in the Liturgy as of the First Sunday of Advent, December 1, 2024, and its use is obligatory as of Ash Wednesday, March 5, 2025. From that date forward, no other English translation of the rite may be used in the dioceses of the United States of America.

Given at the General Secretariat of the United States Conference of Catholic Bishops, Washington, DC, on March 31, 2024, Easter Sunday of the Resurrection of the Lord.

✠ Timothy P. Broglio

Archbishop for the Military Services, USA
President, United States Conference of Catholic Bishops

Rev. Michael J.K. Fuller
General Secretary

UNITED STATES CONFERENCE OF CATHOLIC BISHOPS

DECREE OF PROMULGATION

On November 15, 2023, the Latin Church members of the United States Conference of Catholic Bishops approved *National Statutes for the Christian Initiation of Adults* implementing canon 788 §3 of the Code of Canon Law for the dioceses of the United States of America.

In accord with Article 110 of the Apostolic Constitution of Pope Francis, *Prædicate Evangelium*, the approved Statutes were granted *recognitio* by the Apostolic See, in a decree dated January 9, 2024 (Prot. N° 778/2005) signed by Robert Cardinal Prevost, O.S.A., Prefect of the Dicastery for Bishops, and His Excellency Most Rev. Ilson de Jesus Montanari, Secretary of the Dicastery.

Wherefore, as President of the United States Conference of Catholic Bishops, I hereby decree that the effective date of the *National Statutes for the Christian Initiation of Adults* in the dioceses of the United States of America will be December 1, 2024, the First Sunday of Advent. Following the effective date, the National Statutes for the Catechumenate approved by the National Conference of Catholic Bishops on November 11, 1986 are abrogated.

Given at the offices of the United States Conference of Catholic Bishops, in the city of Washington, the District of Columbia, on April 25, 2024, Feast of Saint Mark, Evangelist.

✠ Timothy P. Broglio
Archbishop for the Military Services, USA
President, United States Conference of Catholic Bishops

Reverend Michael J.K. Fuller
General Secretary,
United States Conference of Catholic Bishops

CHRISTIAN INITIATION

GENERAL INTRODUCTION

1. Through the Sacraments of Christian Initiation all who have been freed from the power of darkness and have died, been buried and been raised with Christ, receive the Spirit of filial adoption and celebrate with the entire People of God the memorial of the Lord's Death and Resurrection.[1]

2. For, having been incorporated into Christ through Baptism, they are formed into the People of God, and, having received the remission of all their sins and been rescued from the power of darkness, they are brought to the status of adopted sons and daughters,[2] being made a new creation by water and the Holy Spirit. Hence they are called, and indeed are, children of God.[3] Sealed with the gift of the same Spirit in Confirmation, they are more perfectly configured to the Lord and filled with the Holy Spirit, so that bearing witness to Christ before the world, they bring the Body of Christ to its full stature without delay.[4] Finally, participating in the Eucharistic assembly (*synaxis*), they eat the Flesh and drink the Blood of the Son of Man, so that they may receive eternal life[5] and show forth the unity of God's people. Offering themselves with Christ, they take part in the universal sacrifice, which is the entire city of the redeemed offered to God through the great High

[1] Second Vatican Council, Decree on the Church's Missionary Activity, *Ad gentes*, no. 14.

[2] Cf. Colossians 1:13; Romans 8:15; Galatians 4:5. Cf. also Council of Trent, sess. 6., *Decr. de iustificatione*, cap. 4: Denz.-Schön. 1524.

[3] Cf. 1 John 3:1.

[4] Cf. Second Vatican Council, Decree on the Church's Missionary Activity, *Ad gentes*, no. 36.

[5] Cf. John 6:55.

Priest;[6] they also pray that, through a fuller outpouring of the Holy Spirit, the whole human race come into the unity of God's family.[7] Thus the three Sacraments of Christian Initiation so work together that they bring to full stature the Christian faithful, who exercise in the Church and in the world the mission of the entire Christian people.[8]

I. Dignity of Baptism

3. Baptism, the door to life and to the Kingdom, is the first Sacrament of the New Law, which Christ offered to all that they might have eternal life[9] and which, together with the Gospel, he later entrusted to his Church, when he commanded his Apostles: "Go, teach all nations, baptizing them in the name of the Father, and of the Son, and of the Holy Spirit."[10] Therefore Baptism is first and foremost the Sacrament of that faith by which human beings, enlightened by the grace of the Holy Spirit, respond to the Gospel of Christ. That is why the Church believes that there is nothing more ancient and nothing more proper for herself than to urge all—catechumens, parents of children who are to be baptized, and godparents—to that true and active faith by which, as they hold fast to Christ, they enter into or confirm the New Covenant. In fact, the pastoral instruction of catechumens and the preparation of parents, as well as the celebration of God's Word and the profession of baptismal faith, are all ordered to this end.

4. Furthermore, Baptism is the Sacrament by which human beings are incorporated into the Church and are built up together into a

[6] Cf. Saint Augustine, *De civitate Dei* 10, 6: PL 41, 284. Vatican Council II, Dogmatic Constitution on the Church, *Lumen gentium*, no. 11; Decree on the Ministry and Life of Priests, *Presbyterorum ordinis*, no. 2.

[7] Cf. Second Vatican Council, Dogmatic Constitution on the Church, *Lumen gentium*, no. 28.

[8] Cf. *ibidem*, no. 31.

[9] Cf. John 3:5.

[10] Matthew 28:19.

dwelling place of God in the Spirit,[11] and into a royal priesthood and a holy nation;[12] it is also a sacramental bond of unity linking all who are signed by it.[13] Because of that unchangeable effect (which the very celebration of the Sacrament in the Latin Liturgy makes clear when the baptized are anointed with Chrism, in the presence of the People of God), the rite of Baptism is held in highest honor by all Christians. Nor is it lawful for anyone to repeat it once it has been validly celebrated, even by separated brethren.

5. Moreover, the washing with water in the word of life,[14] which is what Baptism is, cleanses human beings of every stain of sin, both original and personal, and makes them sharers in the divine nature[15] and in filial adoption.[16] For Baptism, as is proclaimed in the prayers for the blessing of water, is the washing of regeneration[17] of the children of God and of birth from on high. The invocation of the Most Holy Trinity over those who are to be baptized has the effect that, signed with this name, they are consecrated to the Trinity and enter into fellowship with the Father, and the Son, and the Holy Spirit. This is the high point for which the biblical readings, the prayer of the community, and the threefold profession of faith prepare, and to which they lead.

6. Baptism, far superior to the purifications of the Old Law, produces these effects by virtue of the mystery of the Lord's Passion and Resurrection. Those who are baptized are united with Christ in a death like his, are buried with him in death,[18] and also in him are given life and are raised up.[19] For in Baptism nothing other than the Paschal Mystery is recalled and accomplished, because in it human beings pass from the death of sin into life. Therefore,

[11] Cf. Ephesians 2:22.

[12] Cf. 1 Peter 2:9.

[13] Cf. Second Vatican Council, Decree on Ecumenism, *Unitatis redintegratio*, no. 22.

[14] Cf. Ephesians 5:26.

[15] Cf. 2 Peter 1:4.

[16] Cf. Romans 8:15; Galatians 4:5.

[17] Cf. Titus 3:5.

[18] Cf. Romans 6:5, 4.

[19] Cf. Ephesians 2:5-6.

the joy of the resurrection should shine forth in the celebration of Baptism, especially when it takes place during the Easter Vigil or on a Sunday.

II. Duties and Ministries in the Celebration of Baptism

7. Preparation for Baptism and Christian instruction are of the highest concern for the People of God, that is, for the Church, which hands on and nourishes the faith received from the Apostles. Through the ministry of the Church, adults are called to the Gospel by the Holy Spirit and infants are baptized and brought up in her faith. Therefore, it is very important that, in the preparation for Baptism, catechists and other laypersons should work with Priests and Deacons. Furthermore, in the celebration of Baptism, the People of God—represented not only by godparents, parents, and relatives, but also, insofar as possible, by friends, acquaintances, neighbors, and some members of the local Church—should take an active part, in order to show their common faith and to express their shared joy with which the newly baptized are received into the Church.

8. In accordance with a most ancient custom of the Church, an adult is not admitted to Baptism without a godparent: a member of the Christian community who will already have assisted the candidate at least in the final preparation for receiving the Sacrament and who will help the candidate after Baptism to persevere in the faith and in the Christian life.

Likewise, at the Baptism of a child a godparent should be present in order to represent both the wider spiritual family of the one to be baptized and the role of the Church as mother and, as circumstances suggest, to help the parents so that the infant will come to profess the faith and to express it in life.

9. At least in the later rites of the catechumenate and in the celebration of Baptism itself, the role of the godparent is to testify to the faith of the adult candidate or, together with the parents, to profess the Church's faith, in which the infant is baptized.

10. Therefore the godparent, chosen by the catechumen or the family, must, in the judgment of the pastor of souls, be qualified to carry out the proper liturgical functions mentioned in no. **9**, that is:

1) be designated by the one to be baptized or by the parents or by whoever takes their place or, in their absence, by the pastor or the minister of Baptism and have the aptitude and the intention to carry out this responsibility;
2) be mature enough to fulfill this responsibility; a person sixteen years old is presumed to have the requisite maturity, unless a different age has been established by the Diocesan Bishop or it seems to the pastor or minister that an exception is to be made for a just cause;
3) be initiated with the three Sacraments of Baptism, Confirmation, and the Eucharist, and be living a life consistent with faith and the responsibility of a godparent;
4) be neither the father nor the mother of the one to be baptized;
5) be one godparent, male or female; but there may be two, one of each sex;
6) be a member of the Catholic Church, not prohibited by law from carrying out this office. A baptized person who belongs to a non-Catholic ecclesial community may be received only as a witness of the Baptism and only together with a Catholic godparent, at the request of the parents.[20] In the case of separated Eastern Christians, the special discipline for the Eastern Churches is to be respected.

11. The ordinary ministers of Baptism are Bishops, Priests, and Deacons.

1) In every celebration of this Sacrament they should be mindful that they act in the Church in the name of Christ and by the power of the Holy Spirit. They should therefore be

[20] Cf. C.I.C., can. 873 and 874, § 1 and § 2.

diligent in the ministry of the Word of God and in the celebration of the Sacrament.

2) They should avoid any action that the faithful could rightly regard as favoritism.[21]

3) Except in a case of necessity, they are not to confer Baptism in the territory of another, even on their own subjects, without the required permission.

12. Bishops, who are indeed the chief stewards of the mysteries of God, just as they are also the moderators of the entire liturgical life in the Church entrusted to their care,[22] direct the conferring of Baptism, by which a participation in the royal priesthood of Christ is conferred.[23] They themselves should not neglect to celebrate Baptism, especially at the Easter Vigil. The Baptism of adults and care for their preparation are especially entrusted to them.

13. It is the duty of pastors to assist the Bishop in the instruction and Baptism of the adults entrusted to their care, unless the Bishop makes other provisions. It is also their duty, with the assistance of catechists and other qualified laypersons, to prepare and assist the parents and godparents of children to be baptized through appropriate pastoral guidance, and finally to confer the Sacrament on infants.

14. Other Priests and Deacons, since they are co-workers in the ministry of Bishops and pastors, also prepare persons for Baptism, and confer it at the direction or with the consent of the Bishop or pastor.

15. The celebrant of Baptism may be assisted by other Priests or Deacons and also by laypersons in those parts that pertain to them,

[21] Cf. Second Vatican Council, Constitution on the Sacred Liturgy, *Sacrosanctum Concilium*, no. 32; Pastoral Constitution on the Church in the Modern World, *Gaudium et spes*, no. 29.

[22] Cf. Second Vatican Council, Decree on the Pastoral Office of Bishops, *Christus Dominus*, no. 15.

[23] Cf. Second Vatican Council, Dogmatic Constitution on the Church, *Lumen gentium*, no. 26.

especially if there is a large number to be baptized, as is foreseen in respective parts of the ritual.

16. In imminent danger of death and especially at the moment of death, if no Priest or Deacon is present, any member of the faithful, indeed any person who has the requisite intention, can and sometimes must administer Baptism. But if there is only the danger of death, the Sacrament should be administered, if possible, by a member of the faithful and according to the shorter form (nos. 370–399). However, it is desirable that, even in this case, a small community should be gathered, or at least one or two witnesses should be present, if possible.

17. All laypersons, since they are members of the priestly people—but especially parents and, by reason of their work, catechists, midwives, women dedicated to works of social or family assistance or to the care of the sick, as well as physicians and surgeons—should take care to be thoroughly familiar, according to their capacities, with the correct method of baptizing in case of necessity. They should be taught by pastors, Deacons, and catechists, and Bishops should provide appropriate means for their instruction within the diocese.

III. Requisites for the Celebration of Baptism

18. Water used in Baptism should be natural and clean, so that the truth of the sign may be apparent, and also for hygienic reasons.

19. The font in the baptistery, or, as circumstances suggest, the vessel in which water is prepared for a celebration in the sanctuary, should be notable for its cleanliness and beauty.

20. Furthermore, provision should be made for the water to be warmed if the climate requires this.

21. Except in case of necessity, a Priest or Deacon is only to baptize with water that has been blessed for the purpose. If the consecration of water has taken place at the Easter Vigil, the blessed water should, insofar as possible, be kept and used throughout Easter

Time to signify more clearly the relationship between the Sacrament and the Paschal Mystery. However, outside Easter Time, it is desirable that the water be blessed for each celebration, so that the mystery of salvation that the Church remembers and proclaims may be clearly expressed in the words of consecration themselves. If the baptistery is constructed in such a way that the water flows, the source from which it flows should be blessed.

22. Both the rite of immersion, which more suitably signifies participation in the Death and Resurrection of Christ, and the rite of pouring can lawfully be used.

23. The words with which Baptism is conferred in the Latin Church are: ***Ego te baptizo in nomine Patris, et Filii, et Spiritus Sancti*** (*I baptize you in the name of the Father, and of the Son, and of the Holy Spirit*).

24. A suitable place for celebrating the Word of God should be prepared in the baptistery or in the church.

25. The baptistery (the place where the baptismal water flows or the font is located) should be reserved for the Sacrament of Baptism and be clearly worthy to serve as the place for Christians to be reborn of water and the Holy Spirit. Whether it is situated in a chapel inside or outside the church or in some other part of the church within the sight of the faithful, it must be organized so as to be suitable for the participation of a large number of people. After Easter Time, it is fitting for the paschal candle to be kept in a place of honor in the baptistery, so that, when it is lit for the celebration of Baptism, it is easy to light candles from it for the newly baptized.

26. In celebrating Baptism, the rites that are to be performed outside the baptistery should take place in the different areas of the church that best suit both the number of those present and the various parts of the baptismal liturgy. It is also permitted to choose other suitable locations within the church for those parts that are normally celebrated inside the baptistery, if the chapel of the baptistery is unable to accommodate all the catechumens or all of those present.

27. As far as possible, there should be a common celebration of Baptism on the same day for all newborn babies. Except for a just cause, Baptism should not be celebrated twice on the same day in the same church.

28. More will be said concerning the time for Baptism of adults and of children in the appropriate places. But the celebration of the Sacrament should always have a markedly paschal character.

29. Pastors must carefully and without delay record in the baptismal register the names of those baptized, of the minister, parents, and godparents, and of the place and date of the conferral of Baptism.

IV. Adaptations within the Competence of the Conferences of Bishops

30. It is for Conferences of Bishops, by virtue of the Constitution on the Sacred Liturgy (no. 63b), to prepare for inclusion among their particular ritual books an edition corresponding to this one in the Roman Ritual, adapted to the needs of particular regions, so that, once their decisions have been accorded the *recognitio* of the Apostolic See, the edition may be used in the regions to which it pertains.

In this regard, it is for the Conferences of Bishops:

1) to determine the adaptations mentioned in no. 39 of the Constitution on the Sacred Liturgy, once their decisions have been accorded the *recognitio* of the Apostolic See;
2) to consider carefully and prudently what may appropriately be admitted from the traditions and culture of particular peoples, and consequently to propose to the Apostolic See other adaptations considered useful or necessary and, after they have been accorded the *recognitio*, to introduce them;
3) to retain, or to adapt, distinctive elements of any existing local rituals, provided that they conform to the Constitution on the Sacred Liturgy and correspond to contemporary needs, once their decisions have been accorded the *recognitio* of the Apostolic See;

4) to prepare versions of the texts, so that they are truly adapted to the character of various languages and cultures, and also to approve them, once their decisions have been accorded the *confirmatio* of the Apostolic See. They may add, as appropriate, suitable melodies for singing;
5) to adapt and supplement the Introductions contained in the Roman Ritual, so that ministers may fully understand the meaning of the rites and perform them effectively, once their decisions have been accorded the *recognitio* of the Apostolic See;
6) in the various editions of the liturgical books to be prepared under the guidance of the Conferences of Bishops, to arrange the material in a form that seems most suitable for pastoral use.

31. Taking into consideration especially the norms in the Constitution on the Sacred Liturgy, nos. 37–40 and 65, the Conferences of Bishops in mission countries have the responsibility to judge whether the elements of initiation in use among some peoples can be adapted for the rite of Christian Baptism and to decide whether such elements are to be incorporated into it, once their decisions have been accorded the *recognitio* of the Apostolic See.

32. When the Roman Ritual for Baptism gives several optional formulas, local rituals may add other formulas of the same kind, once their decisions have been accorded the *recognitio* of the Apostolic See.

33. Since the celebration of Baptism is greatly enhanced by singing—to stimulate a sense of unity among those present, to foster their common prayer, and to express the paschal joy with which the rite should resound—Conferences of Bishops should encourage and support skilled musicians to compose settings for those liturgical texts that are considered suitable to be sung by the faithful.

V. Adaptations within the Competence of the Minister

34. Taking into account existing circumstances and other needs, as well as the wishes of the faithful, the minister should make generous use of the various options allowed in the rite.

35. In addition to the optional formulas for the dialogue and blessings that are provided in the Roman Ritual itself, the minister may introduce certain adaptations for special circumstances, of which more will be said in the Introductions to Baptism for adults and for children.

NATIONAL STATUTES FOR THE CHRISTIAN INITIATION OF ADULTS

Period of Evangelization and Precatechumenate

Norm 1 The evangelization of unbaptized persons during the Period of Evangelization and Precatechumenate will lead them through Scripture, prayer, and friendly conversation to an encounter with the person of Jesus Christ as the fullness of God's revelation.

Norm 2 Early in the Period of Evangelization and Precatechumenate, a parochial minister will meet inquirers individually to hear of their "first faith" (see *The Order of Christian Initiation of Adults* [OCIA] 42), discern the continuing impact of their encounter with the Lord, and discuss any issues (e.g., an irregular marriage) that could affect their eventual celebration of the Sacraments of Initiation.

Period of the Catechumenate

Norm 3 The term "catechumen" is to be strictly reserved for the unbaptized who have entered the catechumenate and who are joined to the Church in a special way while they strive to lead a life of faith, hope, and charity (CIC c. 206 §1).

Norm 4 Ordinarily, a person who has entered the catechumenate is to remain in it from at least the Easter Time of one year until the beginning of the Easter Time of the next year; preferably it should begin before Lent in one year and extend until Easter of the following year.

Norm 5 §1. As a general rule, the preparation of catechumens for the Sacraments of Initiation takes place in a parochial setting or its equivalent.

§2. Catechumens prepared at a center, school, prison, or other institution are to be introduced into the Christian life of a parish or similar community, insofar as possible from the very beginning of the catechumenate, so that after their Initiation and Mystagogy they will not find themselves isolated from the ordinary life of the Christian people.

Norm 6 The formation of catechumens is to be comprehensive. It is to be:

1° suited to the liturgical year and supported by the Church's liturgy;

2° rooted in Sacred Scripture, the truths of Catholic doctrine and the moral life, and aided by catechetical texts, such as the *Catechism of the Catholic Church,* texts based upon that Catechism, such as the *United States Catholic Catechism for Adults,* and other texts approved by the local ordinary;

3° exercised in works of service and charity (OCIA 75).

Norm 7 While unbaptized persons in irregular marriages can enter the catechumenate, they are not to celebrate the Rite of Election until they are free to enter a canonical marriage.

Norm 8 Upon entry into the catechumenate, catechumens incur the following obligations:

1° They are to participate in the Liturgy of the Word, preferably on Sundays and other holy days of obligation, with the community if possible (see OCIA 81);

2° They will continually purify their motivation for Baptism, live an upright life, and be ready to witness to their conversion to Christ, as they seek to grow in their knowledge of and assent to what the Church believes and teaches (CIC cc. 206 and 865 §1).

Norm 9 §1. In addition to the prerogatives granted in universal law (see CIC cc. 1170 and 1183 §1 and OCIA 47), catechumens may:

1° participate in the apostolic and charitable works of the Church, especially works of mercy;

2° take advantage of opportunities given to Catholic parents in the parish or region concerning the enrollment for their children in Catholic schools;

3° be buried in a Catholic cemetery.

§2. If it seems appropriate, the diocesan bishop can establish other prerogatives.

Norm 10 It is praiseworthy that catechumens be dismissed from the liturgical assembly, at least on Sundays, after the Homily and before the Creed to reflect on the Word of God just proclaimed.

Norm 11 Because liturgical ministries arise from Christian Baptism, it is inappropriate for catechumens to proclaim the Word of God or serve at the altar during the liturgy.

Period of Purification and Enlightenment

Norm 12 The Elect, as well as those who assist them and participate in the celebration of the Easter Vigil with them, are encouraged to keep and extend the paschal fast of Good Friday, as determined by CIC canon 1251, throughout the day of Holy Saturday until the end of the Vigil itself (see *Sacrosanctum Concilium* 110, and OCIA 185/1).

Period of Mystagogy

Norm 13 Following the Period of Mystagogy, and to the extent possible, neophytes may benefit from meeting periodically to deepen their Christian formation, especially through opportunities that enhance their participation in the life of the parish or similar community (see OCIA 244 and 245).

Registration of Initiation-Related Acts

Norm 14 §1. The register of those who have entered the catechumenate is to be kept in the parish archive.

§2. In addition to those things required by OCIA 46, the pastor is to see that the date and place of birth of the catechumens are inscribed in the register.

Norm 15 The Book of the Elect, in which the catechumens enroll their names in anticipation of the Sacraments of Initiation (OCIA 119), is to be kept in the archives of the parish or of the diocese, unless diocesan law directs otherwise.

Norm 16 §1. The register of those received into the full communion of the Catholic Church is to be kept in the parish archive.

§2. In addition to those things required by OCIA 486, the pastor is to see that the date and place of birth of the candidate are inscribed in the register, with mention made of the minister, parents, sponsors, and the date and place of Reception into full communion.

§3. If married, a notation of the spouse, date and place of marriage should be noted in the register. Any future marriage is also to be noted in the register.

Rites for Particular Circumstances

Norm 17 It is for the diocesan bishop:

1° to appoint a qualified person to promote, direct, and coordinate the Christian Initiation of Adults in his diocese;

2° to issue norms concerning the qualifications for and training of catechists;

3° to approve the use of catechetical texts for the formation of catechumens and candidates for Reception into full communion (see Norm 6, 2° above);

4° to issue norms for the Simpler Order of Adult Initiation and for the preparation of baptized but uncatechized adults for Confirmation and Eucharist and for the reception of validly baptized Christians into the full communion of the Catholic Church.

Norm 18 The term "convert" is reserved strictly for those converted to Christian belief and never used of those baptized Christians who are received into the full communion of the Catholic Church.

When these statutes take effect on December 1, 2024, the National Statutes for the Catechumenate approved by the National Conference of Catholic Bishops on November 11, 1986, and confirmed by the Congregation for Divine Worship on June 26, 1988, are abrogated.

THE ORDER OF CHRISTIAN INITIATION OF ADULTS

INTRODUCTION

1. The Order of Christian Initiation described below is designed 1
for adults who, upon hearing the proclamation of the mystery of Christ as the Holy Spirit opens their hearts, consciously and freely seek the living God and undertake the journey of faith and conversion. By God's power and in their own preparation, they will be strengthened with spiritual help and at the proper time will fruitfully receive these Sacraments.

2. For the Order includes not only the celebration of the Sacra- 2
ments of Baptism, Confirmation, and the Eucharist, but also all the rites of the catechumenate, which, commended by the very ancient practice of the Church and suited to contemporary missionary work in all regions, was so widely requested that the Second Vatican Council decreed that it should be restored and revised, and adapted to local traditions.[1]

3. So that it may be better harmonized with the work of the Church 3
and with the circumstances of individuals, parishes and missions, USA
the Order of Initiation presents in Part I of this book the complete or usual form, suitable for the preparation of many (nos. **36–251**), from which, by a simple adaptation, pastors may obtain a form appropriate for one person.

Then Part II of this book provides rites for special cases: the Christian Initiation of children (nos. **252–330**), a simpler form of the rite for adults which may be carried out on one occasion (nos. **331, 336–369**) or in several celebrations (nos. **332–335**), as well as

[1] Cf. Second Vatican Council, Constitution on the Sacred Liturgy, *Sacrosanctum Concilium*, nos. 64–66; Decree on the Missionary Activity of the Church, *Ad gentes*, no. 14; Decree on the Pastoral Office of Bishops in the Church, *Christus Dominus*, no. 14.

a shorter form for those in danger of death (nos. **370–399**). Part II also includes guidelines for preparing uncatechized Catholic adults for Confirmation and the Eucharist (nos. **400–410**) and validly baptized Christians for Reception into the full communion of the Church (nos. **473–486**), along with four optional rites which may be used with such candidates (nos. **411–472**) and the Rite of Reception of baptized Christians into the full communion of the Catholic Church (nos. **487–504**).

Rites for catechumens and validly baptized candidates celebrated in combination are contained in Appendix I (nos. **562–594**). Finally, Appendix II contains acclamations, hymns, and chants (nos. **595–597**).

I. Structure of the Initiation of Adults

4. The Initiation of catechumens takes place step by step in the 4
midst of the community of the faithful, who together with the catechumens reflecting upon the value of the Paschal Mystery and renewing their own conversion, lead them by their own example to obey the Holy Spirit more generously.

5. The Order of Initiation is suited to the spiritual journey of 5
adults, which varies according to the many forms of God's grace, the free cooperation of individuals, the action of the Church, and the circumstances of time and place.

6. On this journey, besides periods of inquiry and maturation (cf. 6
no. **7** below), there are "steps" or stages upon which the catechumen progresses to cross a threshold, as it were, or to climb a step.

a) The first step: approaching initial conversion, the person desires to become a Christian and is accepted by the Church as a catechumen.

b) The second step: having advanced in faith and nearly completed the catechumenate, the person is received to a more intense preparation for the Sacraments.

c) The third step: after the spiritual preparation has been completed, the person receives the Sacraments by which a Christian is initiated.

These, then, are the three steps, stages or doorways that are to be regarded as the major or more intense moments of Initiation. These steps are marked by three liturgical rites: the first by the Rite for Entrance into the Catechumenate (nos. **41–74**), the second by Election (nos. **118–137**), the third by the celebration of the Sacraments (nos. **206–243**).

7. The steps leading to, or preparing for, "periods" of inquiry and 7
maturation are:

a) The first period, which calls for inquiry on the part of an individual, is dedicated by the Church to evangelization and "precatechumenate," and ends with entrance into the order of catechumens;
b) The second period, which begins with entrance into the order of catechumens and can last several years, is taken up with catechesis and the rites associated with it, and ends on the day of Election;
c) The third period, a much shorter one, which normally coincides with the Lenten preparation for the Paschal Solemnities and Sacraments, is designated for purification and enlightenment and includes the rites belonging to this period.
d) The final period, which lasts for the whole of Easter Time, is given to "Mystagogy," that is to gaining experience and spiritual fruits, and to spending time in the company of the faithful and forming stronger links with them.

These, then, are the four consecutive periods: "precatechumenate," marked by initial evangelization (nos. **36–40**); "catechumenate," set aside for the presentation of an integral catechesis (nos. **75–117**); "purification and enlightenment" for the acquisition of a more intense spiritual preparation (nos. **138–205**); and "Mystagogy," marked by new experience, both of the Sacraments and of the community (nos. **244–251**).

8. Furthermore, since the Initiation of Christians is nothing other 8
than their first sacramental participation in the Death and Resurrection of Christ, and since also the time of purification and enlightenment usually falls in Lent[2] and "Mystagogy" in Easter Time, the whole Initiation must show a paschal character. Therefore, Lent will have its full power as a more intense preparation of the elect and the Easter Vigil itself will be considered as the normative time for the Sacraments of Initiation. It is not, however, forbidden to celebrate these Sacraments for pastoral needs outside these times (cf. nos. **26–30**).

II. Ministries and Offices

9. In addition to those things mentioned in *Christian Initiation*, Gen- 41
eral Introduction (no. 7), the People of God, represented by the local 57
Church, should always realize and show that the Initiation of adults is its own concern and a matter for all the baptized.[3] It should therefore show itself always prepared to fulfill its apostolic vocation by helping those who seek Christ. In the varying circumstances of everyday life, as in the apostolate, every disciple of Christ is individually obliged to spread the faith.[4] He or she must therefore help others throughout the course of their Initiation, in the precatechumenate, the catechumenate, the Period of Purification and Enlightenment, and the Period of Mystagogy. In particular:

1) In the time of evangelization and precatechumenate the faithful should remember that the apostolate of the Church and of all her members is principally directed toward making known the message of Christ to the world by words and

[2] Cf. Second Vatican Council, Constitution on the Sacred Liturgy, *Sacrosanctum Concilium*, no. 109.

[3] Cf. Second Vatican Council, Decree on the Missionary Activity of the Church, *Ad gentes*, no. 14.

[4] Cf. Second Vatican Council, Dogmatic Constitution on the Church, *Lumen gentium*, no. 17.

deeds and toward communicating his grace.[5] They should therefore show themselves willing to exhibit a spirit of Christian community, to welcome inquirers into their families, into personal conversations, and also into some of the community's gatherings.

2) They should be willing to attend the celebrations of the catechumenate when possible and take an active part in the responses, prayers, songs and acclamations.

3) On the day of Election, since the addition of members to the community itself is involved, they should take care to give a just and prudent testimony about the catechumens when appropriate.

4) During Lent, which is the Period of Purification and Enlightenment, they should take care to be present at the Rites of the Scrutinies and of Handing On and give the catechumens the example of their own renewal in the spirit of penitence, faith and charity. They should be eager to renew their own baptismal promises at the Easter Vigil.

5) During the Period of Mystagogy they should participate in the Masses for the neophytes (cf. no. **25**), embrace them with charity, and help them to feel more at home in the community of the baptized.

10. A person who applies to be received among the catechumens 42
should be accompanied by a sponsor, that is, by a man or woman who knows and has helped him (her), and is a witness to the individual's character, faith, and intention. It may happen that this sponsor will fulfill the office of godparent during the times of purification and enlightenment and of Mystagogy, but someone else may replace the sponsor for this task.

11. A godparent, however,[6] chosen by the catechumen for his or 43
her example, gifts and friendship, delegated by the local Christian community and approved by a Priest, accompanies the catechumen

[5] Cf. Second Vatican Council, Decree on the Apostolate of the Laity, *Apostolicam actuositatem*, no. 6.

[6] Cf. *Christian Initiation*, General Introduction, nos. 8 and 10.1.

on the day of Election, at the celebration of the Sacraments, and during the Period of Mystagogy. The godparent's task is to show the catechumen in a friendly way how to practice the Gospel in personal and social life, to help at times of doubt or anxiety, to bear witness to and watch over the catechumen's growth in baptismal life. Chosen before the "Election," the godparent exercises his or her office from the day of Election, testifying for the catechumen in the presence of the community. The godparent's task remains important when the neophyte, having received the Sacraments, needs help to remain faithful to the promises of Baptism.

12. It is for the Bishop,[7] either in person or through a delegate, to 44
establish, supervise and encourage the pastoral instruction of 48
catechumens, and to admit them to Election and to the Sacraments. It is desirable that, insofar as possible, presiding over the Lenten liturgy, he himself celebrate the Rite of Election and, during the Easter Vigil, the Sacraments of Initiation at least for the Initiation of those who are fourteen years old or older. Finally, as part of his pastoral care, the Bishop should depute catechists, truly worthy and suitably prepared, to celebrate the Minor Exorcisms (nos. **90–94**) and the Blessings of the catechumens (nos. **95–97**).

13. It is for Priests, in addition to the usual ministry that they 45
exercise in any celebration of Baptism, Confirmation, and the Eucharist,[8] to attend to the pastoral and personal care of catechumens,[9] taking special care of those who seem hesitant or troubled, and to provide for their catechesis with the help of Deacons and catechists. They are to approve the choice of godparents and generously listen to them and help them. Finally they are to see to the complete and appropriate use of the rites throughout the course of the Order of Initiation (cf. no. **35**).

[7] Cf. *ibidem*, no. 12.

[8] Cf. *ibidem*, nos. 13–15.

[9] Cf. Second Vatican Council, Decree on the Ministry and Life of Priests, *Presbyterorum ordinis*, no. 6.

14. A Priest who baptizes an adult or a child of catechetical age in the absence of the Bishop should also confer Confirmation, unless this Sacrament has to be conferred at another time (cf. no. **24**).[10] 46

When those to be confirmed are too numerous, the minister of Confirmation may ask other Priests to join him for the administration of the Sacrament.

It is necessary that these Priests:

a) either exercise a particular role or office in the diocese, being namely, either Vicars General, Episcopal Vicars, or Vicars Forane, or by the mandate of the Ordinary, are considered equal to these because of the office they hold.

b) or are pastors of parishes where Confirmation is conferred, or pastors of parishes where those to be confirmed belong, or Priests who had a special part in the catechetical preparation of those to be confirmed.[11]

15. If there are Deacons, their help should be available. If the Conference of Bishops has decided to establish the permanent diaconate, it should also ensure that their number is sufficient to enable the steps, periods, and exercises of the catechumenate to take place everywhere that pastoral need requires them.[12] 47

16. Catechists, whose role is important for the progress of catechumens and the growth of the community, should have an active part in the rites whenever this is possible. When they teach, they should take care that their teaching is imbued with an evangelical spirit, harmonious with the symbols of the liturgy and the course of the year, suitable for catechumens and, insofar as possible, enriched by local tradition. Furthermore, when delegated by the Bishop, they can perform Minor Exorcisms (cf. no. **12**) and Blessings,[13] for which see the Ritual, nos. **94–97**. 48

[10] Cf. *Order of Confirmation*, Introduction, no. 7b.

[11] Cf. *ibidem*, no. 8.

[12] Cf. Second Vatican Council, Dogmatic Constitution on the Church, *Lumen gentium*, no. 26; Decree on the Missionary Activity of the Church, *Ad gentes*, no. 16.

[13] Cf. Second Vatican Council, Constitution on the Sacred Liturgy, *Sacrosanctum Concilium*, no. 79.

III. Time and Place of Initiation

17. Pastors should normally use the Order of Initiation in such a way that the Sacraments are celebrated during the Easter Vigil and the Election takes place on the First Sunday of Lent. In addition, the other rites should be spaced in accord with the principles set out elsewhere (nos. **6–8, 41–43, 46–47, 75–77, 119–120, 122, 124, 138–141, 147, 185, 206, 209–217, 244–247**). However, for very serious pastoral needs, the course of the entire Order may be arranged differently, as will be more fully explained below (nos. **26–30**). 49

A. Legitimate or Customary Times

18. With regard to the time for celebrating the Rite for Entrance into the Catechumenate (nos. **41–74**), the following should be noted: 50

1) It should not happen too early: it is right to wait until the inquirers, depending on their attitudes and circumstances, have enough time to embrace the beginnings of faith and to show the first signs of conversion (cf. no. **42**).
2) Where the number of those entering is smaller than usual, it is right to wait until a group of sufficient size forms for catechesis and the liturgical rites.
3) Two or, if necessary, three more suitable days or occasions in a year should be set for celebrating the rite.

19. The Rite of "Election" or "Enrollment of Names" (nos. **118–137**) should normally be celebrated on the First Sunday of Lent. When appropriate, it can be celebrated somewhat earlier or on a weekday. 51

20. The "Scrutinies" (nos. **150–156, 164–170, 171–177**) should take place on the Third, Fourth and Fifth Sundays of Lent, or if necessary on other Sundays of the same Lent, or even on weekdays that are found to be more suitable. Three "Scrutinies" should be celebrated. However, the Bishop can dispense from one of them in view of serious impediments or even, in exceptional circumstances, from two (cf. nos. **34.3, 331**). When time is short and the Election has been anticipated, the First Scrutiny should also be 52 anticipated; however, in this case care should be taken to ensure that the "Period of Purification and Enlightenment" is not extended beyond eight weeks.

21. From antiquity the "Rites of Handing On," since they take 53
place after the Scrutinies, belong to the same Period of Purification and Enlightenment; however, they should be celebrated during the week. The Creed is handed on (nos. **157–163**) during the week following the First Scrutiny and the Lord's Prayer (nos. **178–184**) after the Third. If this is pastorally suitable, however, for enrichment of the liturgy of the Period of the Catechumenate, the Rites of Handing On can be transferred and celebrated during the catechumenate as a kind of "rite of passage" (cf. nos. **79**, **104–105**).

22. On Holy Saturday, while the elect, free from work, devote 54
themselves to meditation, various Rites of Immediate Preparation can take place: the Recitation of the Creed, the "Ephphatha" Rite, and the Choosing of a Christian Name (cf. nos. **185–205**).

23. The Sacraments of Initiation of adults (nos. **206–243**) should be 55
celebrated during the Easter Vigil itself (cf. nos. **8** and **17**). But if there is a very large number of catechumens, most of them receive the Sacraments on this very night, but others can be delayed to days within the Octave of Easter and be made new by the Sacraments either in the principal churches or even in secondary ones. In this case either the Mass proper to the day is used or the Ritual Mass for the Conferral of Baptism, with readings taken from the Easter Vigil.

24. In some cases, the conferring of Confirmation can be delayed 56
until around the end of the Period of Mystagogy, for example on Pentecost Sunday (cf. no. **249**).

25. On each and every Sunday of Easter following the First there 57
should take place the so-called "Masses for the neophytes" which both the community and the newly baptized with their godparents are urged to attend (cf. no. **247**).

B. At Other Times

26. Although the Order of Initiation should normally be arranged 58
so that the Sacraments are celebrated during the Easter Vigil, it is

nonetheless permitted, because of unusual circumstances and pastoral needs, that the rites of Election and of the Period of Purification and Enlightenment be celebrated outside Lent and the Sacraments themselves outside the Easter Vigil or Easter Day. Even in ordinary circumstances, but only for serious pastoral needs, for example when the number to be baptized is very large, it is permitted to choose another time, especially Easter Time, for celebrating the Sacraments of Initiation in addition to the course of Initiation normally held during Lent. In such cases, the structure of the entire Order should remain the same, with appropriate intervals, although the times of its insertion into the liturgical year are changed. Moreover, adaptations should be made as follows.

27. Insofar as possible, the Sacraments of Initiation themselves 59
should be celebrated on a Sunday, using, as circumstances suggest, either the Mass of the Sunday or the appropriate Ritual Mass (cf. nos. **23, 208**).

28. The Rite for Entrance into the Catechumenate should take place 60
at an appropriate time, as has been said in no. **18.**

29. The "Election" should be celebrated about six weeks before 61
the Sacraments of Initiation, so that there is enough time for the Scrutinies and Rites of Handing On. Care should be taken that the celebration of Election does not fall on a Solemnity in the liturgical year. For the rite, the readings appointed in the Ritual should be used. The formulary for the Mass will either be that of the day or of the Ritual Mass.

30. The "Scrutinies" should not be celebrated on Solemnities, but 62
on Sundays or weekdays, with the usual intervals between them, using the readings appointed in the Ritual. The formulary for the Mass will either be that of the day or of the Ritual Mass in *The Roman Missal.*

C. Places of Initiation

31. The rites should take place in appropriate locations, as indi- 63
cated in the Ritual. Account must be taken of particular needs that arise in secondary stations of missionary regions.

IV. Adaptations That the Conferences of Bishops Are Permitted to Make Using This Roman Ritual

32. In addition to the adaptations foreseen in *Christian Initiation*, General Introduction (nos. 30–33), the Order of Initiation of adults allows other adaptations to be defined by the Conferences of Bishops, once their decisions have been accorded the *recognitio* of the Apostolic See. 64

33. These Conferences can decide the following: 65

1) To establish a method of welcoming inquirers (the "well-disposed") before the catechumenate, where this is judged appropriate (cf. no. **39**). In the Dioceses of the United States of America, this is done in accord with the *National Statutes for the Christian Initiation of Adults* (cf. Norms 1–2).
2) Where pagan cults flourish and are common, to insert into the Rite for Entrance into the Catechumenate, a first Exorcism and a first Renunciation (cf. nos. **69–72**). In the United States, the Diocesan Bishop has this discretion.
3) To decide that the gesture of signing the forehead be made in front of the forehead, in places where touching is thought improper (nos. **54–55**). In the United States, the Diocesan Bishop has this discretion.
4) Where a new name is given at once to the initiate in the practice of non-Christian religions, to decide that individuals be given their new name during the Rite for Entrance into the Catechumenate (no. **73**). In the United States, the norm is that no new name is to be given, though the Diocesan Bishop has discretion to permit it for catechumens from cultures where it is the practice.
5) In accordance with local customs, to incorporate into the same Order, no. **74**, auxiliary rites to signify reception into the community. In the United States, an optional presentation of a Cross has been included, and the Diocesan Bishop has discretion to include additional rites.
6) In the Period of the Catechumenate, besides the customary rites (nos. **81–97** and **106–117**), to establish "rites of passage," such as anticipated celebrations of the "Rites of Handing

On" (nos. **157–163, 178–184**), the "Ephphatha" Rite, the Recitation of the Creed, or even the Anointing with the Oil of Catechumens (nos. **98–103**). In the United States, the Anointing is permitted in the Period of the Catechumenate, and in appropriate circumstances, the other celebrations mentioned may also be anticipated.

7) To decide that the Anointing with the Oil of Catechumens be omitted, or transferred to take place among the Rites of Immediate Preparation, or used within the Period of the Catechumenate as a kind of "rite of passage" (nos. **98–103**). In the United States, the Anointing is permitted only in the Periods of the Catechumenate and of Purification and Enlightenment, and is thus to be omitted both in the Rites of Immediate Preparation and at the celebration of the Sacraments of Initiation.

8) To make the formulas of Renunciation richer and more forceful (cf. nos. **70–72**). In the United States, the norm is that the formulas should not be adapted, though the Diocesan Bishop has discretion to permit it in the Rite for Entrance into the Catechumenate and at the celebration of the Sacraments of Initiation (cf. no. **224**) for catechumens from cultures where false worship is widespread.

V. Matters Pertaining to the Bishop

34. The Bishop can, for his own diocese: 66

1) Establish instruction for the catechumenate and decide on appropriate norms as necessary (cf. no. **12**).
2) When appropriate, decide whether and when the Order of Initiation can be celebrated at other times (cf. no. **26**).
3) Dispense from one Scrutiny in view of serious impediments or even, in exceptional circumstances, from two (cf. no. **331**).
4) Permit that the Simpler Rite be used partially or entirely (cf. no. **331**).
5) Depute catechists, truly worthy and suitably prepared, to celebrate the Minor Exorcisms and Blessings (cf. nos. **12** and **16**).

6) Preside at the Rite of "Election" and make a judgment, either personally or through a delegate, on the admission of the elect (cf. no. **12**).
7) Stipulate the requisite age for godparents, in keeping with the provisions of law[14] (cf. *Christian Initiation*, General Introduction, no. 10.2).

VI. Adaptations Within the Competence of the Minister

35. It is for the celebrant to use fully and intelligently the freedom that is given to him both in *Christian Initiation*, General Introduction, no. 34, and, later on, in the rubrics of the Order. In many places consulted, the manner of acting and praying has not been determined, or two solutions have been offered, so that the celebrant can adapt the rite to the situation of the individuals and others who are present, according to his prudent pastoral judgment. The greatest freedom has been left in the invitations and intercessions, which can always be shortened or changed according to circumstances, or even enriched with other intentions so as to answer the particular situation either of the individuals (for example grief or joy that has occurred in the family of one of them) or others present (for example grief or joy common to the parish or town). 67

It will also be for the celebrant to adapt the texts, changing gender and number, to suit each circumstance.

Abbreviations

ASPC	*The Order of the Anointing of the Sick and of their Pastoral Care*
R	Appendix of the *Ordo initiationis christianæ adultorum* (Order of Reception into the Full Communion of the Catholic Church of Those Already Validly Baptized)
RM	*The Roman Missal*
USA	Ritual or Textual Adaptation for the Dioceses of the United States of America

[14] Cf. *Code of Canon Law*, can. 874, §1, 2°.

PART I

CHRISTIAN INITIATION OF ADULTS

CHAPTER I

ORDER OF THE CATECHUMENATE ARRANGED IN STEPS

PERIOD OF EVANGELIZATION AND PRECATECHUMENATE

36. Although the Order of Initiation begins with admission into the catechumenate, the period that precedes it, the "precatechumenate," is of great importance and should not normally be omitted. For within it takes place that evangelization in which the living God is confidently and constantly proclaimed, together with the one whom he sent for the salvation of all, Jesus Christ, so that, as the Holy Spirit opens their hearts, non-Christians may be freely converted to the Lord as believers and sincerely hold fast to him who, since he is the way, the truth, and the life, fulfills all their spiritual expectations, and indeed infinitely surpasses them.[1] 9

37. From evangelization, carried out with God's help, arise faith and initial conversion, by which each person feels called away from sin and into the profound mystery of divine love. The entire Period of the Precatechumenate is devoted to this evangelization, so that the will to follow Christ and to seek Baptism may mature. 10

38. Therefore, in this period a suitable explanation of the Gospel should be given to the inquirers by Priests, Deacons or catechists and other lay people; careful help should be offered to them so 11

[1] Cf. Second Vatican Council, Decree on the Missionary Activity of the Church, *Ad gentes*, no. 13.

that they may cooperate with divine grace with a purified and clearer intention, and that the group of inquirers may then more easily meet with Christian families and groups.

39. In addition to the evangelization appropriate for this period, 12
it is for the Conferences of Bishops to provide, if this should be necessary and according to the circumstances of their region, an initial way of receiving the inquirers (who are commonly called the "well-disposed"), that is, those who, even if they do not fully believe, nonetheless show a leaning toward the Christian faith.

1) Their reception, which will be voluntary and without ceremony, shows their right intention, but not yet their faith.
2) It will be adapted to the conditions and possibilities of their region. Some inquirers must primarily be shown the Christian spirit, which they wish to discover and experience; for others, whose catechumenate is for various reasons delayed, some first external act, either of their own or of the community, is appropriate.
3) The reception will take place within the gatherings and meetings of the local community, with suitable time allowed for friendship and conversation. Presented by a friend, the inquirer ("well-disposed") is greeted with generous words and received by a Priest or by another worthy and suitable member of the community.

40. During the Period of the Precatechumenate, pastors are to as- 13
sist the "well-disposed" with appropriate prayers. The Minor 111
Exorcisms and the Blessings may be carried out for their spiritual 120
good (nos. **94, 97**).

FIRST STEP: RITE FOR ENTRANCE INTO THE CATECHUMENATE

41. The rite commonly called "Entrance into the Catechumenate" 14
is most important since that is when, coming together in public for the first time, those entering the catechumenate manifest their will to the Church, and when the Church, fulfilling her apostolic office, receives those who intend to become her members. God grants them his grace, since their desire is expressed openly in this celebration, and their reception and first consecration are marked by the Church.

42. In order for them to take this step, it is necessary for the begin- 15
nings of a spiritual life and the foundations of Christian doctrine 68
to have been planted in the inquirers,[1] namely: the first faith conceived during the Period of the Precatechumenate; an initial conversion and a desire to change their lives and enter a relationship with God in Christ; a consequent beginning of a sense of penitence and of a habit of calling on God and of prayer; a sense of the Church; a first experience of the company and spirit of Christians through contact with a Priest or some members of the community; and preparation for this liturgical order.

43. Before the Rite is celebrated, a period of time is set aside, suit- 16
able and appropriate to each case, for investigating and, if neces- 69
sary, purifying their motives for conversion. It is the particular responsibility of pastors, with the help of sponsors (cf. no. **10** above), catechists and Deacons, to discern the outward signs of their spiritual dispositions.[2] It is also for them, being aware of the power of Sacraments already validly received (cf. *Christian Initiation*, General Introduction, no. 4), to take care lest anybody who is already baptized should wish, for whatever reason, to be baptized again.

[1] Cf. Second Vatican Council, Decree on the Missionary Activity of the Church, *Ad gentes*, no. 14.
[2] Cf. *ibidem*, no. 13.

44. Those entering the catechumenate are to be received on fixed 65
days during the year (cf. no. **18**) in accord with local circumstances. 69
The Rite, which consists of their reception, the Liturgy of the Word 72
and their Dismissal, can also be followed by the Eucharist. USA

When combined with the Eucharist, the Rite of Introduction (nos. **48–60**) replaces the usual Introductory Rites of the Mass. The Gloria, when prescribed, and the Collect of the Mass follow. On days when Ritual Masses are permitted, the readings may be taken from the *Lectionary for Mass*, no. 743. Following the Homily, intercessions are offered for the catechumens (no. **65**), who afterwards are dismissed (no. **67**). Mass continues as usual (no. **68**).

By decision of the Conferences of Bishops, the following can be incorporated into this Rite: a first Exorcism and a first Renunciation (nos. **70–72**), the giving of a new name (no. **73**), and auxiliary rites in accordance with local customs to signify reception into the community (no. **74**). See no. **33** for the decisions made by the United States Conference of Catholic Bishops regarding these matters.

45. It is desirable that either the entire Christian community or 70
some part of it consisting of friends, relatives, catechists and 71
Priests, should take an active part in the celebration. The presiding 73
celebrant is a Priest or a Deacon. Additionally there should be present "sponsors," who, having brought forward those entering the catechumenate, now present them to the Church.

46. After the celebration of the rite, the names of the catechumens 17
should be written in a timely manner in the book kept for this purpose, with mention of the minister and sponsors, and of the day and place of their admission.

47. Thus, from that moment, catechumens, whom Mother Church 18
already embraces as her own with her love and care, and who are joined to her, already belong to the house of Christ,[3] for they are fed by the Church with the word of God and the aid of the liturgy.

[3] Cf. Second Vatican Council, Dogmatic Constitution on the Church, *Lumen gentium*, no. 14; Decree on the Missionary Activity of the Church, *Ad gentes*, no. 14.

For their part, they should have the desire to participate in the Liturgy of the Word and receive Blessings and Sacramentals. Whenever two catechumens contract marriage or a catechumen contracts marriage with an unbaptized person, they should use the appropriate rite.[4] Finally, if they die during their catechumenate, they receive a Christian funeral.

RITE OF INTRODUCTION

48. Those entering the catechumenate together with their sponsors 73
and a group of the faithful gather outside the entrance to the church, or in the vestibule or at the entrance, or even at some other suitable part of the church, or lastly, in another suitable place outside the church. The Priest or Deacon, wearing an alb or a surplice, with a stole, or also a cope of festive color, goes to meet them, while, if circumstances suggest, the faithful sing a psalm or an appropriate hymn.

Preliminary Instruction

49. The celebrant warmly greets those entering the catechumenate. 74
He speaks to them, their sponsors, and all present, pointing out the joy and happiness of the Church. He may also recall for the sponsors and friends the particular experience and religious response by which they, following their own spiritual path, have come to this step on this day.

Then he invites the sponsors and those entering to come forward. As they are taking their places before the celebrant, a suitable chant may be sung, for example, Psalm 63 (62):2-9:

[4] Cf. *Order of Celebrating Matrimony*, second typical edition, no. 118.

Psalm 63 (62):2-9

2 O God, you are my God; at dawn I seek you;
    for you my soul is thirsting.
For you my flesh is pining,
    like a dry, weary land without water.
3 I have come before you in the sanctuary,
    to behold your strength and your glory.

4 Your loving mercy is better than life;
    my lips will speak your praise.
5 I will bless you all my life;
    in your name I will lift up my hands.
6 My soul shall be filled as with a banquet;
    with joyful lips, my mouth shall praise you.

7 When I remember you upon my bed,
    I muse on you through the watches of the night.
8 For you have been my strength;
    in the shadow of your wings I rejoice.
9 My soul clings fast to you;
    your right hand upholds me.

Dialogue

50. Then the celebrant first asks or calls out the civil or family name of the individuals, if necessary, unless their names are already known because of their small number. They should always reply individually, even if the celebrant asks the question only once because of their number. This is done in the following or similar way. 75

A

Celebrant:
What is your name?

The one entering:
N.

B

The celebrant, if he wishes, calls out the name of each entrant, who answers:
Present.

The celebrant continues with the following questions. When there is a large number entering, the remaining questions may be answered by all of them as a group. The celebrant may use other words in asking them about their intentions and may permit them to reply in their own words; for example, after the first question: **What do you ask of God's Church?** or **What do you desire?** or **For what reason have you come?**, he may receive such answers as: **The grace of Christ** or **Entry into the Church** or **Eternal life** or other suitable replies. The celebrant may then adapt his questions to their replies.

Celebrant:
What do you ask of God's Church?

The one entering:
Faith.

Celebrant:
What does faith offer you?

The one entering:
Eternal life.

51. At the discretion of the Diocesan Bishop (cf. no. **33.2**), the Initial Commitment of those entering the catechumenate (no. **52**) may be replaced by the Rite of Exorcism and Renunciation of False Worship (nos. **70–72**). USA

Initial Commitment

52. Then the celebrant, adapting his words, as required, to the replies received, addresses those entering again in these or similar words: 76

A

God enlightens everyone who comes into the world,
and from the created world
he manifests his invisible attributes to each,
that all may learn to give thanks to their Creator.

To you, therefore, who have followed his light,
behold now, the way of the Gospel lies open.
In laying down solid foundations,
may you acknowledge the living God
who truly speaks to human beings.
Walking in the light of Christ,
may you put your trust in his wisdom.
Entrusting your life to him day by day,
may you come to believe in him with your whole heart.

This is the way of faith,
along which Christ will lead you in charity,
that you may have eternal life.
With him to guide you, then,
are you ready to set out on this path today?

Those entering:

I am.

B 370.1

God, who made the world and all of us
and in whom all living things have their being,
enlightens our minds,
so that we may come to know and worship him.
He has sent Jesus Christ, his faithful witness,
to announce to us what he has seen in heaven and
on earth.

Therefore it is now time for you,
who rejoice at Christ's coming,
to listen to his word,
so that, with us, beginning to know God
and to love your neighbor,
you may possess the life of heaven.
Are you ready to lead this life with the help of God?

Those entering:
I am.

C 370.2

This is eternal life:
to know the true God
and Jesus Christ, whom he has sent.
For Christ has been raised from the dead
and established by God
as Prince of life and Lord of all things,
visible and invisible.

If, then, you wish to become his disciples
and members of the Church,
you must be led into the whole truth
that he has revealed to us:
learn to make the mind of Christ Jesus your own,
strive to model your life on the teachings of
the Gospel,
and so, love the Lord your God and your neighbor
as Christ commanded and showed us.

Is each of you ready to accept all of this?

Those entering:

I am.

Affirmation by the Sponsors and the Assembly

53. Then the celebrant turns to the sponsors and all the faithful and questions them in these or similar words: 77

You, the sponsors who are now presenting these men and women to us,
and all of you brothers and sisters gathered here,
are you prepared to help them find Christ and follow him?

All:

We are.

The celebrant, with hands joined, says: 82

To you, most merciful Father,
we give thanks for these your servants,
because they have already been searching for you,
who in diverse ways have gone ahead of them and knocked at their door,
and because they have answered your call today in our presence.
Therefore, we all praise and bless you, Lord.

All:

We praise and bless you, Lord.

Signing of the Forehead and of the Senses

54. Next a Cross is traced on the forehead of those entering (or, at 83
the discretion of the Diocesan Bishop, in front of the forehead for 85
those in whose culture the act of touching may not seem proper; cf. no. **33.3**); at the discretion of the celebrant the signing of one, several, or all of the senses may follow. The celebrant alone says the formulas accompanying each signing.

Signing of the Forehead

55. One of the following options is used, depending on the number of those entering.

A 83

The celebrant invites them (if they are few) and their sponsors in these or similar words:

Dear friends, come forward now with your sponsors
to receive the sign of your new status as catechumens.

With their sponsors, those entering, one by one, approach the celebrant. With his thumb he makes a Cross on the forehead of each person entering. After the celebrant has signed them, the catechists or sponsors, as circumstances so suggest, do the same, unless they are to sign them later, as in no. **56**. The celebrant says:

N., receive the Cross on your forehead.
Christ himself strengthens you
with the sign of his love
(if the renunciation has preceded: **with the sign of his victory**).
Learn now to know him and follow him.

As circumstances suggest, the signing may be concluded with the 86
singing of an acclamation praising Christ, for example:

Glory and praise to you, Lord Jesus Christ!

B 84

If there are a great many to enter the catechumenate, the celebrant addresses them in these or similar words:

Dear friends,
since you are of one mind with us
(if the renunciation has preceded: **and have renounced false worship**),
affirming our life and hope in Christ,
together with your catechists and sponsors,
I now sign you with the sign of Christ's Cross,
that you may become catechumens.
The whole community will embrace you with its love
and accompany you with its help.

Then the celebrant makes the Sign of the Cross over them all together, while the catechists or sponsors make it over each individual, as he says:

Receive the Cross on your forehead.
Christ himself strengthens you
with the sign of his love
(if the renunciation has preceded: **with the sign of his victory**).
Learn now to know him and follow him.

As circumstances suggest, the signing may be concluded with the 86
singing of an acclamation praising Christ, for example:

Glory and praise to you, Lord Jesus Christ!

Signing of the Other Senses

56. Then the signing of the senses takes place (according to the 85
judgment of the celebrant, however, it can partially or even totally 86
be omitted).

The signings are carried out by the catechists or sponsors (and, if required in special circumstances, these may be done by several

Priests or Deacons). As circumstances suggest, the signings each time they are made may be concluded with the singing of an acclamation praising Christ, for example: **Glory and praise to you, Lord Jesus Christ!** The formula, however, is always spoken by the celebrant, who says:

While the ears are being signed: 85

Receive the sign of the Cross on your ears,
that you may hear the voice of the Lord.

While the eyes are being signed:

Receive the sign of the Cross on your eyes,
that you may see the glory of God.

While the lips are being signed:

Receive the sign of the Cross on your lips,
that you may respond to the word of God.

While the chest is being signed:

Receive the sign of the Cross on your chest,
that Christ may dwell in your heart by faith.

While the shoulders are being signed:

Receive the sign of the Cross on your shoulders,
that you may bear the gentle yoke of Christ.

[While the hands are being signed: USA

Receive the sign of the Cross on your hands,
that Christ may be known in the work which you do.

While the feet are being signed:

Receive the sign of the Cross on your feet,
that you may walk in the way of Christ.]

Then, without touching them, the celebrant alone makes the Sign of the Cross over all the catechumens, while he says: 85

I sign all of you
in the name of the Father, and of the Son, ✠ and of the
Holy Spirit,
that you may live for ever and ever.

Catechumens:

Amen.

If there are few catechumens, the rite of signing with the Cross may be done over each catechumen by the celebrant, who says the formulas in the singular.

57. Then the celebrant says: 87

A

Let us pray.

Mercifully hear our prayers, we ask, O Lord,
for these catechumens N. and N.,
whom we have signed with the Cross of the Lord,
and guard them with its power
so that, treasuring what they have come to know of your glory,
they may, by keeping your commandments,
merit to attain the glory of rebirth.
Through Christ our Lord.

℟. Amen.

B

Let us pray.

Almighty God,
who through the Cross and Resurrection of your Son
have given life to your people,

grant, we pray,
that, following in the footsteps of Christ,
your servants, whom we have signed with the Cross,
may possess its saving power in their lives
and show it forth in their deeds.
Through Christ our Lord.

℟. Amen.

58. At the discretion of the Diocesan Bishop, the giving of a new name (no. **73**) may take place at this time. USA

59. At the discretion of the Diocesan Bishop, the invitation to the Celebration of the Word of God may be preceded or followed by additional rites signifying reception into the community, for example, the presentation of a Cross (no. **74**) or some other symbolic act. USA

Introduction into the Church

60. When this has been completed, the celebrant invites the catechumens and their sponsors to enter the church or another suitable place, while saying these or similar words: 90

N. and N., come into the church,
to partake with us at the table of God's word.

Then with a gesture, he invites them to enter.

Meanwhile, the following antiphon is sung with Psalm 34 (33):2-3, 6 and 9, 10-11 and 16 or another suitable chant:

Come, children, and hear me;
I will teach you the fear of the Lord.

Psalm 34 (33):2-3, 6 and 9, 10-11 and 16

2 I will bless the LORD at all times,
praise of him is always in my mouth.
3 In the LORD my soul shall make its boast;
the humble shall hear and be glad. ℟.

6 Look toward him and be radiant;
let your faces not be abashed.
9 Taste and see that the LORD is good.
Blessed the man who seeks refuge in him. ℟.

10 Fear the LORD, you his holy ones.
They lack nothing, those who fear him.
11 The rich suffer want and go hungry,
but those who seek the LORD lack no blessing.
16 The LORD turns his eyes to the just one,
and his ears are open to his cry. ℟.

SACRED CELEBRATION OF THE WORD OF GOD

INSTRUCTION

61. After the catechumens have reached their seats, the celebrant 91
speaks to them briefly, helping them to understand the dignity of God's word, which is proclaimed and heard in the church.

A book of the Sacred Scriptures is carried in procession and set in a place of honor and, as circumstances so suggest, may also be incensed.

The Sacred Celebration of the Word of God follows.

Readings

62. One or more readings suited to the new catechumens may be 92
chosen from those assigned in the *Lectionary for Mass*, no. 743: 372

First Reading

Gen 12:1-4a: *Go forth from the land of your kinsfolk to a land that I will show you.*

Responsorial Psalm

Ps 33 (32):4-5, 12-13, 18-19, 20 and 22

℟. (12b) Blessed the people the Lord has chosen as his heritage.

Or:

℟. (22) May your merciful love be upon us, as we hope in you, O Lord.

Verse before the Gospel

Jn 1:41, 17b

We have found the Messiah: Jesus Christ,
through whom came truth and grace.

Gospel

Jn 1:35-42: *Behold, the Lamb of God. We have found the Messiah.*

Homily

63. The Homily follows. 92

Presentation of the Gospels

64. Then, if the celebrant so wishes, books containing the Gospels are distributed with dignity and reverence to the catechumens; Crosses may also be given, unless they were already handed on to them as a sign of their reception (cf. no. **74**). The celebrant uses a suitable formula, such as: 93

Receive the Gospel of Jesus Christ, the Son of God.

It is fitting for the catechumen to respond with appropriate words to the celebrant's gift and words.

Intercessions for the Catechumens

65. Then the whole congregation of the faithful together with the sponsors prays these Intercessions or other, similar ones for the catechumens. The usual petition for the needs of the Church and of the whole world should be added if, after the catechumens are dismissed, the Universal Prayer (Prayer of the Faithful) is to be omitted in the Eucharistic Celebration (cf. no. **68**). 94

Celebrant:

These catechumens, our brothers and sisters,
have already traveled far.
We rejoice with them in the gentle guidance of God,
which has brought them to this day.

Let us pray for them,
that they may have strength to complete the great journey that lies ahead
toward full participation in our way of life.

Lector:

That the heavenly Father reveal his Christ to them more each day,
let us pray to the Lord:

℟. Lord, hear our prayer.

Lector:

That they embrace with generous heart and willing spirit
the entire will of God,
let us pray to the Lord:

℟. Lord, hear our prayer.

Lector:

That they enjoy our sincere and unfailing support every step of their way,
let us pray to the Lord:

℟. Lord, hear our prayer.

Lector:

That they find in our community
visible signs of unity and generous love,
let us pray to the Lord:

℟. Lord, hear our prayer.

Lector:

That their hearts and ours become
ever more responsive to the needs of others,
let us pray to the Lord:

℟. Lord, hear our prayer.

Lector:

That in due time they be found worthy
of the cleansing waters of rebirth
and of renewal by the Holy Spirit,
let us pray to the Lord:

℟. Lord, hear our prayer.

Concluding Prayer

66. After the Intercessions, the celebrant, extending his hands 95
toward the catechumens, says one of the following prayers:

A

Let us pray.

(God of our Fathers,)
O God, creator of the whole universe,
we humbly ask you
to look with favor on your servants N. and N.,
that they may be ever fervent in spirit,
joyful in hope,
and always obedient to your name.
Lead them, we pray, O Lord,
to the cleansing waters of rebirth,
so that, leading a fruitful life in the company of your faithful,
they may obtain the eternal rewards you have promised.
Through Christ our Lord.

℟. Amen.

B

Let us pray.

Almighty ever-living God,
Father of all creation,
who made man and woman in your own image,
welcome these beloved ones who have taken this step,
and grant that, hearing the word of your Christ among us,
they may be made new by its power,
and by your grace attain at last
complete conformity with him.
Who lives and reigns for ever and ever.

℟. Amen.

Dismissal of the Catechumens

67. If the Eucharist is to be celebrated, the catechumens are normally dismissed at this point by use of option A or B; if the catechumens are to stay for the celebration of the Eucharist, option C USA is used; if the Eucharist is not to be celebrated, the entire assembly is dismissed by use of option D.

A 96

The celebrant recalls briefly the great joy with which the catechumens have just been received and urges them to strive to live according to the word they have just heard. The group of catechumens leaves but does not immediately disperse, but with the guidance of some of the faithful they remain together to share their joy and their spiritual experience. The Deacon or the celebrant dismisses them in these or similar words:

Catechumens, go in peace,
and may the Lord remain with you.

Catechumens:
Thanks be to God.

B USA

As an optional formula for dismissing the catechumens, the Deacon or the celebrant may use these or similar words:

My dear friends, this community now sends you forth to reflect more deeply upon the word of God which you have shared with us today. Be assured of our loving support and prayers for you. We look forward to the day when you will share fully in the Lord's table.

C 96

If, however, for serious reasons the catechumens do not leave (cf. no. **75.3**) and must remain with the faithful, they are to be instructed that, though they are present at the celebration of the Eucharist, they cannot take part as the baptized do. They may be reminded of this by the Deacon or the celebrant in these or similar words: USA

Although you cannot yet participate fully in the Lord's Eucharist, stay with us as a sign of our hope that all God's children will eat and drink with the Lord and work with his Holy Spirit to recreate the face of the earth.

D 96

If, however, the Eucharist is not celebrated, a suitable chant, as circumstances suggest, may be added, and the faithful and the catechumens may be dismissed, using these or similar words:

Go in peace,
and may the Lord remain with you.

All:
Thanks be to God.

CELEBRATION OF THE EUCHARIST

68. If the Eucharist is celebrated after the dismissal, the Universal 97
Prayer (Prayer of the Faithful) for the needs of the Church and the whole world begins at once. Then, if required, the Creed is said and the Preparation of the Gifts follows. But for pastoral reasons it is permissible to omit the Universal Prayer and the Creed.

OPTIONAL RITES

69. By decision of the United States Conference of Catholic Bishops USA
the presentation of a Cross (no. **74**) may be included as a symbol of reception into the community. At the discretion of the Diocesan Bishop, one or more additional rites may be incorporated into the "Rite for Entrance into the Catechumenate": a first Exorcism and Renunciation of False Worship, the giving of a new name, as well as additional rites that symbolize acceptance into the community (cf. no. **33.2, 33.4, 33.5, 33.8**).

EXORCISM AND RENUNCIATION OF FALSE WORSHIP

70. In regions where false worship is widespread, whether in worshiping spiritual powers or in calling on the spirits of the dead or for obtaining benefits from magical arts, a first Exorcism and a first Renunciation may, according to the judgment of the Diocesan Bishop (cf. no. **33.2**), be introduced, in whole or in part, as follows. In this case the Initial Commitment (no. **52**) should be omitted. 78

Exorcism

71. After a very brief, suitable introduction, the celebrant breathes lightly toward the face of each one entering. If the breathing, even done lightly, seems unsuitable, it is omitted; the celebrant, however, should say the formula below, holding up his right hand toward those entering, or in another way accommodated to the customs of the region, or even without any gesture. 79

But if there are a great many entering, the celebrant omits the breathing and says the formula once for all.

Celebrant:
By the breath of your mouth, O Lord,
drive out all evil spirits;
command them to be gone,
for your kingdom is at hand.

Renunciation of False Worship

72. If the Diocesan Bishop judges it suitable to have those entering the catechumenate openly renounce false worship and spirits or magical arts, he should see to the preparation of a formula for the questions and renunciation relevant to the local situation. As long as the language is not offensive to members of non-Christian religions, this may be expressed in one of the following formulas or similar words. 80

A

Celebrant:

Dear friends, since you have been called and helped by God
and are determined to worship and adore only him and
his Christ
and because you now desire to serve God and his Christ alone,
it is now time for you to renounce publicly those powers that
are not God,
and those cults that do not honor God.
Far be it from you, therefore, to abandon God and
his Christ
and serve other powers.

Those entering:

Far be it from us!

Celebrant:

Far be it from you to serve N. and N.

Those entering:

Far be it from us!

He continues in the same way for each cult to be renounced.

B 371

Celebrant:

Dear friends,
you have chosen to worship the true God,
who has called you and led you this far,
and to serve only him and his Son Jesus Christ.
Now, therefore, in the presence of the entire community,
renounce all rites and cults which do not worship the true God.
You must never desert him and his Son, Jesus Christ,
in order to return to the service of other masters.

Those entering:
Far be it from us to serve masters other than the true God!

Celebrant:
Christ Jesus, Lord of the living and the dead,
has dominion over all spirits and demons:
you must never desert him
in order to return to the worship of N. (Here mention is made of the images worshiped in false rites, such as fetishes).

Those entering:
Far be it from us!

Celebrant:
Christ Jesus alone has power to protect human beings:
you must never desert him
in order to seek (wear/use) N. again (Here mention is made of the objects that are used superstitiously, such as amulets).

Those entering:
Far be it from us!

Celebrant:
Christ Jesus alone is the truth:
you must never desert him
in order to approach fortune-tellers, sorcerers, or conjurers again.

Those entering:
Far be it from us!

The celebration then continues with the affirmation by the sponsors and the assembly (no. **53**).

GIVING OF A NEW NAME

73. In regions where non-Christian religions flourish, which im- 88
mediately give a new name to those who are initiated, the Dioc- USA
esan Bishop may decide that for new catechumens the name they already have may be given, or a Christian name, or one familiar in their culture, notwithstanding the precept of canon 855 in the 1983 Code of Canon Law, as long as a Christian meaning can be attached to it (in this case, nos. **200–202** are omitted). In some instances it will be enough to explain the Christian meaning of the name previously received from his (her) parents. If a new name is given, one of the following formulas may be used.

A

Celebrant:

By what name do you wish to be called?

Catechumen:

N.

B

Celebrant:

N., from now on you will also be called N.

Catechumen:

Amen (or another suitable reply).

The celebration then continues with the optional presentation of the Cross (no. **74**), with an additional rite determined by the Diocesan Bishop to symbolize acceptance into the community (cf. no. **33.5**), or with the invitation to the Celebration of the Word of God (no. **60**).

PRESENTATION OF A CROSS

74. The presentation of a Cross on occasion may be incorporated into the rite either before or after the invitation to the Celebration of the Word of God (no. **60**). USA

Celebrant:

You have been marked with the Cross of Christ.
Receive now the sign of his love.

Catechumens:

Amen.

PERIOD OF THE CATECHUMENATE

75. The catechumenate is a lengthy period during which catechumens receive pastoral instruction and practice appropriate disciplines;[1] by the help of these their spiritual frame of mind, already manifested by their entrance, is brought to maturity. There are four ways by which this is achieved: 19

1) Appropriate catechesis, given by Priests, Deacons or catechists and other lay people, divided into steps and fully presented, suited to the liturgical year and supported by Celebrations of the Word, leads them not only to a suitable knowledge of dogmas and precepts, but also to an intimate knowledge of the mystery of salvation, which they desire to make their own.
2) Becoming familiar with the practice of Christian life, helped by the example and support of sponsors and godparents, and indeed of the faithful of the entire community, they grow accustomed to praying more easily to God, witnessing to the faith, keeping an expectation of Christ in all things, following inspiration from above in their works, and showing charity to their neighbor even to renunciation of themselves. Thus instructed, "the newly converted set out on a spiritual journey, by means of which, already sharing through faith in the mystery of Christ's Death and Resurrection, they pass from the old self to the new, perfected in Christ. This passage, bringing with it a progressive change of outlook and morals, must become evident in its social consequences, and must be gradually developed during the Period of the Catechumenate. Since the Lord in whom he or she believes is a sign of contradiction, the convert often experiences an abrupt break in human ties, but he or she also tastes the joy which God gives without measure."[2]

[1] Cf. Second Vatican Council, Decree on the Missionary Activity of the Church, *Ad gentes*, no. 14.
[2] *Ibidem*, no. 13.

3) They are assisted on their journey by Mother Church with suitable liturgical rites and by them they are now gradually cleansed and sustained with divine blessing. It is appropriate to promote Celebrations of the Word for them to attend, and indeed they themselves can already come to the Liturgy of the Word with the faithful to prepare themselves better for their future participation in the Eucharist. However, when they are present with the congregation of the faithful, they must normally be gently dismissed before the Eucharistic Celebration begins, unless there are difficulties that suggest otherwise: for they ought to wait for Baptism, by which they will be incorporated into the priestly people and deputed to participate in the new worship of Christ.

4) Since the life of the Church is apostolic, catechumens too should learn to cooperate actively in evangelization and the building up of the Church by the testimony of their life and their profession of faith.[3]

76. The length of time appropriate for the catechumenate depends 20
both on the grace of God and on various circumstances, namely on the plan of instruction of the catechumenate itself, the number of catechists, Deacons and Priests, the cooperation of individual catechumens, the facilities necessary for finding a place for the catechumenate and occupying it, and the help of the local community. So nothing can be laid down *a priori*.

The catechumenate, or pastoral formation of the catechumens, 98
should last long enough for their conversion and faith to mature, even over several years, if need be. Moreover, by learning about the whole of Christian life over an appropriately extended apprenticeship, the catechumens are suitably initiated by the mysteries of salvation and the exercise of an evangelical way of life and sacred rites that are to be celebrated in the subsequent periods, and are introduced into the faith, liturgy, and charity proper to the People of God.

[3] Cf. *ibidem*, no. 14.

77. It is for the Bishop to determine the duration and to supervise 20
the formation of the catechumenate. It is also appropriate that the Conferences of Bishops make more specific decisions in view of the conditions of people and regions.[4]

In special cases, depending on the spiritual preparation of a 98
catechumen, if the local Ordinary so decides, the Period of the Catechumenate can be shorter (cf. nos. **331–335**) or even, in entirely exceptional cases, completed on a single occasion (cf. nos. **332, 336–369**).

78. During that period instructions are to be given to the catechu- 99
mens in which, as every aspect of Catholic doctrine is explained to them, faith is enlightened, the heart is directed toward God, participation in the liturgical mystery is fostered, apostolic activity is encouraged, and the whole of life is nourished according to the spirit of Christ.

79. During these same years, as the catechumens progress from 103
their first catechetical group to others, passages that occur can sometimes be marked by rites. Among the rites belonging to the Period of the Catechumenate, Celebrations of the Word of God (nos. **81–89**) are foremost. The Minor Exorcisms (nos. **90–94**) and the Blessings of the catechumens (nos. **95–97**) are ordinarily celebrated in conjunction with a Celebration of the Word. It is also permitted when appropriate to anticipate the Handing On of the Creed, even of the Lord's Prayer, and the "Ephphatha" Rite, for which sometimes there will not be enough time during the final preparation of the co-petitioners (nos. **104–105**). Also celebrations of the Rite of Anointing with the Oil of Catechumens can also be offered in places where this is found useful and desirable (cf. nos. **98–103** below).

80. Catechumens should seek those godparents by whom they 104
will be presented to the Church on the day of their Election (cf. no. **11**; also *Christian Initiation*, General Introduction, nos. 8–10).

[4] Cf. Second Vatican Council, Constitution on the Sacred Liturgy, *Sacrosanctum Concilium*, no. 64.

From time to time during the year, care should be taken at some celebrations of the catechumenate and for rites of passage (cf. nos. **98–105**), that the entire community come together, namely Priests, Deacons, catechists, sponsors and godparents, friends and relatives, who have a part to play in the Initiation of catechumens. 105

PERIOD OF THE CATECHUMENATE AND ITS RITES

CELEBRATIONS OF THE WORD OF GOD

81. Celebrations of the Word of God should be held, suited to the 100
liturgical time, which serve both for the instructions of the catechu- USA
mens and for the needs of the community. These Celebrations of the Word are: first, celebrations held specially for the catechumens; second, participation in the Liturgy of the Word at the Sunday Mass; third, celebrations held in connection with catechetical instruction.

82. Special Celebrations of the Word of God should be arranged for 106
the benefit of the catechumens and their main purpose should be:

a) to implant in their hearts the teachings they are receiving: for example, the morality characteristic of the New Testament, the forgiving of injuries and insults, a sense of sin and repentance, the duties Christians must carry out in the world, etc.;

b) to give them instruction and experience in the different aspects and ways of prayer;

c) to explain to them the signs, actions, and seasons of the liturgy;

d) to lead them gradually into the worship of the entire community.

83. To keep holy the Lord's Day, from the very beginning of the Period of the Catechumenate certain provisions should be made: 107

a) The special celebrations for the catechumens just mentioned (no. **82**) should be held regularly on Sunday, so that the catechumens will become accustomed to taking an active and practiced part in these celebrations.

b) The first part of the celebration of the Sunday Mass should gradually be opened to them. After the Liturgy of the Word the Dismissal of the Catechumens should, if possible, take place (cf. no. **67** for formulas of Dismissal), and an intention for them should be included in the Universal Prayer (Prayer of the Faithful).

84. Celebrations of the Word of God may also be held in conjunction with catechetical instruction and may include the Minor Exorcisms. They may also be concluded with the Blessings as stated below (cf. nos. **92** and **96**). 108

Model for a Celebration of the Word of God USA

85. For the Celebrations of the Word of God that are held specially for the benefit of the catechumens (cf. no. **82**), the following structure may be used as a model.

86. Song – An appropriate song may be sung to open the celebration.

87. Readings and Responsorial Psalms – One or more readings from Scripture, chosen for their relevance to the formation of the catechumens, are proclaimed by a baptized member of the community. A sung responsorial psalm should ordinarily follow each reading.

88. Homily – A brief Homily that explains and applies the readings should be given.

89. Concluding Rites – The Celebration of the Word may conclude with a Minor Exorcism (no. **94**) or with a Blessing of the catechumens (no. **97**). When the Minor Exorcism is used, it may be followed by one of the Blessings (no. **97**) or, on occasion, by the Rite of Anointing (nos. **102–103**).*

MINOR EXORCISMS

90. The first or Minor Exorcisms, which have been drawn up in a deprecatory or positive form, should put before the catechumens the true character of the spiritual life, the battle between flesh and spirit, the importance of renunciation in order to obtain the beatitudes of the Kingdom of God, and the continual need for divine help. 101

91. The Minor Exorcisms are celebrated by a Priest, a Deacon, or by a worthy and suitable catechist appointed by the Bishop to carry out this ministry (cf. no. **16**). 109

92. The Minor Exorcisms take place in a church, a chapel, or in a center for the catechumenate during a Celebration of the Word. According to circumstances they may also take place at the beginning or end of a meeting for catechetical instruction; finally, for some special need, they may be done privately for individual catechumens. 110

93. Nothing prevents the formulas for the Minor Exorcisms from being used on several occasions in various circumstances. 112

* Celebrations of the Word that are held in connection with instructional sessions may include, along with an appropriate reading, a Minor Exorcism (no. **94**) or a Blessing of the catechumens (no. **97**). When the Minor Exorcism is used, it may be followed by one of the Blessings (no. **97**) or, on occasion, by the Rite of Anointing (nos. **102–103**).

The meetings of the catechumens after the Liturgy of the Word of the Sunday Mass may also include a Minor Exorcism (no. **94**) or a Blessing (no. **97**). Likewise, when the Minor Exorcism is used, it may be followed by one of the Blessings (no. **97**) or, on occasion, by the Rite of Anointing (nos. **102–103**).

Prayers of Exorcism

94. As the catechumens bow or kneel, the celebrant, with hands extended over them, says one or other of the prayers printed below (options A–K). 109

A 113

Let us pray.

Almighty ever-living God,
who through your Only Begotten Son
promised us the Holy Spirit,
we humbly pray to you for these catechumens,
who offer themselves to you:
drive far from them every evil spirit
and every working of error and sin,
that they may be found worthy
to become the temple of your Holy Spirit.
And, confirming the word of our faith,
grant that our speech may not be empty,
but full of the power and grace
by which your Only Begotten Son
has freed the world from evil.
Through Christ our Lord.

All:
Amen.

B 114

Let us pray.

O Lord our God, by whom true life is revealed,
corruption is taken away, faith is strengthened,
hope is raised up, and charity is nourished,
we ask you in the name of your beloved Son
our Lord Jesus Christ
and in the power of the Holy Spirit:
dispel from these your servants
unbelief and doubt,

(idol worship and sorcery,
witchcraft and necromancy,)
the love of money and the lure of passions,
enmities and dissensions,
and every form of wickedness.
And since you have called them
to be holy and spotless in your sight,
renew in them the spirit of faith and devotion,
of patience and hope,
of temperance and purity,
of charity and peace.
Through Christ our Lord.

All:
Amen.

115

C

Let us pray.

Lord God almighty,
who made man and woman in holiness and justice
after your own image and likeness
and, not forsaking the sinner,
wisely provided for their salvation
through the Incarnation of your Son,
save these your servants,
free them from slavery to all that is evil and harmful,
and take from them the spirit of falsehood, greed, and
wickedness.
Receive them into your kingdom,
open the eyes of their heart to understand your Gospel,
so that, as children of light,
they may be members of your holy Church,
bear witness to the truth,
and perform works of charity according to your commandments.
Through Christ our Lord.

All:
Amen.

D

116

Let us pray.

Lord Jesus Christ,
in your desire to turn your disciples from the way
of sin
you went up the mountain
and revealed the beatitudes of the Kingdom of Heaven;
grant that your servants
who hear the word of the Gospel
may be kept safe from the spirit of greed and avarice,
lust and pride.
Like your disciples,
may they consider themselves blessed to be poor
and hungry,
merciful and pure in heart.
May they be peacemakers and bear persecution joyfully,
so as to become partakers of your kingdom,
and, receiving the mercy promised them,
to enjoy with gladness the vision of God in heaven.
Who live and reign for ever and ever.

All:

Amen.

E 117

Let us pray.

O God, Creator and Savior of all flesh,
who tenderly fashioned these beloved ones,
mercifully received them,
and graciously called them to yourself,
watch over them today,
searching their hearts as they await your Son.
Preserve them by your providence,
and, as you bring the plan of your love to completion,
grant that they may hold firmly to Christ,
so as to be numbered among his disciples on earth
and joyfully hear him acknowledge them in heaven.
Through Christ our Lord.

All:

Amen.

F 118

Let us pray.

O God, who search our hearts and reward our works,
look kindly on the endeavor and progress of your servants.
Steady their steps,
increase their faith,
accept their repentance,
and, opening wide the store of your righteousness and
goodness,
grant that they may be found worthy
to partake of your Sacraments on earth
and to enjoy eternal fellowship with you.
Through Christ our Lord.

All:

Amen.

G 373.1

Let us pray.

Lord Jesus Christ, lover and redeemer of humanity,
on whose name all depend for salvation,
to whom all bend the knee
in heaven, on earth, and under the earth,
we humbly beseech you for these your servants,
who adore you as true God:
illumine and search their hearts,
remove from them all temptation and malice of
the enemy,
heal their sins and weaknesses,
so that, discerning what is pleasing and perfect according to
your will,
they may constantly obey your Gospel
and be made a worthy dwelling-place for the
Holy Spirit.
Who live and reign for ever and ever.

All:
Amen.

H 373.2

Let us pray.

Lord Jesus Christ, sent by the Father and anointed by the
Holy Spirit,
who willed in the synagogue to fulfill the words of the Prophet
by preaching liberty to captives and a year acceptable to God,
we humbly beseech you for these your servants,
who open their ears and hearts to you:
grant that they may profit from this season of grace.
Let them not remain distressed in mind,
caught up in the desires of the flesh,
estranged from the hope of the promises,
or enslaved by the spirit of unbelief.

But rather, let them believe in you,
to whom the Father has subjected all things
and whom he has set over all people,
and let them submit themselves to the Spirit of faith and grace,
so that, steadfast in the hope of their calling,
they may attain the dignity of a priestly people
and exult with the overflowing joy of the new Jerusalem.
Who live and reign for ever and ever.

All:

Amen.

I 373.3

Let us pray.

Lord Jesus Christ,
who, after calming the storm and freeing those possessed
by devils,
called to yourself Matthew the tax-collector
that he might be offered as an example of your mercy,
and that he might record for the ages
your command to teach all nations:
we humbly pray for these your servants,
who confess that they are sinners.
Restrain the menacing power of the enemy
and grant that they may experience your mercy
by being healed of the wounds of sin
and finding peace in their hearts.
May they delight in the newness of the Gospel,
and wholeheartedly follow your call.
Who live and reign for ever and ever.

All:

Amen.

J 373.4

Let us pray.

God of highest wisdom,
who called the Apostle Paul
to proclaim the good news of your Son among the nations,
we humbly pray to you for these your servants
who desire holy Baptism:
grant that, imitating the Apostle of the Gentiles,
they will not yield to flesh and blood,
but will submit to your grace.
Therefore, search and cleanse their hearts,
so that, freed of all falsehood,
forgetting what lies behind,
and pressing forward to what lies ahead,
they may count all things as loss
because of the surpassing knowledge of Christ your Son,
and so may gain him.
Who lives and reigns for ever and ever.

All:

Amen.

K 373.5

Let us pray.

O God, Creator and Redeemer of your holy people,
who have drawn these catechumens to you with a
wonderful love:
today as you look upon them and purify their hearts,
fulfill in them the unfolding of your mystery,
so that, following Christ with sincere hearts,
they may come to draw the water of salvation.
Through Christ our Lord.

All:

Amen.

BLESSINGS OF THE CATECHUMENS

95. Blessings, which are also signs of the charity of God and the care of the Church, may be offered to the catechumens so that, while they still lack the grace of the Sacraments, nonetheless, they may receive from the Church courage, joy, and peace in pursuing their task and journey. 102

96. The Blessings may be given by a Priest, a Deacon, or even by a catechist (cf. no. **16**). The Blessings are usually given at the end of a Celebration of the Word; they may also be given at the end of a meeting for catechetical instruction; finally, for some special need, they may be given privately for individual catechumens. 119

Prayers of Blessing

97. The celebrant extends his hands toward the catechumens and says one of the prayers printed below (options A–I). After the Prayer of Blessing, the catechumens, if this can be done conveniently, approach the celebrant, who lays hands on each of them. Then they leave. 119

A 121

Let us pray.

Grant to our catechumens, we pray, O Lord,
that, instructed in the holy mysteries,
they may be made new in the font of Baptism
and be numbered among the members of your Church.
Through Christ our Lord.

All:

Amen.

B 122

Let us pray.

O God, who through your holy Prophets
commanded those who approach you,
"Wash and be clean,"
and who through Christ have established spiritual rebirth:
look now on these servants,
who are carefully preparing themselves for Baptism.
Bless them and, in faithfulness to your promises,
prepare and sanctify them,
so that they may be made fit to receive your gifts
and be found worthy of adoption as your children
and of fellowship in your Church.
Through Christ our Lord.

All:

Amen.

C 123

Let us pray.

Lord God almighty,
look upon your servants
who are being instructed in the Gospel of your Christ:
grant that, knowing and loving you,
they may always do your will wholeheartedly and eagerly.
Graciously teach them through the holy rites of Initiation;
join them to your Church,
that they may become partakers of the divine mysteries
and of an inheritance
both on earth and in heaven.
Through Christ our Lord.

All:

Amen.

D 124

Let us pray.

O God, who in your providence have freed the world
from error
by the coming of your Only Begotten Son Jesus Christ,
hear us and give to your catechumens
mature understanding, unwavering faith,
and a firm grasp of the truth,
so that day by day they may go from strength to strength.
In due time, may they receive new birth for the forgiveness
of sins,
and glorify your name with us.
Through Christ our Lord.

All:

Amen.

E 374.1

Let us pray.

Lord our God,
who dwell on high and look upon the lowly,
who for the salvation of the human race sent your Son,
our Lord and God, Jesus Christ,
look upon your servants the catechumens,
who humbly bow their heads before you:
make them worthy of the cleansing waters of rebirth,
of the remission of sins, and of the clothing with incorruption;
gather them into your holy catholic and apostolic Church,
so that with us they may glorify your name.
Through Christ our Lord.

All:

Amen.

F 374.2

Let us pray.

O God, Lord of all,
who through your Only Begotten Son cast down Satan
and broke his bonds, freeing captive humanity,
we thank you for the catechumens you have called:
may they be confirmed in faith,
so that they may know you, the only true God,
and Jesus Christ whom you have sent;
keep them pure in heart and let them grow in virtue,
that they may be made worthy of the cleansing waters of rebirth
and of the holy mysteries.
Through Christ our Lord.

All:
Amen.

G 374.3

Let us pray.

O God, who will that all be saved
and come to knowledge of the truth,
in your kindness pour your faith into the hearts
of those being prepared for Baptism,
and in your mercy gather them into your holy Church,
that they may be made worthy of the gift of immortality.
Through Christ our Lord.

All:
Amen.

H 374.4

Let us pray.

Lord God almighty,
Father of our Savior Jesus Christ,
look mercifully on these your servants:
drive from their minds every trace of idolatry,
strengthen your law and teachings in their hearts,
lead them to full knowledge of the truth,
and prepare them, that through the rebirth of Baptism,
they may become a temple of the Holy Spirit.
Through Christ our Lord.

All:
Amen.

I 374.5

Let us pray.

Look, Lord, on your servants
who hold fast to your holy name
and bow their heads before you:
assist them in every good work;
rouse their hearts,
so that, mindful of your works and commandments,
they may hasten eagerly toward all that is yours.
Through Christ our Lord.

All:
Amen.

ANOINTING OF THE CATECHUMENS

98. During these same years, as the catechumens progress from 103
their first catechetical group to others, celebrations of the Rite of 127
Anointing with the Oil of Catechumens can be offered in places where this is found useful and desirable. If it seems appropriate to strengthen the catechumens with the first Anointing, it must always be administered by a Priest or Deacon.

99. The Anointing with the Oil of Catechumens is intended to 212
signify the need for divine strength, so that the one to be baptized, unhindered by the bonds of his or her past life and having overcome the opposition of the Devil, may steadfastly take the step of professing faith and hold it unfailingly throughout his or her life.

100. The Anointing is conferred at the end of the Celebration of 128
the Word of God and is given to all the catechumens (cf. no. **89**). For special reasons, the Anointing may be conferred privately on individual catechumens. Furthermore, as circumstances suggest, it is permissible to anoint the catechumens several times.

101. In this rite the Oil of Catechumens blessed by the Bishop at 129
the Chrism Mass should be used; for pastoral reasons, it may be blessed by the Priest immediately before the Anointing.[1]

PRAYER OF EXORCISM OR BLESSING OF OIL

102. If the celebrant is using oil customarily blessed before by the 33.7
Bishop, he first says the prayer of exorcism given as option A (or 130
one of the other formulas of the Minor Exorcisms in no. **94**). If, 131
however, the oil is to be blessed by the Priest, the Priest blesses it, 206
saying the prayer given as option B. 207
218

[1] Cf. *The Order of Blessing the Oil of Catechumens and of the Sick and of Consecrating the Chrism*, Introduction, no. 7.

A 373.2

Prayer of Exorcism

Let us pray.

Lord Jesus Christ, sent by the Father and anointed by the
Holy Spirit,
who willed in the synagogue to fulfill the words of the Prophet
by preaching liberty to captives and a year acceptable to God,
we humbly beseech you for these your servants,
who open their ears and hearts to you:
grant that they may profit from this season of grace.
Let them not remain distressed in mind,
caught up in the desires of the flesh,
estranged from the hope of the promises,
or enslaved by the spirit of unbelief.
But rather, let them believe in you,
to whom the Father has subjected all things
and whom he has set over all people,
and let them submit themselves to the Spirit of faith and grace,
so that, steadfast in the hope of their calling,
they may attain the dignity of a priestly people
and exult with the overflowing joy of the new Jerusalem.
Who live and reign for ever and ever.

All:

Amen.

B 131

BLESSING OF OIL

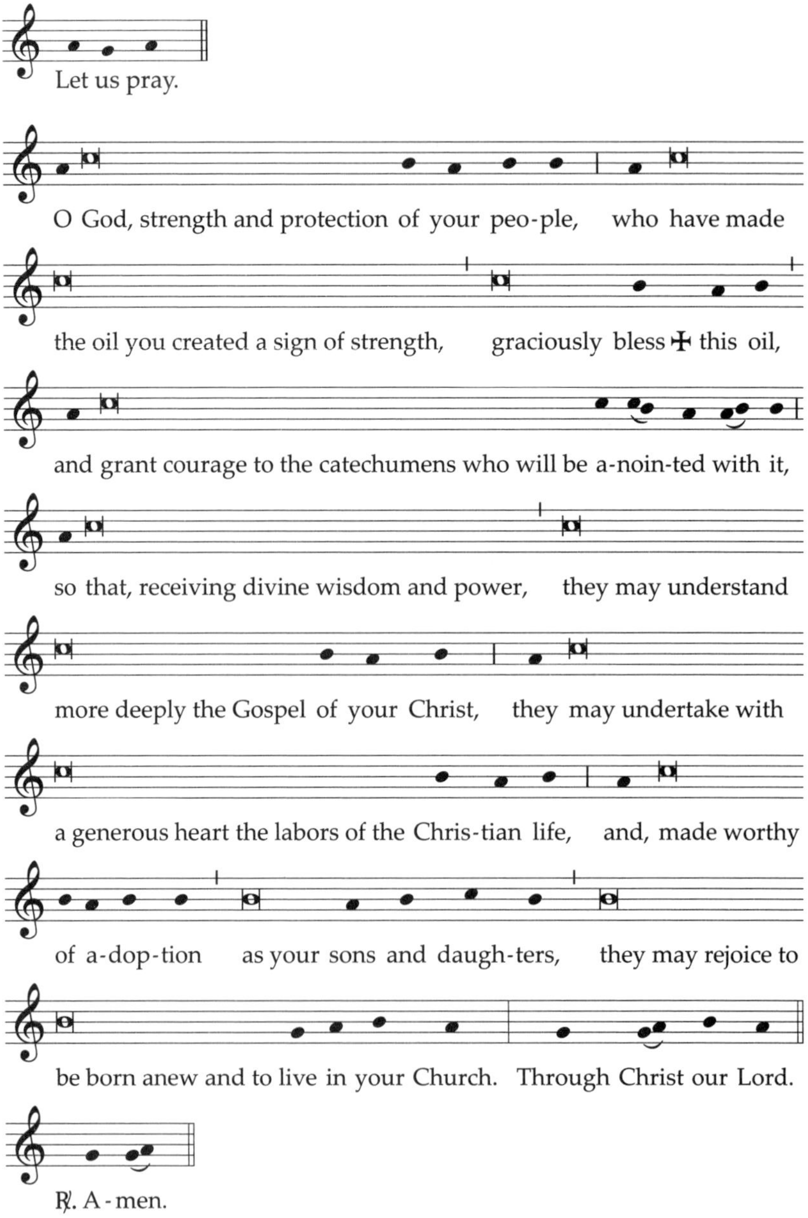

O God, strength and protection of your peo-ple, who have made

the oil you created a sign of strength, graciously bless ✠ this oil,

and grant courage to the catechumens who will be a-noin-ted with it,

so that, receiving divine wisdom and power, they may understand

more deeply the Gospel of your Christ, they may undertake with

a generous heart the labors of the Chris-tian life, and, made worthy

of a-dop-tion as your sons and daugh-ters, they may rejoice to

be born anew and to live in your Church. Through Christ our Lord.

℟. A - men.

Let us pray.

O God, strength and protection of your people,
who have made the oil you created a sign of strength,
graciously bless ✠ this oil,
and grant courage to the catechumens
who will be anointed with it,
so that, receiving divine wisdom and power,
they may understand more deeply
the Gospel of your Christ,
they may undertake with a generous heart
the labors of the Christian life,
and, made worthy of adoption
as your sons and daughters,
they may rejoice to be born anew and to live in your Church.
Through Christ our Lord.

All:

Amen.

Anointing

103. Then facing the catechumens, the celebrant says: 132

May the strength of Christ the Savior protect you.
As a sign of this we anoint you with the oil of salvation
in the same Christ our Lord,
who lives and reigns for ever and ever.

Catechumens:
Amen.

Each catechumen is anointed with the Oil of Catechumens on the breast or on each hand or even on other parts of the body, if this seems appropriate. If there are a large number of catechumens, it is permissible to use several ministers.

The anointing may be followed by a Blessing of the catechumens USA
(no. **97**).

OPTIONAL RITES DURING THE PERIOD OF THE CATECHUMENATE

104. The Rites for Handing On of the Creed and of the Lord's Prayer 125
may be anticipated both for the benefit of the Period of the Catechumenate and because of the brevity of the Period of Purification and Enlightenment. They should be celebrated when the catechumens seem to be mature; otherwise they should not take place.

105. Each may be concluded with the Ephphatha Rite (cf. nos. 126
197–199).[2] In these cases care is to be taken to substitute the term "catechumens" for the term "elect" in the formulas.

[2] If the Recitation of the Creed (nos. **193–196**) is also anticipated as one of the "rites of passage," (cf. no. **33.6**), the Ephphatha Rite is used only to begin the Recitation of the Creed and not with the Rites of Handing On.

Optional Rites

The Handing On of the Creed – cf. nos. **157–162**.

The Handing On of the Lord's Prayer – cf. nos. **178–183**.

The Ephphatha Rite – cf. nos. **197–199**.

RITE OF SENDING CATECHUMENS FOR ELECTION (Optional)

USA

106. At the conclusion of the Period of the Catechumenate, a Rite of Sending Catechumens for Election by the Bishop may be celebrated in parishes wherever this seems beneficial or desirable. When Election will take place in the parish, this rite is not used.

107. As the focal point of the Church's concern for the catechumens, admission to Election belongs to the Bishop who is usually its presiding celebrant. It is within the parish community, however, that the preliminary judgment is made concerning the catechumens' state of formation and progress.

This rite offers that local community the opportunity to express its approval of the catechumens and to send them forth to the celebration of Election assured of the parish's care and support.

108. The rite is celebrated in the parish church at a suitable time prior to the Rite of Election.

109. The rite takes place after the Homily in a Celebration of the Word of God (cf. no. **89**) or at Mass.

110. When the Rite of Sending Catechumens for Election is combined with the Rite of Sending Candidates for the Calling to Continuing Conversion, the alternate rite given in Appendix I, 2 is used (nos. **530–546**).

Presentation of the Catechumens

111. After the Homily, the Priest in charge of the catechumens' Initiation, or a Deacon, a catechist, or a representative of the community, presents the catechumens, using the following or similar words:

Reverend Father, these catechumens, whom I now present to you,
are beginning their final period of preparation and purification
leading to their Initiation.
They have found strength in God's grace
and support in our community's prayers and example.

Now they ask that they be recognized
for the progress they have made in their spiritual formation
and that they receive the assurance of our blessings and prayers
as they go forth to the Rite of Election
celebrated this afternoon (or: **next Sunday** [or specify the day])
by Bishop N.

The celebrant replies:
Those who are to be sent to the celebration of Election in Christ,
come forward, together with those who will be your
godparents.

One by one, the catechumens are called by name. Each catechumen, accompanied by a godparent (or godparents), comes forward and stands before the celebrant.

Affirmation by the Godparents (and the Assembly)

112. Then the celebrant addresses the assembly in these or similar words:

My dear friends, these catechumens
who have been preparing for the Sacraments of Initiation
hope that they will be found ready to participate in the Rite of
Election

and be chosen in Christ for the Paschal Sacraments.
It is the responsibility of this community to inquire about their readiness
before they are presented to the Bishop.

He addresses the godparents:

I turn to you, godparents,
for your testimony about these catechumens.
Have they taken their formation in the Gospel
and in the Catholic way of life seriously?

Godparents:

They have.

Celebrant:

Have they given evidence of their conversion by the example of their lives?

Godparents:

They have.

Celebrant:

Do you judge them to be ready
to be presented to the Bishop for the Rite of Election?

Godparents:

We do.

When appropriate in the circumstances, the celebrant may also ask the entire assembly to express its approval of the catechumens.

The celebrant concludes the affirmation by the following:

My dear catechumens, this community gladly recommends you to the Bishop,
who, in the name of Christ, will call you to the Paschal Sacraments.
May God who has begun the good work in you bring it to fulfillment.

113. If the signing of the Book of the Elect is to take place in the presence of the Bishop, it is omitted here. However, if the signed Book of the Elect is to be presented to the Bishop in the Rite of Election, the catechumens may now come forward to sign it or they should sign it after the celebration or at another time prior to the Rite of Election.

Intercessions for the Catechumens

114. Then the community prays for the catechumens by use of the following or a similar formula. The celebrant may adapt the introduction and the intentions to fit various circumstances. Moreover, the usual intentions for the Church and the whole world should be added if the catechumens are to be dismissed after the Intercessions and the Universal Prayer (Prayer of the Faithful) is omitted during Mass (cf. no. **117**).

Celebrant:

Dear brothers and sisters,
today we begin the Lenten journey
looking forward to the saving mysteries of the Passion and Resurrection.
The catechumens, whom we are bringing to the Paschal Sacraments,
look to us for an example of renewal.

Therefore let us pray to the Lord for them and for ourselves,
that being encouraged by our mutual renewal,
we may be made worthy of the paschal graces.

Lector:

That these catechumens may renounce self-centeredness
and think of others rather than themselves,
let us pray to the Lord:

℟. Lord, hear our prayer.

Lector:

For their godparents, that they may show to the catechumens
a constant application of the Gospel
both in their private and in their public lives,
let us pray to the Lord:

℟. Lord, hear our prayer.

Lector:

For their catechists, that they may convey the sweetness of God's word
to those who search for it,
let us pray to the Lord:

℟. Lord, hear our prayer.

Lector:

That they may share with others
the happiness they have found in their faith,
let us pray to the Lord:

℟. Lord, hear our prayer.

Lector:

For our community, that during this (or: **the coming**) Lenten season,
it may be radiant with the fullness of charity and with constancy in prayer,
let us pray to the Lord:

℟. Lord, hear our prayer.

Prayer over the Catechumens

115. The celebrant, extending his hands over the catechumens, concludes the Intercessions with this prayer:

Almighty, most beloved Father,
whose will it is to renew all things in Christ
and who draw all people to him,

graciously guide these catechumens of the Church
and grant that, faithful to the calling they have received,
they may be built up into the kingdom of your Son
and be sealed with the promised Holy Spirit.
Through Christ our Lord.

℟. Amen.

Dismissal of the Catechumens

116. If the Eucharist is to be celebrated, the catechumens are normally dismissed at this point by use of option A or B; if the catechumens are to stay for the celebration of the Eucharist, option C is used; if the Eucharist is not to be celebrated, the entire assembly is dismissed by use of option D.

A

The Deacon or the celebrant dismisses the catechumens in these or similar words:

My dear friends, you are about to enter with us on the Lenten journey. Christ will be for you the way, the truth, and the life. In his name we send you forth from this community to celebrate with the Bishop the Lord's choice of you to be numbered among his elect. Until we gather again for the Scrutinies, go in peace.

Catechumens:
Amen.

B

As an optional formula for dismissing the catechumens, the Deacon or the celebrant may use these or similar words:

My dear friends, this community now sends you forth to reflect more deeply upon the word of God which you have shared with us today. Be assured of our loving support and prayers for you. We look forward to the day when you will share fully in the Lord's table.

C

If, however, for serious reasons the catechumens do not leave (cf. no. **75.3**) and must remain with the faithful, they are to be instructed that, though they are present at the celebration of the Eucharist, they cannot take part as the baptized do. They may be reminded of this by the Deacon or the celebrant in these or similar words:

Although you cannot yet participate fully in the Lord's Eucharist, stay with us as a sign of our hope that all God's children will eat and drink with the Lord and work with his Holy Spirit to recreate the face of the earth.

D

If, however, the Eucharist is not celebrated, a suitable chant, as circumstances suggest, may be added, and the faithful and the catechumens may be dismissed, using these or similar words:

Go in peace,
and may the Lord remain with you.

All:
Thanks be to God.

CELEBRATION OF THE EUCHARIST

117. After the dismissal, the Eucharist is celebrated. The Universal Prayer (Prayer of the Faithful) for the needs of the Church and the whole world begins immediately. Then, if required, the Creed is said, and the Preparation of the Gifts follows. But for pastoral reasons the Universal Prayer (Prayer of the Faithful) and the Creed may be omitted.

SECOND STEP: RITE OF ELECTION OR ENROLLMENT OF NAMES

118. At the celebration of the "Election" the catechumenate itself 134
comes to an end, and with it a long period of formation of heart and mind. Therefore, in order that a person may be enrolled among the "elect," an enlightened faith and a considered intention to receive the Sacraments of the Church is required. Moreover, once enrollment has taken place, the person will be encouraged to follow Christ with greater generosity.

119. At the beginning of Lent, which is the proximate preparation 22
for Sacramental Initiation, is held the "Election" or "Enrollment 133
of Names," at which, having heard the testimony of godparents and catechists, with the catechumens confirming their intention, the Church discerns their state of preparation and decides whether they may proceed to the Paschal Sacraments. In this step the Church makes her "Election," or the choice and admission of catechumens, who by their dispositions are fit to take part in the next celebration of the Sacraments of Initiation. It is called "Election" because the admission made by the Church is founded on election by God, in whose name the Church acts; it is also called "Enrollment of Names" because the catechumens write their names in the Book of the Elect as a pledge of their faithfulness.

120. Before "Election" is celebrated, the catechumens are ques- 23
tioned regarding their conversion of mind and morals, a sufficient knowledge of Christian doctrine, and their sense of faith and charity; deliberation is especially required regarding their suitability. Then, during the actual celebration of the rite, the manifestation of their will and the judgment of the Bishop or his delegate are made in the presence of the community. Therefore it is clear that the Election, which is endowed with such solemnity, is as it were the hinge of the whole catechumenate.

121. As regards the Church, the "Election" is, as it were, the center 135
of her attentive care for these catechumens. Admission to Election USA
therefore belongs to the Bishop, and the presiding celebrant for the Rite of Election is the Bishop himself or a Priest or a Deacon who acts as the Bishop's delegate (cf. no. **12**). The Bishop, Priests, Deacons, catechists, godparents, and the entire local community, according to each one's own order and manner, should render a judgment on the instruction and progress of the catechumens, having considered the matter with the greatest care. Then they embrace the elect with prayer, so that the whole Church takes them with her to meet Christ.

122. In order to arrive at a wise decision about the suitability of 137
the candidates, a discussion must be held before the liturgical celebration by those in charge of the instruction of the catechumenate, that is, Priests, Deacons and catechists as well as godparents and delegates of the local community; indeed, if this is appropriate, the group of catechumens can take part. This discussion may take various forms, depending on local conditions and pastoral demands. The acceptance itself should be announced subsequently by the celebrant during the liturgical rite.

123. Then the godparents, who have been previously chosen by 136
the catechumens with the consent of the Priest, and, insofar as possible, accepted by the local community (cf. no. **11**), publicly exercise their ministry: they are now called by name at the beginning of the rite and come forward with the catechumens (no. **130**), they give testimony for them in the presence of the community (no. **131**) and, if appropriate, enroll the catechumen's name with them (no. **132**).

124. From the day of their "Election" and admission, catechumens 24
are called "elect." They are also called "co-petitioners" because together they strive or petition to receive the Sacraments of Christ and the gift of the Holy Spirit. They are also called "those to be enlightened" because Baptism itself is called "enlightenment," and by it the neophytes are flooded with the light of faith. But it is permitted in our days also to use other words that, in view of

the diversity of regions and secular culture, are more suited to the understanding of all and to the character of languages.

125. It is the task of the celebrant, that is, the Bishop or the one who takes his place, whether or not he has been closely involved in the preceding discussion, to explain the religious and ecclesiastical character of the "Election," either in the Homily or during the course of the Rite. For it is for him to proclaim the judgment of the Church in the presence of those attending and, if appropriate, to hear their judgment, to require a personal declaration of intent from the catechumens and, acting in the name of Christ and the Church, to carry out the admission of the "elect." Furthermore he should explain to everyone the divine mystery that is contained in the call of the Church and in her liturgical celebration; and he should encourage the faithful to prepare themselves, together with the elect, who offer an example, for the Paschal Solemnities. 138

126. Since the Sacraments of Initiation are celebrated during the Paschal Solemnities and preparation for them belongs to the particular character of Lent, the Rite of Election should normally take place on the First Sunday of Lent, and the period of final preparation of the co-petitioners should coincide with the season of Lent, the course of which will benefit the elect, both because of its liturgical structure and because of the participation of the community. However, when pastoral reasons suggest this (especially in mission stations), the Rite can be celebrated in the previous or following week. 139

When, because of unusual circumstances and pastoral needs, the Rite of Election is celebrated outside Lent, it is to be celebrated about six weeks before the Sacraments of Initiation, in order to allow sufficient time for the Scrutinies and Rites of Handing On. The Rite is not to be celebrated on a Solemnity of the liturgical year (cf. no. **29**). USA

127. The Rite should take place in the cathedral church, in a parish church or, if necessary, in some other suitable and fitting place. 140 USA

128. The Rite should be celebrated within the Mass of the First 140
Sunday of Lent, after the Homily. If the Rite happens to be cele- 141
brated on another day, it begins with the Liturgy of the Word. In RM
this case, if the readings for the day are not suitable, they should be chosen from those assigned to the First Sunday of Lent (cf. *Lectionary for Mass*, nos. 22–24), or other suitable texts. The proper Ritual Mass for the Election or Enrollment of Names may be celebrated with the color violet on any day except those listed in nos. 1–4 of the Table of Liturgical Days. The Mass of the Friday of the Fourth Week of Lent may also be used. If, however, the Eucharist is not celebrated, the Rite is concluded with the Dismissal of both the elect and the faithful.

An optional parish Rite of Sending Catechumens for Election USA
by the Bishop precedes the Rite of Election and is found at no. **106**.

LITURGY OF THE WORD

Homily

129. The Homily, suited to the actual situation, should address not 142
only the catechumens but the entire community of the faithful, so that, striving to give good example, they may, together with the elect, embark on the path of the Paschal Mystery.

Presentation of the Catechumens

130. After the Homily, the Priest responsible for the Initiation of 143
the catechumens, or a Deacon, a catechist, or a representative of the community, presents the catechumens for Election, in these or similar words:

(Most) Reverend Father,
as the solemn paschal celebrations approach once more,
the catechumens present here,
relying on divine grace
and supported by the prayers and example of the community,

humbly request that, after due preparation and celebration of
the Scrutinies,
they be admitted to participate
in the Sacraments of Baptism, Confirmation, and the Eucharist.

The celebrant replies:
Let those who are to be chosen as the elect
come forward with their godparents.

One by one, they are called by name. Each catechumen, accompanied by a godparent, comes forward and stands before the celebrant.

If there are a large number of catechumens, all are presented together, for example, each group by its own catechist. But in this case, the catechists should be advised to call each catechumen forward by name in a special celebration held before they come to the common rite.

Affirmation by the Godparents (and the Assembly)

131. Then the celebrant addresses the assembly. If he took part in 144
the previous deliberation about the catechumens' suitability (cf. 145
no. **122**), he may use either option A or option B or similar words; if he has not taken part in the earlier deliberation, he uses option B or similar words.

A 145

Celebrant:
My dear brothers and sisters,
these catechumens have asked to be initiated
into the sacramental life of the Church this Easter.

Those who know them have judged
that they are sincere in their desire.
For some time they have listened to Christ's word

and have tried to live according to his commands;
they have shared in fraternal communion and in the prayers.
Now I make known to the whole congregation
that it is the mind of the community to call them to the Sacraments.
As I inform you of this judgment and speak to the godparents,
I ask them to give their recommendation again, in your presence.

He, then, turns toward the godparents:

With God as your witness,
do you judge these catechumens to be worthy of admission
to the Sacraments of Christian Initiation?

Godparents:

We do.

Then if the circumstances warrant, the celebrant may ask the entire 145
congregation for its assent: USA

Now I ask you, the members of this community:
Are you willing to affirm the testimony expressed about these catechumens
and support them in faith, prayer, and example
as we prepare to celebrate the Paschal Sacraments?

All:

We are.

B 144

Celebrant:

The holy Church of God now wishes to ascertain
whether these catechumens are sufficiently prepared
to be received into the order of the elect
for the solemn paschal celebrations to come.

He, then, turns toward the godparents:

And so, first I ask you their godparents to testify.
Have they faithfully listened to God's word proclaimed by the Church?

Godparents:

They have.

Celebrant:

Have they begun to walk in God's presence,
treasuring the word they have received?

Godparents:

They have.

Celebrant:

Have they persevered in fraternal communion and in the prayers?

Godparents:

They have.

Then if the circumstances warrant, the celebrant may ask the entire congregation for its assent: 145 USA

Now I ask you, the members of this community:
Are you willing to affirm the testimony expressed about these catechumens
and include them in your prayer and affection as we move toward Easter?

All:

We are.

Questioning and Petitioning of the Catechumens

132. Next, the celebrant, looking at the catechumens, addresses and questions them in these or similar words: 146 USA

And now, my dear catechumens, I address you.
Your godparents and catechists (and the entire community)
have testified favorably on your behalf.
Trusting in their judgment,
the Church calls you in the name of Christ to the Paschal Sacraments.
Now it falls to you who have long listened to the voice of Christ
to respond in the presence of the Church by stating your intentions.
Is it your will to be initiated into Christ's Sacraments
of Baptism, Confirmation, and the Eucharist?

Catechumens:
It is.

Celebrant:
Then offer your names for enrollment.

The catechumens give their names, either going with their godparents to the celebrant or while remaining in place, and the actual inscription of the names may be carried out in various ways. The catechumens may inscribe their names themselves or they may call out their names, which are inscribed by the godparents or by the one who presented them (cf. no. **130**). As the Enrollment is taking place, a suitable chant, for example, Psalm 16 (15) may be sung.

If, however, there are a large number of catechumens a list of names may be given to the celebrant, with these or similar words: **These are the names of those seeking Initiation**, or, when the Bishop is celebrant and catechumens from several parishes have been presented to him: **These are the names of the catechumens from the parish of** N. **seeking Initiation**.

Psalm 16 (15)

1 Preserve me, O God, for in you I take refuge.
  2 I say to the LORD, "You are my Lord.
  You, you alone are my good."

3 As for the holy ones who dwell in the land,
  they are noble, and in them is all my delight.
4 Those who choose other gods increase their sorrows.
  I will not take part in their offerings of blood.
  Nor will I take their names upon my lips.

5 O LORD, it is you who are my portion and cup;
  you yourself who secure my lot.
6 Pleasant places are marked out for me:
  a pleasing heritage indeed is mine!

7 I will bless the LORD who gives me counsel,
  who even at night directs my heart.
8 I keep the LORD before me always;
  with him at my right hand, I shall not be moved.

9 And so, my heart rejoices, my soul is glad;
  even my flesh shall rest in hope.
10 For you will not abandon my soul to Sheol,
  nor let your holy one see corruption.

11 You will show me the path of life,
  the fullness of joy in your presence,
  at your right hand, bliss forever.

RECEPTION OR ELECTION

133. At the conclusion of the Enrollment of Names, the celebrant, 147
after he has briefly explained the meaning of the rite that has taken

place, turns toward the catechumens, addressing them in these or similar words:

N. and N., you have been chosen for Initiation
into the sacred mysteries at the forthcoming Easter Vigil.

Elect:

Thanks be to God.

The celebrant continues:

Now, with divine help,
your duty, like ours, is to be faithful to God,
who is faithful to his call,
and to strive with generous spirit
to reach the full truth of your Election.

Then, turning toward the godparents, the celebrant addresses them in these or similar words:

Godparents, you have spoken in favor of these elect;
receive them now as chosen in the Lord
and accompany them with your help and example,
until they come to share in the Sacraments of divine life.

And he invites them to place their hand on the shoulder of the elect whom they are receiving into their care, or to make some other gesture to indicate the same intent.

Intercessions for the Elect

134. Then, the community prays for the elect using either of the following formulas, options A or B. The celebrant may adapt the introduction and the intentions to fit various circumstances. Moreover, the usual intentions for the Church and the whole world should be added if the elect are to be dismissed after the Intercessions and the Universal Prayer (Prayer of the Faithful) is omitted during Mass (cf. no. **137**). 148

Celebrant:

Dear brothers and sisters,
today we begin the Lenten journey
looking forward to the saving mysteries of the Passion and Resurrection.
The elect, whom we are bringing to the Paschal Sacraments,
look to us for an example of renewal.

Therefore let us pray to the Lord for them and for ourselves,
that being encouraged by our mutual renewal,
we may be made worthy of the paschal graces.

A 148

Lector:

For our elect, that, remembering this day,
they may remain ever grateful for heavenly blessings,
let us pray to the Lord:

℟. Lord, hear our prayer.

Lector:

That they may make good use of this season
by persevering in self-denial and by joining us in works of sanctification,
let us pray to the Lord:

℟. Lord, hear our prayer.

Lector:

For their catechists, that they may convey the sweetness of God's word
to those who search for it,
let us pray to the Lord:

℟. Lord, hear our prayer.

Lector:

For their godparents, that they may show to the elect
a constant application of the Gospel

both in their private and in their public lives,
let us pray to the Lord:

℟. Lord, hear our prayer.

Lector:

For their families,
that they may help them to follow the promptings of the Spirit
without placing any obstacles in their way,
let us pray to the Lord:

℟. Lord, hear our prayer.

Lector:

For our community, that during this Lenten season,
it may be radiant with the fullness of charity and with
constancy in prayer,
let us pray to the Lord:

℟. Lord, hear our prayer.

Lector:

For those who are still held back by doubts,
that they may trust in Christ
and come without hesitation to join us in fraternal communion,
let us pray to the Lord:

℟. Lord, hear our prayer.

B 375

Lector:

That our elect may draw joy from daily prayer:
℟. Lord, we ask you, hear our prayer.

Lector:

That, by praying to you often,
they may live in ever closer union with you:

℟. Lord, we ask you, hear our prayer.

Lector:
That they may rejoice to read your word
and to ponder it in their hearts:

℟. Lord, we ask you, hear our prayer.

Lector:
That they may humbly acknowledge their faults
and undertake wholeheartedly to correct them:

℟. Lord, we ask you, hear our prayer.

Lector:
That they may transform their daily work
into a pleasing offering to you:

℟. Lord, we ask you, hear our prayer.

Lector:
That each day of Lent
they may undertake something that is consecrated to you:

℟. Lord, we ask you, hear our prayer.

Lector:
That with firm resolve
they may abstain from everything that defiles purity of heart:

℟. Lord, we ask you, hear our prayer.

Lector:
That they will acquire the habit
of cherishing and preserving virtue and holiness of life:

℟. Lord, we ask you, hear our prayer.

Lector:
That they may renounce self-centeredness
and think of others rather than themselves:

℟. Lord, we ask you, hear our prayer.

Lector:
That you will graciously protect and bless their families:

℟. Lord, we ask you, hear our prayer.

Lector:
That they may share with others
the happiness they have found in their faith:

℟. Lord, we ask you, hear our prayer.

135. The celebrant, extending his hands over the elect, concludes 149
the Intercessions with one of the following prayers:

A

O God, Creator of the human race,
who fashion it anew,
show mercy to the children of adoption
and enroll them in the New Covenant
as offspring of a new people.
Made children of the promise,
may they rejoice that,
what they could not obtain by nature,
they have received by grace.
Through Christ our Lord.

℟. Amen.

B

Almighty, most beloved Father,
whose will it is to renew all things in Christ
and who draw all people to him,
graciously guide these elect of the Church
and grant that, faithful to the calling they have received,
they may be built up into the kingdom of your Son
and be sealed with the promised Holy Spirit.
Through Christ our Lord.

℟. Amen.

Dismissal of the Elect

136. If the Eucharist is to be celebrated, the elect are normally dismissed at this point by use of option A or B; if the elect are to stay for the celebration of the Eucharist, option C is used; if the Eucharist is not to be celebrated, the entire assembly is dismissed by use of option D. USA

A 150

The Deacon or the celebrant dismisses the elect with this or a similar instruction:

My dear elect,
you have entered with us on the Lenten journey.
Christ will be for you the way, the truth, and the life,
especially when you gather with us
at the forthcoming Scrutinies.
Now go in peace.

Elect:
Amen.

The elect go out.

B USA

As an optional formula for dismissing the elect, the Deacon or the celebrant may use these or similar words:

My dear friends, this community now sends you forth to reflect more deeply upon the word of God which you have shared with us today. Be assured of our loving support and prayers for you. We look forward to the day when you will share fully in the Lord's table.

C 150

If, however, for serious reasons the elect do not leave (cf. no. **75.3**) USA
and must remain with the faithful, they are to be instructed that though they are present at the celebration of the Eucharist, they cannot take part as the baptized do. They may be reminded of this by the Deacon or the celebrant in these or similar words:

Although you cannot yet participate fully in the Lord's Eucharist, stay with us as a sign of our hope that all God's children will eat and drink with the Lord and work with his Holy Spirit to recreate the face of the earth.

D 150

If, however, the Eucharist is not celebrated, a suitable chant, as 96
circumstances suggest, may be added, and the faithful and the elect may be dismissed, using these or similar words:

Go in peace,
and may the Lord remain with you.

All:

Thanks be to God.

CELEBRATION OF THE EUCHARIST

137. After the dismissal, the Eucharist is celebrated. The Universal 151
Prayer (Prayer of the Faithful) for the needs of the Church and the whole world begins immediately. Then, if required, the Creed is said, and the Preparation of the Gifts follows. But for pastoral reasons the Universal Prayer (Prayer of the Faithful) and the Creed may be omitted.

PERIOD OF PURIFICATION AND ENLIGHTENMENT

138. The Period of Purification and Enlightenment of the elect 21
normally coincides with Lent and begins with "Election." Both in 152
the liturgy and in liturgical catechesis, through remembrance of Baptism or preparation for it, and by penitence,[1] Lent renews the community of the faithful together with the elect and disposes them to recall the Paschal Mystery, which the Sacraments of Initiation apply to individuals.[2] In this period, the elect together with the local community give themselves to spiritual recollection, so that they may prepare themselves for the Paschal Feasts and for Initiation by the Sacraments. To this end the Scrutinies, the Rites of Handing On, and the Rites of Immediate Preparation are provided for them.

139. The time of purification and enlightenment is given to a more 22
intense preparation of spirit and heart, which has the character of 25
recollection rather than of catechesis, and is intended to purify 153
hearts and minds by examination of conscience and penitence. This period is intended as well to enlighten the minds and hearts of the elect with a deeper knowledge of Christ the Savior. The Scrutinies (cf. nos. **141–146**) and Rites of Handing On (cf. nos. **147–149**) take place during the Lent that precedes the Sacraments of Initiation. The spiritual and catechetical preparation of the elect, or the "co-petitioners," is completed by these rites and extends throughout the entire Time of Lent.

[1] Cf. Second Vatican Council, Constitution on the Sacred Liturgy, *Sacrosanctum Concilium*, no. 109.

[2] Cf. Second Vatican Council, Decree on the Missionary Activity of the Church, *Ad gentes*, no. 14.

140. Holy Saturday is the day of immediate preparation for the 26
celebration of the Sacraments of Initiation and on that day the Rites of Immediate Preparation (cf. nos. **185–192**) may be celebrated.

PERIOD OF PURIFICATION AND ENLIGHTENMENT AND ITS RITES

SCRUTINIES

141. The "Scrutinies," which are celebrated solemnly on Sundays, 25
have the double purpose mentioned earlier, namely to reveal what 154
is weak, sick and sinful in the hearts of the elect so that it can be healed; and what is honorable, strong and holy, so that it can be strengthened. The purpose of the Scrutinies, which are brought to completion with the help of the Exorcisms, is mainly spiritual. For the Scrutinies are ordered toward liberation from sin and the Devil, and they give strength in Christ, who is the way, the truth, and the life of the elect. Moreover, the Scrutinies are set forth to purify minds and hearts, to fortify against temptations, to convert intentions, and to awaken the will, so that the elect may cling more closely to Christ and pursue more vigorously their desire to love God.

142. Co-petitioners should resolve to achieve an intimate sense of 155
Christ and the Church. Above all, they are expected to progress in genuine self-knowledge through a serious examination of their lives and true penitence.

143. In order to awaken a desire for purification and redemption 157
by Christ, three Scrutinies take place, both to teach the elect gradually about that mystery of sin from which the whole world and every person longs to be rescued in order to be saved from its present and future consequences, and to fill their spirit with the sense of Christ the Redeemer, who is living water (cf. the Gospel

of the Samaritan Woman), light (cf. the Gospel of the Man Born Blind), resurrection and life (cf. the Gospel of the Raising of Lazarus). From the first to the final Scrutiny, they must grow in the awareness of sin and in the desire for salvation.

144. In the Rite of Exorcism (nos. **154, 168, 175**), celebrated by 156
Priests or Deacons, the elect, who have been taught by Mother Church about the mystery of Christ who frees from sin, are set free from the effects of sin and from the influence of the Devil; they are strengthened in their spiritual journey, and they open their hearts to receive the gifts of the Savior.

145. The Scrutinies should be celebrated by a Priest or Deacon 158
presiding over the community, so that the faithful may also benefit from the liturgy of the Scrutinies and intercede for the elect in the Intercessions.

146. The Scrutinies should take place within the Ritual Masses for 159
the Celebration of the Scrutinies, which are held on the Third, USA
Fourth, and Fifth Sundays of Lent; the readings and their chants from Year A are chosen, as designated in the *Lectionary for Mass*, nos. 28, 31 and 34. If for pastoral reasons the Scrutinies cannot take place on these Sundays, other Sundays in Lent or even more convenient weekdays may be chosen.

When, because of unusual circumstances and pastoral needs, the Period of Purification and Enlightenment takes place outside Lent, the Scrutinies are celebrated on Sundays or even on weekdays, with the usual intervals between celebrations. They are not celebrated on Solemnities of the liturgical year (cf. no. **30**).

The first Mass of the Scrutinies should, however, always be the Mass of the Samaritan Woman, the second, of the Man Born Blind, and the third, of Lazarus.

RITES OF HANDING ON

147. The Rites of Handing On of the Creed and of the Lord's Prayer 25
are to be celebrated after the Scrutinies, if they have not already 181
taken place (cf. nos. **79, 104–105**). In these rites, with the formation of the elect completed or underway for a suitable time, the Church lovingly entrusts to them the texts regarded from antiquity as a summary of its faith and prayer. The "Rites of Handing On," by which the Church entrusts to the elect ancient texts of faith and prayer, that is, the Creed and the Lord's Prayer, have the purpose of enlightening them. In the case of the Creed, in which the mighty deeds of God for the salvation of humans are recalled, their eyes are filled with faith and joy. Furthermore, in the Lord's Prayer they discover more deeply the new spirit of sons and daughters by which they call God their Father, especially in the midst of the Eucharistic Assembly.

148. Handing On of the Creed – First comes the Rite of Handing 183
On of the Creed during the week following the First Scrutiny. The 184
elect are to memorize and then recite the Creed in public (cf. nos. **193–196**) prior to professing their faith in accordance with that Creed on the day of their Baptism. If appropriate, this rite can also be celebrated during the Period of the Catechumenate (cf. nos. **79, 104–105**).

149. Handing On of the Lord's Prayer – The Handing On of the 188
Lord's Prayer takes place during the week following the Third 189
Scrutiny. From antiquity it has been the prayer proper to those who in Baptism have received the spirit of adoption. When the neophytes take part in their first celebration of the Eucharist, they will say it together with the rest of the baptized. If circumstances suggest, this rite may also be celebrated during the Period of the Catechumenate (cf. nos. **79, 104–105**). If necessary, it may be deferred for inclusion in Rites of Immediate Preparation (cf. no. **185**).

FIRST SCRUTINY

LITURGY OF THE WORD

Readings

150. The First Scrutiny is celebrated on the Third Sunday of Lent using the formulas designated in the Missal (Ritual Masses: For the Celebration of the Scrutinies) and Lectionary (no. 745). 160

Homily

151. Guided by the readings from Sacred Scripture, the celebrant explains in the Homily the meaning of the First Scrutiny in the light of the Lenten liturgy and of the spiritual journey of the elect. 161

Prayer in Silence

152. After the Homily, the elect with their godparents come forward and stand before the celebrant. 162

Looking at the faithful, he invites them to pray in silence for the elect and ask that they be given a spirit of repentance, a sense of sin, and the true freedom of the children of God.

Then he turns toward the elect and, at the same time, invites them to pray in silence and instructs them to show their spirit of repentance by bowing or kneeling. Then he concludes in these or similar words:

Elect of God, bow your heads (or: **kneel**) and pray.

Then the elect bow or kneel and all pray in silence for a while. Then, as circumstances suggest, all stand.

Intercessions for the Elect

153. Either of the following formulas, options A or B, may be used for the Intercessions for the elect and both the introduction and the intentions may be adapted to fit various circumstances. During the Intercessions for the elect, the godparents place their right hand on the shoulder of the elect they are sponsoring. Moreover, the usual intentions for the Church and the whole world should be added if the elect are to be dismissed after the Intercessions and the Universal Prayer (Prayer of the Faithful) is omitted during Mass (cf. no. **156**). 163 USA

Celebrant: 163

Let us pray for these elect,
who have already made a long journey
and whom the Church has confidently chosen,
that when their preparation is complete,
they may find Christ in his Sacraments at the Paschal Feasts.

A 163

Lector:

That they may ponder the word of God in their hearts
and savor it more fully day by day,
let us pray to the Lord:

℟. Lord, hear our prayer.

Lector:

That they may know Christ,
who came to save what was lost,
let us pray to the Lord:

℟. Lord, hear our prayer.

Lector:

That with humble hearts they may confess that they are sinners,
let us pray to the Lord:

℟. Lord, hear our prayer.

Lector:

That they may sincerely reject anything in their conduct
that has displeased Christ and is contrary to him,
let us pray to the Lord:

℟. Lord, hear our prayer.

Lector:

That the Holy Spirit, who searches every heart,
may strengthen them in their weakness with his power,
let us pray to the Lord:

℟. Lord, hear our prayer.

Lector:

That from the same Spirit
they may learn the things that are of God and are pleasing to God,
let us pray to the Lord:

℟. Lord, hear our prayer.

Lector:

That their families also may put their hope in Christ
and find peace and holiness in him,
let us pray to the Lord:

℟. Lord, hear our prayer.

Lector:

That we ourselves, in preparation for the Paschal Feasts,
may correct our minds, raise our hearts, and perform works of charity,
let us pray to the Lord:

℟. Lord, hear our prayer.

Lector:

That throughout the whole world
the weak may be strengthened, the broken restored,

the lost found, and the found redeemed,
let us pray to the Lord:

℟. Lord, hear our prayer.

B 378

Lector:

That, like the Samaritan woman,
our elect may review their lives in Christ's presence
and acknowledge their sins,
let us pray to the Lord:

℟. Lord, hear our prayer.

Lector:

That they may be freed from the spirit of mistrust
that turns people's footsteps from the way of Christ,
let us pray to the Lord:

℟. Lord, hear our prayer.

Lector:

That as they await the gift of God
they may long with all their hearts
for the living water that springs up to eternal life,
let us pray to the Lord:

℟. Lord, hear our prayer.

Lector:

That by accepting the Son of God as their teacher,
they may become true worshipers of God the Father
in spirit and in truth,
let us pray to the Lord:

℟. Lord, hear our prayer.

Lector:

That, having experienced the wonder of an encounter with Christ,
they may bring the joyful news of him
to their friends and neighbors,
let us pray to the Lord:

℟. Lord, hear our prayer.

Lector:

That all in the world who are poor
for want of God's word
may be able to come to the Gospel of Christ,
let us pray to the Lord:

℟. Lord, hear our prayer.

Lector:

That all of us may be taught by Christ
and, delighting in the Father's will,
lovingly accomplish his work,
let us pray to the Lord:

℟. Lord, hear our prayer.

Exorcism

154. After the Intercessions, the celebrant faces the elect and, with hands joined, says: 164

A

Let us pray.

O God, who sent your Son to us as Savior,
grant that these elect,
who desire to draw living water like the Samaritan woman
and have been converted by the word of the Lord,
may acknowledge the hindrance
of their own sins and weaknesses.

Do not permit them, we pray,
to rely on a vain confidence in themselves
and to be deceived by the power of the devil,
but free them from the spirit of untruth,
so that, recognizing their sinfulness,
they may be cleansed inwardly
and advance on the way of salvation.
Through Christ our Lord.

All:
Amen.

Then, if this can be done conveniently, the celebrant lays hands in silence on each one of the elect.

Then, with hands extended over the elect, the celebrant continues:

Lord Jesus, you are the fountain
for which these chosen ones thirst
and the master whom they seek.
Before you, who alone are holy,
they dare not call themselves innocent.
They open their hearts to you in faith,
they acknowledge what has defiled them,
they uncover their hidden wounds.
Therefore in your love free them from their infirmities,
heal their sickness, quench their thirst, and give them peace.
Be present now to save them by the power of your name,
which we invoke in faith.
Restrain the evil spirit,
whom you conquered by rising again.
Show your elect the way forward in the Holy Spirit,
so that they may come to the Father
and worship him in truth.
Who live and reign for ever and ever.

All:
Amen.

B 379

Let us pray.

Father of mercies,
who through your Son graciously took pity
on the Samaritan woman
and, moved by the same fatherly care,
offered salvation to all sinners,
look with your unbounded love on these elect,
who desire to receive adoption as your children
through the Sacraments.
Free them from the slavery of sin and from Satan's heavy yoke,
that they may take up the gentle yoke of Jesus.
Protect them in every danger,
that, serving you faithfully in peace and joy,
they may render you thanks for ever.
Through Christ our Lord.

All:
Amen.

Then, if this can be done conveniently, the celebrant lays hands in silence on each one of the elect.

Then, with hands extended over the elect, the celebrant continues:

Lord Jesus,
who in the marvelous plan of your mercy
converted the sinful woman
that she might thereafter
worship the Father in spirit and in truth,
now, by your power,
free these elect from Satan's wicked cunning,
as they draw near to the fountain of living water.
In the power of the Holy Spirit, convert their hearts,
that they may come to know your Father
in sincere faith, which expresses itself in charity.
Who live and reign for ever and ever.

All:

Amen.

If circumstances suggest, a suitable chant may be sung, for example, Psalms 6, 26 (25), 32 (31), 38 (37), 39 (38), 40 (39), 51 (50), 116:1-9 (114), 130 (129), 139 (138), or 142 (141).

Dismissal of the Elect

155. If the Eucharist is to be celebrated, the elect are normally dismissed at this point by use of option A or B; if the elect are to stay for the celebration of the Eucharist, option C is used; if the Eucharist is not to be celebrated, the entire assembly is dismissed by use of option D. USA

A 165

The Deacon or the celebrant dismisses the elect, saying:

Go in peace,
and return for the next Scrutiny.
May the Lord be with you always.

Elect:

Amen.

B USA

As an optional formula for dismissing the elect, the Deacon or the celebrant may use these or similar words:

My dear friends, this community now sends you forth to reflect more deeply upon the word of God which you have shared with us today. Be assured of our loving support and prayers for you. We look forward to the day when you will share fully in the Lord's table.

C

165

If, however, for serious reasons the elect do not leave (cf. no. **75.3**) USA
and must remain with the faithful, they are to be instructed that though they are present at the celebration of the Eucharist, they cannot take part as the baptized do. They may be reminded of this by the Deacon or the celebrant in these or similar words:

Although you cannot yet participate fully in the Lord's Eucharist, stay with us as a sign of our hope that all God's children will eat and drink with the Lord and work with his Holy Spirit to recreate the face of the earth.

D

165

If, however, the Eucharist is not celebrated, a suitable chant, as 96
circumstances suggest, may be added, and the faithful and the elect may be dismissed, using these or similar words:

Go in peace,
and may the Lord remain with you.

All:
Thanks be to God.

CELEBRATION OF THE EUCHARIST

156. After the dismissal, the Eucharist is celebrated. The Universal 166
Prayer (Prayer of the Faithful) for the needs of the Church and the whole world begins immediately. Then if required, the Creed is said, and the Preparation of the Gifts follows. But for pastoral reasons the Universal Prayer (Prayer of the Faithful) and the Creed may be omitted. In the Eucharistic Prayer there is to be a remembrance of the elect and their godparents (cf. Ritual Masses: For the Celebration of the Scrutinies).

HANDING ON OF THE CREED

157. The Rite of Handing On of the Creed takes place during the 182
week following the First Scrutiny. It is desirable that the Rite of 184
Handing On of the Creed takes place in the presence of the community of the faithful after the Liturgy of the Word at a weekday Mass with the appropriate readings for these Rites. If appropriate, it can also be celebrated during the Period of the Catechumenate (cf. nos. **104–105**).

LITURGY OF THE WORD

Readings

158. In place of the readings assigned for the weekday Mass, the 185
following appropriate passages may be read, as indicated in the *Lectionary for Mass*, no. 748 (Ritual Masses: Presentation of the Creed):

First Reading

Dt 6:1-7: *Hear, O Israel! You shall love the Lord, your God, with all your heart.*

Responsorial Psalm

Ps 19 (18):8, 9, 10, 11

℟. (Jn 6:68c) Lord, you have the words of everlasting life.

Second Reading

Rom 10:8-13: *The confession of faith of those believing in Christ.*

Or:

1 Cor 15:1-8a (Long Form) or 1-4 (Short Form): *Through the Gospel you are also being saved if you hold fast to the word I preached to you.*

Verse before the Gospel

Jn 3:16

God so loved the world that he gave his only-begotten Son,
so that everyone who believes in him might have eternal life.

Gospel

Mt 16:13-18: *You are Peter, and upon this rock I will build my Church.*
Or:
Jn 12:44-50: *I came into the world as light, so that anyone who believes in me might not remain in darkness.*

Homily

159. The Homily follows, in which the celebrant relies on the sacred text to explain the meaning and importance of the Creed in relation to the teaching that the elect have already received and to the Profession of Faith that they must make at their Baptism and uphold throughout their lives. 185

Handing On of the Creed

160. After the Homily, the Deacon or other minister says: 186

Let the elect come forward
to receive from the Church the Creed, the Profession of Faith.

Before beginning the Apostles' Creed (option A) or the Niceno-Constantinopolitan Creed (option B), the celebrant addresses the elect in these or similar words:

My dear friends,
listen carefully to the words of that faith by which you will be justified.
The words are few, but the mysteries they contain are great.
Receive them with a sincere heart and treasure them.

A
Apostles' Creed

Then, the celebrant alone begins the Creed:

I believe in God,

And he continues alone or with the community of the faithful:

the Father almighty,
Creator of heaven and earth,
and in Jesus Christ, his only Son, our Lord,

At the words that follow, up to and including **the Virgin Mary**, all bow.

who was conceived by the Holy Spirit,
born of the Virgin Mary,
suffered under Pontius Pilate,
was crucified, died and was buried;
he descended into hell;
on the third day he rose again from the dead;
he ascended into heaven,
and is seated at the right hand of God the Father almighty;
from there he will come to judge the living and the dead.

I believe in the Holy Spirit,
the holy catholic Church,
the communion of saints,
the forgiveness of sins,
the resurrection of the body,
and life everlasting. Amen.

B
NICENO-CONSTANTINOPOLITAN CREED

As circumstances so suggest, the Niceno-Constantinopolitan Creed can be used.

The celebrant alone begins:
I believe in one God,

And he continues alone or with the community of the faithful:
the Father almighty,
maker of heaven and earth,
of all things visible and invisible.

I believe in one Lord Jesus Christ,
the Only Begotten Son of God,
born of the Father before all ages.
God from God, Light from Light,
true God from true God,
begotten, not made, consubstantial with the Father;
through him all things were made.
For us men and for our salvation
he came down from heaven,

At the words that follow, up to and including **and became man**, all bow.
and by the Holy Spirit was incarnate of the Virgin Mary,
and became man.

For our sake he was crucified under Pontius Pilate,
he suffered death and was buried,
and rose again on the third day
in accordance with the Scriptures.
He ascended into heaven
and is seated at the right hand of the Father.
He will come again in glory
to judge the living and the dead
and his kingdom will have no end.

I believe in the Holy Spirit, the Lord, the giver of life,
who proceeds from the Father and the Son,
who with the Father and the Son is adored and glorified,
who has spoken through the prophets.

I believe in one, holy, catholic and apostolic Church.
I confess one Baptism for the forgiveness of sins
and I look forward to the resurrection of the dead
and the life of the world to come. Amen.

Prayer over the Elect

161. Afterwards, the celebrant invites the faithful to pray in these 187
or similar words:

Let us pray for our elect,
that our God and Lord
will open the ears of their innermost hearts
and the gate of mercy,
so that, receiving remission of all sins
through the cleansing waters of rebirth,
they too may be found in Christ Jesus our Lord.

All pray in silence.

Then the celebrant, with hands extended over the elect, says:

O Lord, fount of light and truth,
we invoke your eternal and supremely just compassion
upon these your servants N. and N.:
cleanse and sanctify them,
bestow on them true knowledge, firm hope, and holy doctrine,
that they may be made worthy of attaining the grace of
Baptism.
Through Christ our Lord.

All:

Amen.

Dismissal of the Elect

162. If the Eucharist is to be celebrated, the elect are normally USA
dismissed at this point by use of option A or B; if the elect are to stay for the celebration of the Eucharist, option C is used; if the Eucharist is not to be celebrated, the entire assembly is dismissed by use of option D.

A 150

The Deacon or the celebrant dismisses the elect with this or a USA
similar instruction:

Dear elect, go in peace,
and may the Lord remain with you.

Elect:

Amen.

B USA

As an optional formula for dismissing the elect, the Deacon or the celebrant may use these or similar words:

My dear friends, this community now sends you forth to reflect more deeply upon the word of God which you have shared with us today. Be assured of our loving support and prayers for you. We look forward to the day when you will share fully in the Lord's table.

C 150

If, however, for serious reasons the elect do not leave (cf. no. **75.3**) USA
and must remain with the faithful, they are to be instructed that, though they are present at the celebration of the Eucharist, they cannot take part as the baptized do. They may be reminded of this by the Deacon or the celebrant in these or similar words:

Although you cannot yet participate fully in the Lord's Eucharist, stay with us as a sign of our hope that all God's children will eat and drink with the Lord and work with his Holy Spirit to recreate the face of the earth.

D 150

If, however, the Eucharist is not celebrated, a suitable chant, as circumstances suggest, may be added, and the faithful and the elect may be dismissed, using these or similar words: 96

Go in peace,
and may the Lord remain with you.

All:

Thanks be to God.

CELEBRATION OF THE EUCHARIST

163. After the dismissal, the Eucharist is celebrated. USA

SECOND SCRUTINY

LITURGY OF THE WORD

Readings

164. The Second Scrutiny is celebrated on the Fourth Sunday of Lent using the formulas designated in the Missal (Ritual Masses: For the Celebration of the Scrutinies) and Lectionary (no. 746). 167

Homily

165. Guided by the readings from Sacred Scripture, the celebrant explains in the Homily the meaning of the Second Scrutiny in the light of the Lenten liturgy and of the spiritual journey of the elect. 168

Prayer in Silence

166. After the Homily, the elect with their godparents come forward and stand before the celebrant. 169

Looking at the faithful, he invites them to pray in silence for the elect and ask that they be given a spirit of repentance, a sense of sin, and the true freedom of the children of God.

Then he turns toward the elect and, at the same time, invites them to pray in silence and instructs them to show their spirit of repentance by bowing or kneeling. Then he concludes in these or similar words:

Elect of God, bow your heads (or: **kneel**) and pray.

Then the elect bow or kneel and all pray in silence for a while. Then, as circumstances suggest, all stand.

Intercessions for the Elect

167. Either of the following formulas, options A or B, may be used for the Intercessions for the elect and both the introduction and the intentions may be adapted to fit various circumstances. During the Intercessions for the elect, the godparents place their right hand on the shoulder of the elect they are sponsoring. Moreover, the usual intentions for the Church and the whole world should be added if the elect are to be dismissed after the Intercessions and the Universal Prayer (Prayer of the Faithful) is omitted during Mass (cf. no. **170**). 170 USA

Celebrant: 170

Let us pray for these elect, whom God has called,
that in him they may remain holy
and give strong testimony to the words of eternal life.

A 170

Lector:

That, trusting in the truth of Christ,
they may attain and ever preserve freedom of mind and heart,
let us pray to the Lord:

℟. Lord, hear our prayer.

Lector:

That, contemplating the wisdom of the Cross,
they may learn to glory in God,
who confounds the wisdom of this world,
let us pray to the Lord:

℟. Lord, hear our prayer.

Lector:

That, set free in the power of the Holy Spirit,
they may be converted from fear to trust,
let us pray to the Lord:

℟. Lord, hear our prayer.

Lector:

That, being made spiritual,
they may discern those things that are holy and just,
let us pray to the Lord:

℟. Lord, hear our prayer.

Lector:

That all who suffer persecution for the name of Christ
may receive his help,
let us pray to the Lord:

℟. Lord, hear our prayer.

Lector:

That those families and peoples
who are prevented from embracing the faith
may be granted freedom to believe the Gospel,
let us pray to the Lord:

℟. Lord, hear our prayer.

Lector:

That we, who are occupied with the concerns of this world,
may remain faithful to the spirit of the Gospel,
let us pray to the Lord:

℟. Lord, hear our prayer.

Lector:

That the whole world, beloved by the Father,
may come to full spiritual freedom in the Church,
let us pray to the Lord:

℟. Lord, hear our prayer.

B 382

Lector:
That, having put darkness to flight,
he may enlighten the hearts of our elect,
let us pray to the Lord:

℟. Lord, hear our prayer.

Lector:
That in his goodness he may lead them to his Christ,
who has become the light of this world,
let us pray to the Lord:

℟. Lord, hear our prayer.

Lector:
That as our elect open their hearts
they may confess God
as the source of light and the witness of truth,
let us pray to the Lord:

℟. Lord, hear our prayer.

Lector:
That, healed by him, they may be preserved
from the unbelief of this world,
let us pray to the Lord:

℟. Lord, hear our prayer.

Lector:
That, saved by him who takes away the sin of the world,
they may be freed from the contagion and affliction of that sin,
let us pray to the Lord:

℟. Lord, hear our prayer.

Lector:
That, enlightened by the Holy Spirit,
they may never fail to profess the Gospel of salvation
and may hand it on to others,
let us pray to the Lord:

℟. Lord, hear our prayer.

Lector:
That all of us, by the example of our conduct,
may become in Christ a light for the world,
let us pray to the Lord:

℟. Lord, hear our prayer.

Lector:
That all who dwell on earth
may acknowledge the true God, Creator of all things,
who bestows upon us spirit and life,
let us pray to the Lord:

℟. Lord, hear our prayer.

Exorcism

168. After the Intercessions, the celebrant faces the elect and, with hands joined, says: 171

A

Let us pray.

Most merciful Father,
who granted the man born blind to believe in your Son,
and through this faith to come to the kingdom of your light,
grant also that your elect here present
may be freed from deceits that surround and blind them,
so that, firmly grounded in the truth,
they may become children of light
and remain so for ever.
Through Christ our Lord.

All:

Amen.

Then, if this can be done conveniently, the celebrant lays hands in silence on each one of the elect.

Then, with hands extended over the elect, the celebrant continues:

Lord Jesus, true light who enlighten all people,
by the Spirit of truth free all who are oppressed
beneath the yoke of the Father of lies,
and stir up good will in those you have chosen for your
Sacraments,
that, delighting in the joy of your light,
and, like the blind man you once restored to sight,
they may prove to be staunch and fearless witnesses to the faith.
Who live and reign for ever and ever.

All:

Amen.

B 383

Let us pray.

O God,
unfailing light and Father of lights,
who by the Death and Resurrection of your Christ
have cast out the darkness of hatred and lies
and poured forth upon the human family
the light of love and truth,
grant, we pray, that your elect,
whom you have called to be your adopted children,
may pass from darkness to light
and, delivered from the power of the prince of darkness,
may always remain children of the light.
Through Christ our Lord.

All:

Amen.

Then, if this can be done conveniently, the celebrant lays hands in silence on each one of the elect.

Then, with hands extended over the elect, the celebrant continues:

Lord Jesus,
at your own baptism
the heavens were opened
and you received the Holy Spirit
to proclaim the Good News to the poor
and restore sight to the blind.
Pour out the same Holy Spirit on these elect,
who long for your Sacraments.
Guide them along the paths of right faith,
safe from the contagion of error, doubt, and unbelief,
so that with eyes unsealed
they may come to see you face to face.
Who live and reign for ever and ever.

All:

Amen.

If circumstances suggest, a suitable chant may be sung, for example, Psalms 6, 26 (25), 32 (31), 38 (37), 39 (38), 40 (39), 51 (50), 116:1-9 (114), 130 (129), 139 (138), or 142 (141).

Dismissal of the Elect

169. If the Eucharist is to be celebrated, the elect are normally dismissed at this point by use of option A or B; if the elect are to stay for the celebration of the Eucharist, option C is used; if the Eucharist is not to be celebrated, the entire assembly is dismissed by use of option D. USA

A 172

The Deacon or the celebrant dismisses the elect, saying:

Go in peace,
and return for the next Scrutiny.
May the Lord be with you always.

Elect:

Amen.

B USA

As an optional formula for dismissing the elect, the Deacon or the celebrant may use these or similar words:

My dear friends, this community now sends you forth to reflect more deeply upon the word of God which you have shared with us today. Be assured of our loving support and prayers for you. We look forward to the day when you will share fully in the Lord's table.

C 172

If, however, for serious reasons the elect do not leave (cf. no. **75.3**) USA
and must remain with the faithful, they are to be instructed that, though they are present at the celebration of the Eucharist, they cannot take part as the baptized do. They may be reminded of this by the Deacon or the celebrant in these or similar words:

Although you cannot yet participate fully in the Lord's Eucharist, stay with us as a sign of our hope that all God's children will eat and drink with the Lord and work with his Holy Spirit to recreate the face of the earth.

D 172

If, however, the Eucharist is not celebrated, a suitable chant, as circumstances suggest, may be added, and the faithful and the elect may be dismissed, using these or similar words: 96

Go in peace,
and may the Lord remain with you.

All:
Thanks be to God.

CELEBRATION OF THE EUCHARIST

170. After the dismissal, the Eucharist is celebrated. The Universal Prayer (Prayer of the Faithful) for the needs of the Church and the whole world begins immediately. Then if required, the Creed is said, and the Preparation of the Gifts follows. But for pastoral reasons the Universal Prayer (Prayer of the Faithful) and the Creed may be omitted. In the Eucharistic Prayer there is to be a remembrance of the elect and their godparents (cf. Ritual Masses: For the Celebration of the Scrutinies). 173

THIRD SCRUTINY

LITURGY OF THE WORD

Readings

171. The Third Scrutiny is celebrated on the Fifth Sunday of Lent using the formulas designated in the Missal (Ritual Masses: For the Celebration of the Scrutinies) and Lectionary (no. 747). 174

Homily

172. Guided by the readings from Sacred Scripture, the celebrant explains in the Homily the meaning of the Third Scrutiny in the light of the Lenten liturgy and of the spiritual journey of the elect. 175

Prayer in Silence

173. After the Homily, the elect with their godparents come forward and stand before the celebrant. 176

Looking at the faithful, he invites them to pray in silence for the elect and ask that they be given a spirit of repentance, a sense of sin, and the true freedom of the children of God.

Then he turns toward the elect and, at the same time, invites them to pray in silence and instructs them to show their spirit of repentance by bowing or kneeling. Then he concludes in these or similar words:

Elect of God, bow your heads (or: **kneel**) and pray.

Then the elect bow or kneel and all pray in silence for a while. Then, as circumstances suggest, all stand.

INTERCESSIONS FOR THE ELECT

174. Either of the following formulas, options A or B, may be used for the Intercessions for the elect and both the introduction and the intentions may be adapted to fit various circumstances. During the Intercessions for the elect, the godparents place their right hand on the shoulder of the elect they are sponsoring. Moreover, the usual intentions for the Church and the whole world should be added if the elect are to be dismissed after the Intercessions and the Universal Prayer (Prayer of the Faithful) is omitted during Mass (cf. no. **177**). 177 USA

Celebrant: 177

Let us pray for these servants whom God has chosen,
that, being conformed to the Death and Resurrection of Christ,
they may have strength to overcome the bitter legacy of death
by the grace of the Sacraments.

A 177

Lector:
That they may be strengthened by faith
against all the falsehoods of the world,
let us pray to the Lord:

℟. Lord, hear our prayer.

Lector:
That they may remain thankful,
because they have been rescued by God's election
from their ignorance of eternal hope
and have set out on the way of salvation,
let us pray to the Lord:

℟. Lord, hear our prayer.

Lector:

That they may be encouraged to hope for eternal life
by the example and intercession of catechumens
who have shed their blood for Christ,
let us pray to the Lord:

℟. Lord, hear our prayer.

Lector:

That they may all hate sin, which destroys life,
let us pray to the Lord:

℟. Lord, hear our prayer.

Lector:

That those who are saddened
by the death of those they love
may find comfort in Christ,
let us pray to the Lord:

℟. Lord, hear our prayer.

Lector:

That we ourselves,
as the Paschal Solemnities draw near,
may be strengthened in the hope of rising again with Christ,
let us pray to the Lord:

℟. Lord, hear our prayer.

Lector:

That the whole world, created by God out of love,
may be enlivened through growth in faith and charity,
let us pray to the Lord:

℟. Lord, hear our prayer.

B 386

Lector:
That faith may be given to these elect
for them to acknowledge Christ
as the resurrection and the life,
let us pray to the Lord:

℟. Lord, hear our prayer.

Lector:
That, freed from sin,
they may bear fruit for holiness and eternal life,
let us pray to the Lord:

℟. Lord, hear our prayer.

Lector:
That, released by repentance from the chains of sin,
they may be conformed to Christ by Baptism
and they may be dead to sin and alive to God for ever,
let us pray to the Lord:

℟. Lord, hear our prayer.

Lector:
That, in hope of the life-giving Spirit,
they may prepare earnestly for the renewal of life,
let us pray to the Lord:

℟. Lord, hear our prayer.

Lector:
That through the Eucharistic Food,
which they will soon taste,
they may be united to the Author of life and resurrection,
let us pray to the Lord:

℟. Lord, hear our prayer.

Lector:

That all of us, walking in newness of life,
may show to the world the power of Christ's Resurrection,
let us pray to the Lord:

℟. Lord, hear our prayer.

Lector:

That all who dwell on earth, finding Christ,
may recognize in him the promises of life eternal,
let us pray to the Lord:

℟. Lord, hear our prayer.

Exorcism

175. After the Intercessions, the celebrant faces the elect and, with hands joined, says: 178

A

Let us pray.

Father of eternal life,
who are God not of the dead but of the living
and who sent your Son as the herald of life
so that you might rescue human beings
from the kingdom of death
and lead them to the resurrection,
free these chosen ones, we pray,
from the deadly power of the evil spirit,
so that they may receive the new life of the risen Christ
and bear witness to it.
Through Christ our Lord.

All:

Amen.

Then if this can be done conveniently, the celebrant lays hands in silence on each one of the elect.

Then, with hands extended over the elect, the celebrant continues:

Lord Jesus, who in raising Lazarus from the dead
gave a sign that you had come,
that people might have life
and have it more abundantly,
free from death those who seek life through your Sacraments,
release them from the spirit of wickedness,
and endow them with faith, hope, and charity
through your life-giving Spirit,
so that they may live with you always
and share in the glory of your Resurrection.
Who live and reign for ever and ever.

All:

Amen.

B 387

Let us pray.

Father, source of all life,
who seek your glory in man fully alive
and reveal your omnipotence in the resurrection of the dead,
graciously rescue from the domain of death
these elect who desire to come to life through Baptism.
Free them from slavery to the Devil,
who brought death through sin
and who seeks to corrupt the world you created as good.
Subject them to the authority of your beloved Son,
so that they may receive from him the power of the resurrection
and may give witness to your glory before others.
Through Christ our Lord.

All:

Amen.

Then if this can be done conveniently, the celebrant lays hands in silence on each one of the elect.

Then, with hands extended over the elect, the celebrant continues:

Lord Jesus Christ,
who commanded Lazarus to come forth alive from the tomb
and by your own Resurrection freed all people from death,
we humbly pray to you for your servants,
who hasten to the waters of rebirth
and the banquet of life.
Do not let the power of death hold back those
who by their faith
will share in the triumph of your Resurrection.
Who live and reign for ever and ever.

All:

Amen.

If circumstances suggest, a suitable chant may be sung, for example, Psalms 6, 26 (25), 32 (31), 38 (37), 39 (38), 40 (39), 51 (50), 116:1-9 (114), 130 (129), 139 (138), or 142 (141).

Dismissal of the Elect

176. If the Eucharist is to be celebrated, the elect are normally dismissed at this point by use of option A or B; if the elect are to stay for the celebration of the Eucharist, option C is used; if the Eucharist is not to be celebrated, the entire assembly is dismissed by use of option D. USA

A 179

The Deacon or the celebrant dismisses the elect, saying:

Go in peace,
and may the Lord be with you always.

Elect:

Amen.

B USA

As an optional formula for dismissing the elect, the Deacon or the celebrant may use these or similar words:

My dear friends, this community now sends you forth to reflect more deeply upon the word of God which you have shared with us today. Be assured of our loving support and prayers for you. We look forward to the day when you will share fully in the Lord's table.

C 179

If, however, for serious reasons the elect do not leave (cf. no. **75.3**) USA
and must remain with the faithful, they are to be instructed that, though they are present at the celebration of the Eucharist, they cannot take part as the baptized do. They may be reminded of this by the Deacon or the celebrant in these or similar words:

Although you cannot yet participate fully in the Lord's Eucharist, stay with us as a sign of our hope that all God's children will eat and drink with the Lord and work with his Holy Spirit to recreate the face of the earth.

D 179

If, however, the Eucharist is not celebrated, a suitable chant, as 96
circumstances suggest, may be added, and the faithful and the elect may be dismissed, using these or similar words:

Go in peace,
and may the Lord remain with you.

All:
Thanks be to God.

CELEBRATION OF THE EUCHARIST

177. After the dismissal, the Eucharist is celebrated. The Universal Prayer (Prayer of the Faithful) for the needs of the Church and the whole world begins immediately. Then if required, the Creed is said, and the Preparation of the Gifts follows. But for pastoral reasons the Universal Prayer (Prayer of the Faithful) and the Creed may be omitted. In the Eucharistic Prayer there is to be a remembrance of the elect and their godparents (cf. Ritual Masses: For the Celebration of the Scrutinies). 180

HANDING ON OF THE LORD'S PRAYER

178. The Handing On of the Lord's Prayer takes place during the 182
week following the Third Scrutiny. It is desirable that the Rite take 189
place in the presence of the community of the faithful after the Liturgy of the Word at a weekday Mass with the appropriate readings for these Rites. If circumstances suggest, it may also be celebrated during the Period of the Catechumenate (cf. nos. **104–105**). If necessary, it may be deferred for inclusion in Rites of Immediate Preparation (cf. no. **185 ff**).

LITURGY OF THE WORD

Readings and Chants

179. In place of the readings assigned for the weekday Mass, the following appropriate passages may be read, as indicated in the *Lectionary for Mass*, no. 749 (Ritual Masses: Presentation of the Lord's Prayer): 190

First Reading

Hos 11:1b, 3-4, 8e-9: *I drew them with human cords, with bands of love.*

Responsorial Psalm

Ps 23 (22):1b-3a, 3b-4, 5, 6
℟. (1) The Lord is my shepherd; there is nothing I shall want.
Or:
Ps 103 (102):1-2, 8 and 10, 11-12, 13 and 14
℟. (13) As a father has compassion on his children, the Lord's compassion is on those who fear him.

Second Reading

Rom 8:14-17, 26-27: *You received a spirit of adoption, through which we cry,* "Abba!"
Or:
Gal 4:4-7: *God sent the Spirit of his Son into our hearts, crying out,* "Abba! *Father!"*

Verse before the Gospel

Rom 8:15

For you did not receive a spirit of slavery to fall back into fear,
but you received a spirit of adoption, through which we cry,
"Abba! Father!"

Gospel

180. The Deacon says: 191

Let those who are to receive the Lord's Prayer
now come forward.

Then the celebrant addresses the elect in these or similar words:

Now hear how the Lord taught his disciples to pray.

✠ A reading from the holy Gospel according to Matthew *6:9-13*

Jesus said to his disciples:
"This is how you are to pray:
Our Father, who art in heaven,
hallowed be thy name;
thy Kingdom come,
thy will be done
on earth as it is in heaven.
Give us this day our daily bread,
and forgive us our trespasses,
as we forgive those who trespass against us;
and lead us not into temptation,
but deliver us from evil."

The Gospel of the Lord.

Homily

181. The Homily follows in which the celebrant explains the meaning and importance of the Lord's Prayer. 191

Prayer over the Elect

182. Afterwards, the celebrant invites the faithful to pray in these or similar words: 192

Let us pray for our elect,
that our God and Lord
will open the ears of their innermost hearts
and the gate of mercy,
so that, receiving remission of all sins
through the cleansing waters of rebirth,
they too may be found
in Christ Jesus our Lord.

All pray in silence.

Then the celebrant, with hands extended over the elect, says:

Almighty ever-living God,
who make your Church ever fruitful with new offspring,
increase the faith and understanding of our elect,
that, reborn in the font of Baptism,
they may be added to the number of your adopted children.
Through Christ our Lord.

All:

Amen.

Dismissal of the Elect

183. If the Eucharist is to be celebrated, the elect are normally USA
dismissed at this point by use of option A or B; if the elect are to stay for the celebration of the Eucharist, option C is used; if the Eucharist is not to be celebrated, the entire assembly is dismissed by use of option D.

A 150

The Deacon or the celebrant dismisses the elect with this or a similar instruction:

Dear elect, go in peace,
and may the Lord remain with you.

Elect:

Amen.

B USA

As an optional formula for dismissing the elect, the Deacon or the celebrant may use these or similar words:

My dear friends, this community now sends you forth to reflect more deeply upon the word of God which you have shared with us today. Be assured of our loving support and prayers for you. We look forward to the day when you will share fully in the Lord's table.

C 150

If, however, for serious reasons the elect do not leave (cf. no. **75.3**) USA
and must remain with the faithful, they are to be instructed that, though they are present at the celebration of the Eucharist, they cannot take part as the baptized do. They may be reminded of this by the Deacon or the celebrant in these or similar words:

Although you cannot yet participate fully in the Lord's Eucharist, stay with us as a sign of our hope that all God's children will eat and drink with the Lord and work with his Holy Spirit to recreate the face of the earth.

D 150

If, however, the Eucharist is not celebrated, a suitable chant, as 96
circumstances suggest, may be added, and the faithful and the elect may be dismissed, using these or similar words:

Go in peace,
and may the Lord remain with you.

All:
Thanks be to God.

CELEBRATION OF THE EUCHARIST

184. After the dismissal, the Eucharist is celebrated. USA

RITES OF IMMEDIATE PREPARATION

185. For immediate preparation for the Sacraments: 26
1) The elect are to be reminded to keep themselves free on Holy 193
Saturday as far as possible from their usual tasks, and to give time to prayer and recollection and to fast insofar as they are able.
2) Whenever the elect can be gathered on Holy Saturday to prepare themselves, by recollection and prayer, to receive the Sacraments, the following rites are set forth. As circumstances suggest, all or some of the rites may be used: the Recitation of the Creed (nos. **193–196**), "Ephphatha" (nos. **197–199**), and the Choosing of a Christian Name (nos. **200–202**).

186. The choice and arrangement of these rites should be guided 195
by what best suits the particular circumstances of the elect, but the 197
following should be observed with regard to their celebration: USA
1) If because of necessity the Creed could not be handed on, it is not recited.
2) When both the recitation of the Creed and the Ephphatha Rite are celebrated, the Ephphatha Rite immediately precedes the "Prayer for the Recitation of the Creed" (no. **194**).

Model for a Celebration of the Rites USA
of Immediate Preparation

187. Song – When the elect have gathered, the celebration begins with a suitable song.

188. Greeting – After the singing, the celebrant greets the elect and any of the faithful who are present, using one of the greetings for Mass or other suitable words.

189. Reading of the Word of God – Where indicated in the particular rites, the reading of the word of God follows; the readings may be chosen from those suggested for each rite. If more than one reading is used, a suitable psalm or hymn may be sung between the readings.

190. Homily – Where indicated in the particular rites, a brief Homily or an explanation of the text follows the reading of the word of God.

191. Celebration of the Rites Chosen – Cf. nos. **193–202**.

192. Concluding Rites – The celebration may be concluded with the prayer of Blessing and Dismissal given in nos. **204–205**.

RECITATION OF THE CREED

193. With this rite the elect are prepared for the baptismal Profession of Faith (no. **225**) and are instructed in their duty to proclaim the message of the Gospel. 194

Reading and Homily

194. At the beginning a suitable chant is sung. Then one of the following passages or another appropriate one is read: 196

Mt 16:13-17: *You are Christ, the Son of the living God.*
Mk 7:31-37: *Ephphatha, that is, Be opened* (when the Ephphatha Rite is celebrated at this time).
Jn 6:35, 63-71: *To whom shall we go? You have the words of eternal life.*

A brief Homily follows.

If the Ephphatha Rite is carried out at this time, the celebration continues with no. **199**. 197

Prayer for the Recitation of the Creed

195. The celebrant, with hands outstretched, says the following prayer: 198

Let us pray.

Grant, O Lord, to our elect,
who have accepted your loving plan
and the mysteries of the life of your Christ,
that they may profess them with their lips,
hold on to them with faith,
and accomplish your will in their works.
Through Christ our Lord.

All:
Amen.

Recitation of the Creed

196. The elect then recite the Creed. Depending on the version 199
that was entrusted to them at the Handing On of the Creed, they recite either the Apostles' Creed (option A) or the Niceno-Constantinopolitan Creed (option B).

A
Apostles' Creed

Elect:
I believe in God,
the Father almighty,
Creator of heaven and earth,
and in Jesus Christ, his only Son, our Lord,

At the words that follow, up to and including **the Virgin Mary,** all bow.

who was conceived by the Holy Spirit,
born of the Virgin Mary,
suffered under Pontius Pilate,
was crucified, died and was buried;
he descended into hell;
on the third day he rose again from the dead;
he ascended into heaven,
and is seated at the right hand of God the Father almighty;
from there he will come to judge the living and the dead.

I believe in the Holy Spirit,
the holy catholic Church,
the communion of saints,
the forgiveness of sins,
the resurrection of the body,
and life everlasting. Amen.

B
Niceno-Constantinopolitan Creed

Elect:
I believe in one God,
the Father almighty,
maker of heaven and earth,
of all things visible and invisible.

I believe in one Lord Jesus Christ,
the Only Begotten Son of God,
born of the Father before all ages.
God from God, Light from Light,
true God from true God,
begotten, not made, consubstantial with the Father;
through him all things were made.
For us men and for our salvation
he came down from heaven,

At the words that follow, up to and including **and became man**, all bow.

and by the Holy Spirit was incarnate of the Virgin Mary,
and became man.

For our sake he was crucified under Pontius Pilate,
he suffered death and was buried,
and rose again on the third day
in accordance with the Scriptures.
He ascended into heaven
and is seated at the right hand of the Father.
He will come again in glory
to judge the living and the dead
and his kingdom will have no end.

I believe in the Holy Spirit, the Lord, the giver of life,
who proceeds from the Father and the Son,
who with the Father and the Son is adored and glorified,
who has spoken through the prophets.

I believe in one, holy, catholic and apostolic Church.
I confess one Baptism for the forgiveness of sins
and I look forward to the resurrection of the dead
and the life of the world to come. Amen.

EPHPHATHA RITE

197. By the power of its symbolism the Ephphatha Rite impresses on the elect the need of grace in order to be able to hear the word of God and profess it for their salvation. 200

Reading

198. After a suitable chant, Mark 7:31-37 is read, and the celebrant explains it briefly. 201

Ephphatha Rite

199. A suitable song may be sung as the celebrant touches the right and left ear and the closed lips of each of the elect with his thumb and says the following formula: 202 USA

Ephphatha, that is, be opened,
that you may profess the faith you have heard,
to the praise and glory of God.

If, however, there are a great many elect, he should use the entire formula only for the first of the elect; for the rest the celebrant should say:

Ephphatha, that is, be opened.

If there are a great many elect, additional Priests or Deacons may assist in carrying out the rite.

CHOOSING OF A CHRISTIAN NAME

200. At the discretion of the Diocesan Bishop, a new name may now be chosen, unless a name was given in the celebration of the Rite for Entrance into the Catechumenate (cf. nos. **33.4** and **73**). It must be either a Christian name or a name of regional usage that is not incompatible with Christian beliefs. Where it seems better suited to the circumstances and the elect are not too numerous, it will be enough to explain to each of the elect the Christian meaning of the name received before from his (her) parents. 203

Reading

201. After an appropriate chant, if circumstances suggest, there is a reading, which the celebrant briefly explains, for example: 204

Gen 17:1-7: *Your name shall be Abraham.*
Is 62:1-5: *You shall be called by a new name.*
Rev 3:11-13: *I will write my new name upon him.*
Mt 16:13-18: *You are Peter.*
Jn 1:40-42: *You will be called Cephas.*

Choosing of a Name

202. If as baptismal names the elect have chosen new names, option A is used; if they are to use their given names, option B is used. 205

A

The celebrant asks each of the elect to state the new name chosen; then, if circumstances suggest, he says:

N., from now on you will be called N.

Elect:
Amen (or another suitable reply).

B

If the occasion should suggest, the celebrant explains the Christian significance of the name received before from his (her) parents.

CONCLUDING RITES

203. The Rites of Immediate Preparation may be concluded with a prayer of Blessing over the elect and a Dismissal. USA

Prayer of Blessing

204. The celebrant invites those present to pray: 122

Let us pray.

Then, with hands outstretched over the elect, the celebrant says the following prayer:

O God, who through your holy Prophets
commanded those who approach you,
"Wash and be clean,"
and who through Christ have established spiritual rebirth:
look now on these servants,
who are carefully preparing themselves for Baptism.
Bless them and, in faithfulness to your promises,
prepare and sanctify them,
so that they may be made fit to receive your gifts
and be found worthy of adoption as your children
and of fellowship in your Church.
Through Christ our Lord.

All:
Amen.

Dismissal

205. The Deacon or the celebrant may inform the elect of the time and place they are to meet for the Easter Vigil; he then dismisses them, using the following or another suitable formula: USA

May the Lord be with you
until we gather again to celebrate his Paschal Mystery.

Elect:
Amen.

THIRD STEP: CELEBRATION OF THE SACRAMENTS OF INITIATION

206. These Sacraments, namely Baptism, Confirmation, and the 27
Eucharist, are the final step by which the elect, proceeding with their sins forgiven, are incorporated into the People of God, receive the adoption of the children of God, and are led by the Holy Spirit into the promised fullness of time, and indeed into a foretaste of the Kingdom of God through the Eucharistic Sacrifice and Banquet.

207. Because the Initiation of adults is ordinarily celebrated on the 208
holy night of the Easter Vigil (cf. no. **23**), at which preferably the USA
Bishop himself presides as celebrant, at least for the Initiation of those who are fourteen years old or older (cf. no. **12**), these Sacraments are conferred after the Blessing of Water, as noted in the Order of the Easter Vigil, no. 48.

208. However, if it takes place outside the customary times (cf. 209
nos. **26–27**), the celebration should reflect a paschal character (cf. *Christian Initiation*, General Introduction, no. 6), using the Ritual Mass for the Conferral of Baptism that is provided in the Missal, and the readings from those given in the *Lectionary for Mass*, Christian Initiation Apart from the Easter Vigil (nos. 751–755).

Celebration of Baptism

209. The celebration of Baptism, which is brought as it were to its 28
high point in the washing with water with the invocation of the USA
Most Holy Trinity, is prepared by the Blessing of Water and the Profession of Faith, which are intimately connected with the rite of water. Following the baptismal washing, the effects received through this Sacrament are given expression in the Explanatory Rites: the Anointing with Chrism after Baptism (when Confirma-

tion does not immediately follow Baptism), the white garment, and the lighted candle.

210. Prayer over the Water – Moreover, by the Blessing of Water, 29
in which the unfolding of the Paschal Mystery and the choice of 210
water to make it sacramentally effective are recalled, and the Most Holy Trinity is now invoked for the first time, created water receives a religious meaning and the beginning of the mystery of God is made visible to all present. Even when the Sacraments of Initiation are celebrated outside the Paschal Solemnity, the Rite of Blessing of Water is to be included (cf. *Christian Initiation*, General Introduction, no. 21), by which the mystery of God's charity is brought to mind through the remembrance of the wondrous works of God from the very beginning of the world and the creation of the human race; and then, by invoking the Holy Spirit and proclaiming the Death and Resurrection of Christ, it reinforces the newness of the Lord's bath of regeneration, by which we share his Death and Resurrection and receive divine holiness.

211. Renunciation of Sin and Profession of Faith – By the Rites 30
of Renunciation and of the Profession of Faith, the same Paschal Mystery that has been commemorated over the water, and will subsequently be briefly professed by the celebrant in the words of Baptism, is proclaimed with active faith by those about to be baptized. For adults are not saved unless, coming forward by their own choice, they are willing to receive the gift of God with faith. The faith they receive in the Sacrament is not only that of the Church, but also their very own, and is expected to be active in them. When they are baptized, by no means do they receive the Sacrament merely passively; they willingly enter a covenant with Christ by renouncing errors so as to adhere to the true God.

The Renunciation of Satan and the Profession of Faith are a 211
single rite that gains its full force in the Baptism of adults. Since Baptism is the Sacrament of that faith by which the elect hold fast to God and at the same time receive new birth from him, individuals at this bath therefore fittingly make a statement, by which, as was prefigured in the first covenant with the Patriarchs, they now completely renounce sin and Satan in order to hold on for

ever to the promise of the Savior and the mystery of the Trinity. By this Profession, which they make in the presence of the celebrant and the community, they express the intention, which has matured during the Period of the Catechumenate, to enter the New Covenant with Christ. In this faith, which the Church has handed down with God's help, and which they have embraced, adults are baptized.

212. **Baptism** – Having confessed the Paschal Mystery of Christ 31
with living faith, they immediately come forward to receive that mystery expressed in the washing with water and, after they have professed the Most Holy Trinity, that same Trinity, invoked by the celebrant, brings it about that the elect are numbered among the children of adoption and are made members of the People of God.

213. For this reason the washing with water, which signifies mysti- 32
cal participation in the Death and Resurrection of Christ, by which those who believe in his name die to sins and rise again to eternal life, should be given full prominence in the celebration of Baptism. Thus, the choice between the rites of immersion and pouring should be made to suit each individual case, so that, among the variety of traditions and circumstances, it may be better understood that washing is not merely a rite of purification, but a Sacrament of union with Christ.

214. **Explanatory Rites** – The baptismal washing is followed by 33
rites that give expression to the effects of the Sacrament just re- USA
ceived. The Anointing with Chrism after Baptism signifies the royal priesthood of the baptized and their enrollment in the fellowship of God's people. The white garment is a symbol of their new dignity. The lighted candle sheds light on their vocation to walk as befits children of light.

Celebration of Confirmation of Adults

215. According to an ancient practice preserved in the Roman 34
Liturgy itself, an adult may not be baptized without receiving Confirmation immediately after Baptism, unless very serious rea-

sons stand in the way (cf. no. **14**). This linking indicates the unity of the Paschal Mystery, the connection between the mission of the Son and the outpouring of the Holy Spirit, and the unity of the Sacraments by means of which both of these divine Persons come together with the Father to those baptized.

216. Therefore after the complementary rites of Baptism, though 35
with the omission of the Anointing with Chrism after Baptism (no. **228**), Confirmation is conferred.

First Full Participation of the Neophytes in the Eucharist

217. Finally the celebration of the Eucharist takes place, during 36
which on this day for the first time the neophytes take part with full entitlement and reach the completion of their Initiation. For in it the same neophytes, having been raised to the dignity of the royal priesthood, take an active part in the Prayer of the Faithful and, insofar as possible, in the rite of bringing the offerings to the altar. They take part with the whole community in the sacrificial action and recite the Lord's Prayer, by which they manifest the spirit of adoption as God's children which they have received in Baptism. Then, receiving Communion in the Body given up and the Blood poured out, they confirm the gifts they have received and receive a foretaste of eternal gifts.

CELEBRATION OF BAPTISM

218. After the Homily the Baptismal Liturgy begins. The Priest RM
goes with the ministers to the baptismal font, if this can be seen by the faithful. Otherwise a vessel with water is placed in the sanctuary.

Presentation of Those to Be Baptized

219. Accordingly, one of the following procedures, options A, B, or C, is chosen for the presentation of those to be baptized. 213 RM USA

A

When Baptism Is Celebrated Immediately at the Baptismal Font

The Priest goes with the ministers to the baptismal font. The elect are called forward and presented by their godparents in front of the assembled Church. Those to be baptized and their godparents go to the font, which they stand around in such a way that they do not block the view of the faithful. The celebrant's Instruction (no. **220**) and the Litany (no. **221**) follow.

If, however, there are many to be baptized, they may approach while the Litany is being sung.

B

When Baptism Is Celebrated after a Procession to the Font

The elect are called forward and presented by their godparents in front of the assembled Church. The procession to the baptistery or to the font forms immediately. A minister with the paschal candle leads off (unless outside the Easter Vigil, it already rests at the baptismal font), and those to be baptized follow him with their godparents, then the ministers, the Deacon, and the Priest. During the procession, the Litany (no. **221**) is sung. When the procession has reached the font, those to be baptized and their godparents stand around the font in such a way that they do not block the view of the faithful. When the Litany is completed, the Priest gives the address (no. **220**).

If there are a great many to be baptized, they and their godparents simply take their place in the procession.

C

When Baptism Is Celebrated in the Sanctuary

The elect are called forward and presented by their godparents in front of the assembled Church. Those to be baptized and their godparents take their place before the celebrant in the sanctuary, in such a way that they do not block the view of the faithful. The celebrant's Instruction (no. **220**) and the Litany (no. **221**) follow.

If, however, there are many to be baptized, they may approach while the Litany is being sung.

Celebrant's Instruction

220. The celebrant, addressing those present, makes use of one of the following or a similar instruction: 213

A

Dear brothers and sisters,
let us beg the mercy of God the almighty Father,
for these servants of God N. and N.,
who are seeking holy Baptism.
May God bestow light and strength
on those whom he has called and led to this hour,
that they may hold fast to Christ with resolute spirit
and profess the faith of the Church.
May he also give them renewal by the Holy Spirit,
whom we will fervently invoke upon this water.

B RM

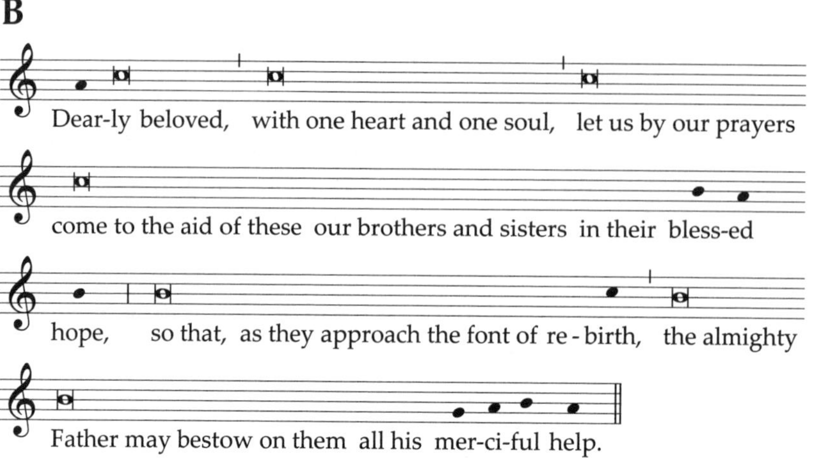
Dear-ly beloved, with one heart and one soul, let us by our prayers
come to the aid of these our brothers and sisters in their bless-ed
hope, so that, as they approach the font of re-birth, the almighty
Father may bestow on them all his mer-ci-ful help.

Dearly beloved,
with one heart and one soul, let us by our prayers
come to the aid of these our brothers and sisters in their
blessed hope,
so that, as they approach the font of rebirth,
the almighty Father may bestow on them
all his merciful help.

Litany

221. The Litany is sung by two cantors, with all standing (because it is Easter Time) and responding. In the Litany the names of some Saints may be added, especially the Titular Saint of the church and the Patron Saints of the place and of those to be baptized. 214 RM

℣. Lord, have mer-cy. ℟. Lord, have mer-cy.
℣. Christ, have mer-cy. ℟. Christ, have mer-cy.
℣. Lord, have mer-cy. ℟. Lord, have mer-cy.

Holy Mary, Mother of God, [ ] ℟. pray for us.
Saint Mich - ael,
Holy Angels of God, [ ]
Saint John the Bap - tist,
Saint Jo - seph,
Saint Peter and Saint Paul, [ ]
Saint An - drew,
Saint John, [ ]
Saint Mary Mag - da - lene,
Saint Ste - phen,
Saint Ignatius of An - ti - och,
Saint Law - rence,
Saint Perpetua and Saint Fe - li - ci - ty,
Saint Ag - nes,
Saint Gre - go - ry,
Saint Au - gus - tine,
Saint Atha - na - sius,
Saint Bas - il,
Saint Mar - tin,
Saint Ben - e - dict,
Saint Francis and Saint Dom - i - nic,
Saint Francis Xa - vi - er,
Saint John Vi - an - ney,
Saint Catherine of Si - e - na,
Saint Teresa of Je - sus,
All holy men
and women, Saints of God, [ ]

Lord, be mer-ci-ful, ℟. Lord, de-liv-er us, we pray.

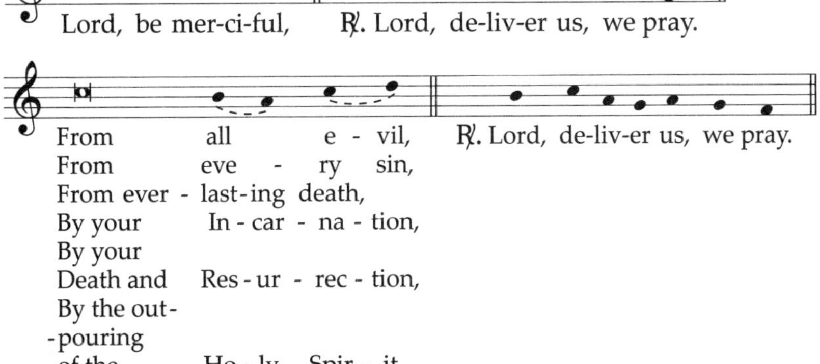
From all e - vil, ℟. Lord, de-liv-er us, we pray.
From eve - ry sin,
From ever - last-ing death,
By your In - car - na - tion,
By your
Death and Res - ur - rec - tion,
By the out-
-pouring
of the Ho - ly Spir - it,

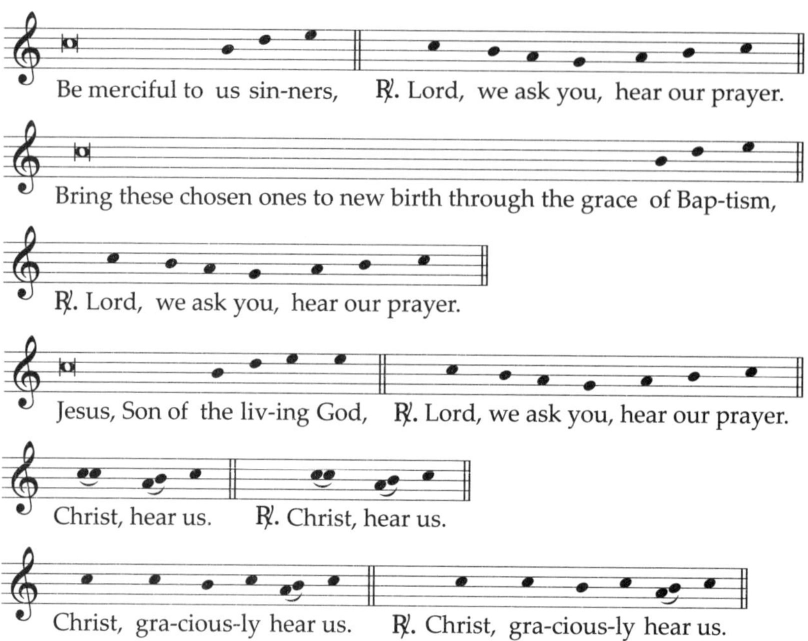
Be merciful to us sin-ners,
℟. Lord, we ask you, hear our prayer.
Bring these chosen ones to new birth through the grace of Bap-tism,
℟. Lord, we ask you, hear our prayer.
Jesus, Son of the liv-ing God,
℟. Lord, we ask you, hear our prayer.
Christ, hear us.
℟. Christ, hear us.
Christ, gra-cious-ly hear us.
℟. Christ, gra-cious-ly hear us.

Text without music:

Lord, have mercy.	Lord, have mercy.
Christ, have mercy.	Christ, have mercy.
Lord, have mercy.	Lord, have mercy.

Holy Mary, Mother of God,	pray for us.
Saint Michael,	pray for us.
Holy Angels of God,	pray for us.
Saint John the Baptist,	pray for us.
Saint Joseph,	pray for us.
Saint Peter and Saint Paul,	pray for us.
Saint Andrew,	pray for us.
Saint John,	pray for us.
Saint Mary Magdalene,	pray for us.
Saint Stephen,	pray for us.
Saint Ignatius of Antioch,	pray for us.
Saint Lawrence,	pray for us.

Saint Perpetua and Saint Felicity, pray for us.
Saint Agnes, pray for us.
Saint Gregory, pray for us.
Saint Augustine, pray for us.
Saint Athanasius, pray for us.
Saint Basil, pray for us.
Saint Martin, pray for us.
Saint Benedict, pray for us.
Saint Francis and Saint Dominic, pray for us.
Saint Francis Xavier, pray for us.
Saint John Vianney, pray for us.
Saint Catherine of Siena, pray for us.
Saint Teresa of Jesus, pray for us.
All holy men and women, Saints of God, pray for us.

Lord, be merciful, Lord, deliver us, we pray.
From all evil, Lord, deliver us, we pray.
From every sin, Lord, deliver us, we pray.
From everlasting death, Lord, deliver us, we pray.
By your Incarnation, Lord, deliver us, we pray.
By your Death and Resurrection, Lord, deliver us, we pray.
By the outpouring of the Holy Spirit, Lord, deliver us, we pray.

Be merciful to us sinners, Lord, we ask you, hear our prayer.

Bring these chosen ones to new birth through the grace of Baptism, Lord, we ask you, hear our prayer.

Jesus, Son of the living God, Lord, we ask you, hear our prayer.

Christ, hear us, Christ, hear us.
Christ, graciously hear us. Christ, graciously hear us.

The Priest, with hands extended, says the following prayer:

Almighty ever-living God,
be present by the mysteries of your great love
and send forth the spirit of adoption
to create the new peoples
brought to birth for you in the font of Baptism,
so that what is to be carried out by our humble service
may be brought to fulfillment by your mighty power.
Through Christ our Lord.

℟. Amen.

Blessing of Water

222. Next, the celebrant turns toward the font and says the Blessing given in option A with hands extended. 215

When Baptism is celebrated outside the Easter Vigil (cf. no. **26**), the celebrant may use any of the blessing formulas given in options A, B, and C.

During Easter Time (cf. no. **26**), however, if baptismal water blessed at the Easter Vigil is available, so that the Baptism may not lack an element of thanksgiving and petition, the Blessing and Invocation of God over the Water takes place in accordance with the formulas given in option D or option E. 216

A
215

Blessing of Water: The celebrant turns toward the font and says the following Blessing with hands extended. RM

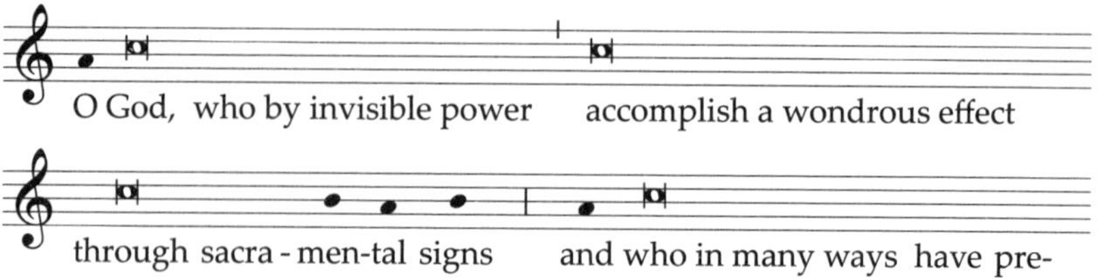
O God, who by invisible power accomplish a wondrous effect
through sacra - men-tal signs and who in many ways have pre-

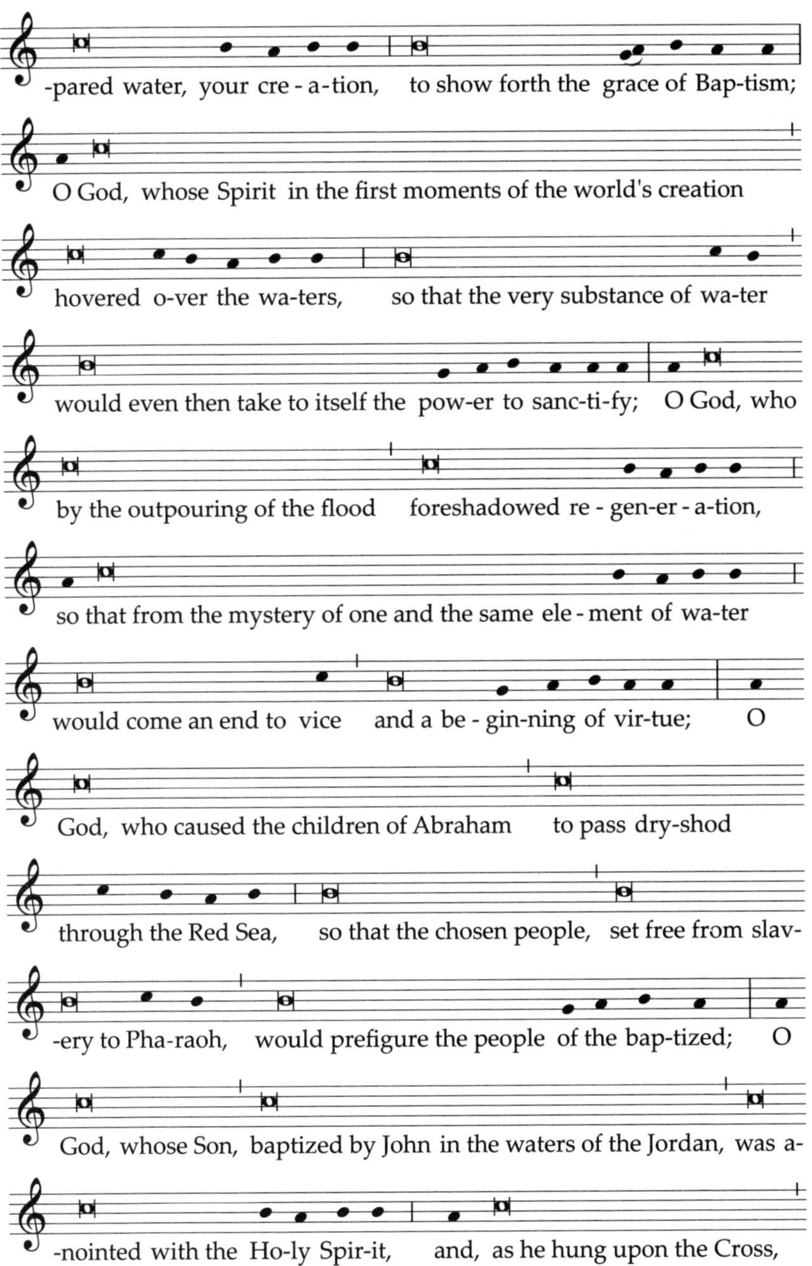
-pared water, your cre - a-tion, to show forth the grace of Bap-tism;
O God, whose Spirit in the first moments of the world's creation
hovered o-ver the wa-ters, so that the very substance of wa-ter
would even then take to itself the pow-er to sanc-ti-fy; O God, who
by the outpouring of the flood foreshadowed re - gen-er - a-tion,
so that from the mystery of one and the same ele - ment of wa-ter
would come an end to vice and a be - gin-ning of vir-tue; O
God, who caused the children of Abraham to pass dry-shod
through the Red Sea, so that the chosen people, set free from slav-
-ery to Pha-raoh, would prefigure the people of the bap-tized; O
God, whose Son, baptized by John in the waters of the Jordan, was a-
-nointed with the Ho-ly Spir-it, and, as he hung upon the Cross,

gave forth water from his side a-long with blood, and after his Res-
-urrection, commanded his dis-ci-ples: "Go forth, teach all na-tions,
baptizing them in the name of the Father and of the Son and of the
Ho-ly Spir-it," look now, we pray, upon the face of your Church
and graciously un-seal for her the foun-tain of Bap-tism. May
this water receive by the Holy Spirit the grace of your Only Be-
-got-ten Son, so that human nature, created in your im-age
and washed clean through the Sacrament of Baptism from all the
squalor of the life of old, may be found worthy to rise to the life of
new-born chil-dren through water and the Ho-ly Spir-it.

And, if appropriate, lowering the paschal candle into the water either once or three times, he continues:

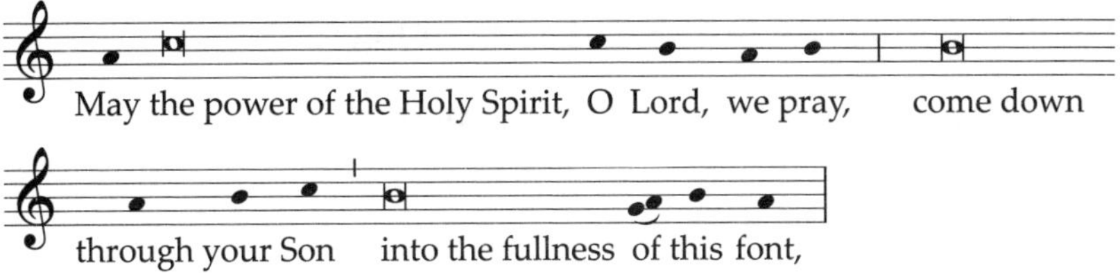
May the power of the Holy Spirit, O Lord, we pray, come down
through your Son into the fullness of this font,

and, holding the candle in the water, he continues:

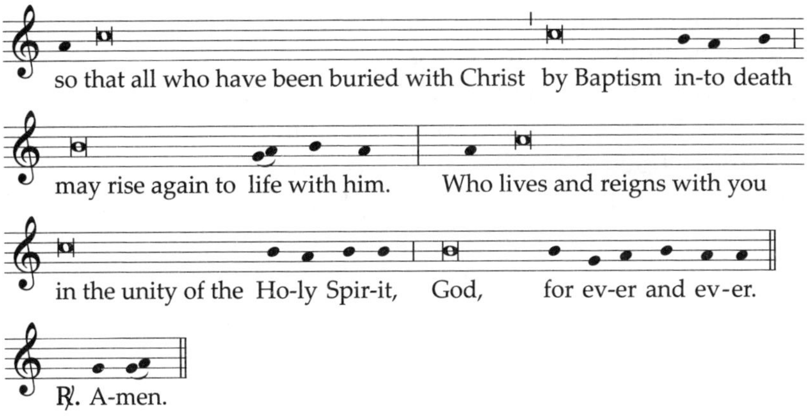
so that all who have been buried with Christ by Baptism in-to death
may rise again to life with him. Who lives and reigns with you
in the unity of the Ho-ly Spir-it, God, for ev-er and ev-er.
℟. A-men.

Text without music:

O God, who by invisible power
accomplish a wondrous effect
through sacramental signs
and who in many ways have prepared water, your creation,
to show forth the grace of Baptism;

O God, whose Spirit
in the first moments of the world's creation
hovered over the waters,
so that the very substance of water
would even then take to itself the power to sanctify;

O God, who by the outpouring of the flood
foreshadowed regeneration,
so that from the mystery of one and the same element of water
would come an end to vice and a beginning of virtue;

O God, who caused the children of Abraham
to pass dry-shod through the Red Sea,
so that the chosen people,
set free from slavery to Pharaoh,
would prefigure the people of the baptized;

O God, whose Son,
baptized by John in the waters of the Jordan,
was anointed with the Holy Spirit,
and, as he hung upon the Cross,
gave forth water from his side along with blood,
and after his Resurrection, commanded his disciples:
"Go forth, teach all nations, baptizing them
in the name of the Father and of the Son and of the Holy Spirit,"
look now, we pray, upon the face of your Church
and graciously unseal for her the fountain of Baptism.

May this water receive by the Holy Spirit
the grace of your Only Begotten Son,
so that human nature, created in your image
and washed clean through the Sacrament of Baptism
from all the squalor of the life of old,
may be found worthy to rise to the life of newborn children
through water and the Holy Spirit.

And if appropriate, lowering the paschal candle into the water either once or three times, he continues:

May the power of the Holy Spirit,
O Lord, we pray,
come down through your Son
into the fullness of this font,

and, holding the candle in the water, he continues:

so that all who have been buried with Christ
by Baptism into death
may rise again to life with him.
Who lives and reigns with you in the unity of the Holy Spirit,
God, for ever and ever.

℟. Amen.

Then the candle is lifted out of the water, as the people acclaim:

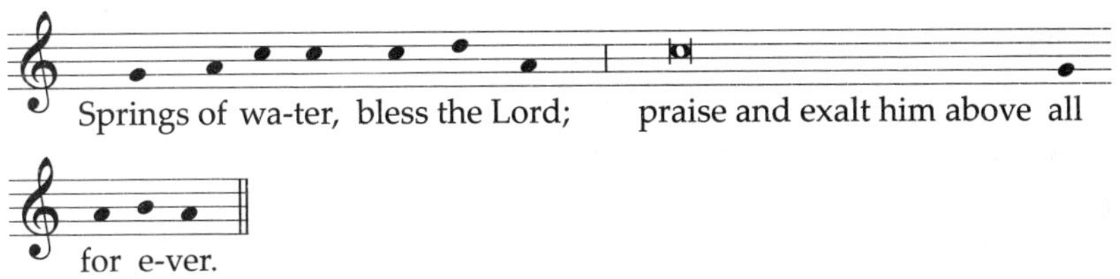
Springs of wa-ter, bless the Lord; praise and exalt him above all
for e-ver.

Springs of water, bless the Lord;
praise and exalt him above all for ever.

B 389.1

Blessing of Water: The celebrant turns toward the font and says the following Blessing with hands extended:

Blessed are you, God the almighty Father,
for you have created water to cleanse and give life.

All:
Blessed be God (or another suitable acclamation of the people).

Celebrant:
Blessed are you, God the Only Begotten Son, Jesus Christ,
for you poured forth water with blood from your side,
so that from your Death and Resurrection the Church might
be born.

All:
Blessed be God.

Celebrant:

Blessed are you, God the Holy Spirit,
for you anointed Christ at his baptism in the waters of the Jordan,
that we might all be baptized into you.

All:

Blessed be God.

Celebrant:

Draw near to us, Lord, the one Father,
and sanctify this water you have created,
that those baptized in it may be washed clean of sin
and be born again to the life of your adopted children.

All:

Hear us, O Lord (or another suitable invocation of the people).

Celebrant:

Sanctify this water you have created,
that those baptized through it
into Christ's Death and Resurrection
may be conformed to the image of your Son.

All:

Hear us, O Lord.

The celebrant touches the water with his right hand and continues:

Sanctify this water you have created,
that those you have chosen
may be born again by the Holy Spirit
and have a portion among your holy people.

All:

Hear us, O Lord.

C 389.2

Blessing of Water: The celebrant turns toward the font and says the following Blessing with hands extended:

Most merciful Father,
from the font of Baptism,
you have made the new life of your children
well up within us.

All:

Blessed be God (or another suitable acclamation of the people).

Celebrant:

You have been pleased to unite
by water and the Holy Spirit
all the baptized into one people in your Son Jesus Christ.

All:

Blessed be God.

Celebrant:

You free us by the Spirit of your love,
whom you pour into our hearts,
so that we may delight in your peace.

All:

Blessed be God.

Celebrant:

You choose the baptized,
that they may joyfully proclaim to all the nations
the Gospel of your Christ.

All:

Blessed be God.

Celebrant:

Be pleased now to bless ✠ this water,
by which your servants (N. and N.) are to be baptized,
for you have called them to this cleansing water of rebirth
in the faith of the Church,
that they may have eternal life.
Through Christ our Lord.

All:

Amen.

D 389.1

Easter Time Thanksgiving over Water Already Blessed: The celebrant turns toward the font containing the blessed water and says the following:

Blessed are you, God the almighty Father,
for you have created water to cleanse and give life.

All:

Blessed be God (or another suitable acclamation of the people).

Celebrant:

Blessed are you, God the Only Begotten Son,
Jesus Christ,
for you poured forth water with blood from your side,
so that from your Death and Resurrection the Church might
be born.

All:

Blessed be God.

Celebrant:

Blessed are you, God the Holy Spirit,
for you anointed Christ at his baptism in the waters of the Jordan,
that we might all be baptized into you.

All:

Blessed be God.

Celebrant:

By the mystery of this blessed water,
graciously lead to spiritual rebirth your servants (N. and N.),
whom you have called to this cleansing water,
that they may have eternal life.
Through Christ our Lord.

All:

Amen.

E

389.2

Easter Time Thanksgiving over Water Already Blessed: The celebrant turns toward the font containing the blessed water and says the following:

Most merciful Father,
from the font of Baptism,
you have made the new life of your children
well up within us.

All:

Blessed be God (or another suitable acclamation).

Celebrant:

You have been pleased to unite
by water and the Holy Spirit
all the baptized into one people in your Son Jesus Christ.

All:

Blessed be God.

Celebrant:

You free us by the Spirit of your love,
whom you pour into our hearts,
so that we may delight in your peace.

All:

Blessed be God.

Celebrant:

You choose the baptized,
that they may joyfully proclaim to all the nations
the Gospel of your Christ.

All:

Blessed be God.

Celebrant:

By the mystery of this blessed water,
graciously lead to spiritual rebirth your servants (N. and N.),
whom you have called to this cleansing water,
that they may have eternal life.
Through Christ our Lord.

All:

Amen.

Profession of Faith

223. After the consecration of the font (or prayer of thanksgiving), 217
the celebrant continues with the Profession of Faith, which in- USA
cludes the Renunciation of Sin and the Profession itself.

Renunciation of Sin

224. As circumstances suggest, the celebrant, informed by the godparents of the name of each person to be baptized, asks each of them, choosing any one of the three formulas below; or he may use the same formulas to question all of the elect together. 217 USA

At the discretion of the Diocesan Bishop, the formulas for the Renunciation of Sin may be made more specific and detailed as circumstances might require (cf. no. **33.8**).

A

Celebrant:

Do you renounce sin,
so as to live in the freedom of the children of God?

Elect:

I do.

Celebrant:

Do you renounce the lure of evil,
so that sin may have no mastery over you?

Elect:

I do.

Celebrant:

Do you renounce Satan,
the author and prince of sin?

Elect:

I do.

B

Celebrant:
Do you renounce Satan,
and all his works and empty promises?

Elect:
I do.

C

Celebrant:
Do you renounce Satan?

Elect:
I do.

Celebrant:
And all his works?

Elect:
I do.

Celebrant:
And all his empty show?

Elect:
I do.

Profession of Faith

225. Then the celebrant, informed again by the godparents of the name of each to be baptized, questions the elect individually. 219

When there are a great many to be baptized, the Profession of Faith may be made simultaneously either by all together or group by group.

Celebrant:

N., do you believe in God,
the Father almighty,
Creator of heaven and earth?

Elect:

I do.

Celebrant:

Do you believe in Jesus Christ, his only Son, our Lord,
who was born of the Virgin Mary,
suffered death and was buried,
rose again from the dead
and is seated at the right hand of the Father?

Elect:

I do.

Celebrant:

Do you believe in the Holy Spirit,
the holy catholic Church,
the communion of saints,
the forgiveness of sins,
the resurrection of the body,
and life everlasting?

Elect:

I do.

Rite of Baptism

226. After the Profession of Faith, each elect is immediately bap- 219
tized by immersion (option A) or by the pouring of water (option 220
B). After the Baptism of each adult, a brief acclamation (cf. Appendix II, nos. **595–597**) may be sung by the people.

When there are a great number of the elect to be baptized, if there 222
are several Priests or Deacons present, those to be baptized may be divided into groups among the individual ministers. In baptizing, either by immersion (option A) or by the pouring of water (option B) these ministers say the sacramental formula for each one. While the rite is taking place, singing by the people is desirable; it is also permitted to have readings or to observe sacred silence.

A 220

If Baptism is by immersion of the whole body or of the head only, decency and decorum should be observed. Either or both godparents touch the one to be baptized. Touching the elect, the celebrant immerses him (her) or his (her) head three times, raising the elect out of the water each time and baptizing him (her) by calling upon the Most Holy Trinity only once:

N., I baptize you in the name of the Father,

He immerses the elect the first time.

and of the Son,

He immerses the elect the second time.

and of the Holy Spirit.

He immerses the elect the third time.

B 221

If, however, Baptism is by the pouring of water, either or both godparents place the right hand on the right shoulder of the one to be baptized, and the celebrant, taking baptismal water and pouring it three times on the person's bowed head, baptizes him (her) in the name of the Most Holy Trinity:

N., I BAPTIZE YOU IN THE NAME OF THE FATHER,

He pours water the first time.

AND OF THE SON,

He pours water the second time.

AND OF THE HOLY SPIRIT.

He pours water the third time.

EXPLANATORY RITES

227. The Explanatory Rites (nos. **228–230**) are carried out immediately after Baptism. After these rites, Confirmation normally is celebrated, as described below (nos. **231–235**), in which case the Anointing after Baptism is omitted. 223

ANOINTING AFTER BAPTISM

228. If for some special reason, the celebration of Confirmation is separated from the Baptism (cf. no. **215**), then, after the immersion or the pouring of water, the celebrant administers the Anointing with Chrism in the usual way. If, however, there are a large number of newly baptized and several Priests or Deacons are present, each of them may anoint some of the newly baptized with Chrism. 224

The celebrant says the following over all the newly baptized:

Almighty God, the Father of our Lord Jesus Christ,
has given you new birth by water and the Holy Spirit,
granted you the remission of all sins,
and joined you to his people.
He now anoints you with the Chrism of salvation,
so that you may remain members of Christ,
Priest, Prophet and King,
unto eternal life.

The newly baptized:

Amen.

Then, in silence, the celebrant anoints each of the newly baptized with sacred Chrism on the crown of the head.

Clothing with a White Garment

229. The celebrant says the following formula. At the words **Receive, therefore, the white garment** the godparents place the white garment on the newly baptized, unless another color more suited to local custom should be required. If circumstances suggest, this rite can be omitted. 225

Celebrant:

N. and N., you have become a new creation
and have clothed yourselves in Christ.
Receive, therefore, the white garment
and bring it unstained
before the judgment seat of our Lord Jesus Christ,
that you may have eternal life.

The newly baptized:

Amen.

Handing On of a Lighted Candle

230. The celebrant then takes the paschal candle in his hands or touches it, saying: 226

Come forward, godfathers and godmothers,
that you may hand on the light to the newly baptized.

A godparent of each of the neophytes goes to the celebrant, lights a candle from the paschal candle, and presents it to the neophyte.

Then the celebrant says:
You have been made light in Christ.
Walk always as children of light,
that persevering in faith
you may run to meet the Lord when he comes
with all the Saints in the heavenly court.

The newly baptized:
Amen.

If the celebration of Confirmation is to be deferred, the renewal of baptismal promises, as in *The Roman Missal*, The Easter Vigil (no. 55), now takes place; then the neophytes are led back to their places among the faithful. USA

Outside the Easter Vigil if Confirmation is to be deferred, the neophytes are led back to their places among the faithful after the presentation of a lighted candle.

CELEBRATION OF CONFIRMATION

231. Unless the baptismal washing and the other Explanatory Rites have occurred in the sanctuary, a procession returns to the sanctuary, formed as before, with the newly baptized or the godparents or parents carrying lighted candles. During this procession, the baptismal canticle **Vidi aquam (I saw water)** or another appropriate chant is sung (*The Roman Missal*, The Easter Vigil, no. 56). RM

232. If the Bishop has conferred Baptism, he should now also administer Confirmation. If the Bishop is not present, Confirmation is to be given by the Priest who conferred Baptism (cf. *Code of Canon Law*, can. 866). 228

When those to be confirmed are too numerous, Priests who may be designated for this role can be associated to the minister of Confirmation to administer the Sacrament (cf. no. **14**).

Invitation

233. The celebrant briefly addresses the neophytes, in these or similar words: 229

Dear neophytes, you have been born again in Christ,
and have become members of Christ and of his priestly people.
Now you are to share
in the outpouring among us of the Holy Spirit,
who was sent by the Lord upon the Apostles at Pentecost
to be given by them and their successors to the baptized.

Therefore, you also are to receive the promised power of the
Holy Spirit,
so that, being more perfectly conformed to Christ,
you may bear witness to the Lord's Passion and Resurrection
and become an active member of the Church
for the building up of the Body of Christ in faith and charity.

Then the celebrant (while the Priests associated with him remain by his side) standing, facing the people, with hands joined, says:

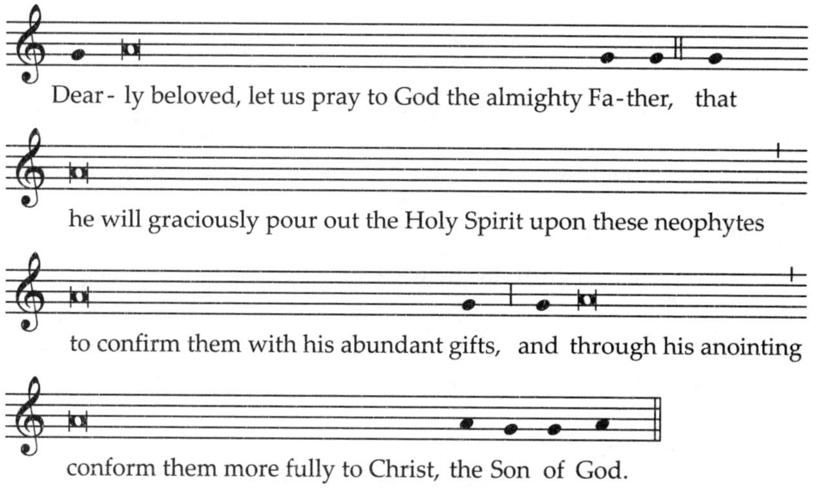
Dear- ly beloved, let us pray to God the almighty Fa-ther, that
he will graciously pour out the Holy Spirit upon these neophytes
to confirm them with his abundant gifts, and through his anointing
conform them more fully to Christ, the Son of God.

Dearly beloved,
let us pray to God the almighty Father,
that he will graciously pour out the Holy Spirit
upon these neophytes
to confirm them with his abundant gifts,
and through his anointing
conform them more fully to Christ, the Son of God.

And all pray in silence for a while.

The Laying On of Hands

234. Then the celebrant lays hands over all those to be confirmed (as do the Priests who are associated with him). But the celebrant alone says: 230

Al-mighty God, Father of our Lord Je-sus Christ, who brought these
your servants to new birth by water and the Holy Spirit, freeing
them from sin: send upon them, O Lord, the Holy Spir-it, the
Par-a-clete; give them the spirit of wisdom and understanding,
the spirit of coun-sel and for-ti-tude, the spirit of knowl-edge and
pi-e-ty; fill them with the spirit of the fear of the Lord.
Through Christ our Lord. ℟. A-men.

Almighty God, Father of our Lord Jesus Christ,
who brought these your servants to new birth
by water and the Holy Spirit,
freeing them from sin:
send upon them, O Lord, the Holy Spirit, the Paraclete;
give them the spirit of wisdom and understanding,
the spirit of counsel and fortitude,

the spirit of knowledge and piety;
fill them with the spirit of the fear of the Lord.
Through Christ our Lord.

All:
Amen.

The Anointing with Chrism

235. The sacred Chrism is brought by a minister to the celebrant. 231

If other Priests are associated with the celebrant in conferring the Sacrament, the vessels of sacred Chrism are given to them by the Bishop, if he is present.

Each of those to be confirmed goes to the celebrant (or to the Priests); or, if appropriate, the celebrant (and the Priests) goes to each of those to be confirmed. In addition, the godparent places his (her) right hand on the shoulder of the one to be confirmed and says his (her) name to the celebrant; or the one to be confirmed alone says his (her) own name. During the anointing a suitable chant may be sung.

The celebrant dips the tip of the thumb of his right hand in the Chrism and, with the thumb, makes the Sign of the Cross on the forehead of the one to be confirmed, as he says:

N., BE SEALED WITH THE GIFT OF THE HOLY SPIRIT.

The newly confirmed:
Amen.

The celebrant adds:
Peace be with you.

The newly confirmed:
And with your spirit.

236. At the Easter Vigil the renewal of baptismal promises by the congregation follows the celebration of Confirmation (nos. **237–240** below; *The Roman Missal*, The Easter Vigil, no. 55). Then the neophytes are led to their places among the faithful. RM

Outside the Easter Vigil, the neophytes are led to their places among the faithful immediately after Confirmation. The Universal Prayer (Prayer of the Faithful) then begins (cf. no. **241**).

RENEWAL OF BAPTISMAL PROMISES (at the Easter Vigil)

Invitation

237. When the Rite of Baptism (and Confirmation) has been completed all stand, holding lighted candles in their hands, and renew the promise of baptismal faith, unless this has already been done together with those to be baptized (cf. *The Roman Missal*, The Easter Vigil, no. 49). The Priest addresses the faithful in these or similar words: RM

Dear brethren (brothers and sisters), through the Paschal Mystery
we have been buried with Christ in Baptism,
so that we may walk with him in newness of life.
And so, now that our Lenten observance is concluded,
let us renew the promises of Holy Baptism,
by which we once renounced Satan and his works
and promised to serve God in the holy catholic Church.
And so I ask you:

Renunciation of Sin

238. The celebrant continues with one of the following formulas of renunciation. RM

If the situation warrants, formula A may be adapted by the Conference of Bishops according to local needs.

A

Celebrant:
Do you renounce sin,
so as to live in the freedom of the children of God?

All: I do.

Celebrant:
Do you renounce the lure of evil,
so that sin may have no mastery over you?

All: I do.

Celebrant:
Do you renounce Satan,
the author and prince of sin?

All: I do.

B

Celebrant:
Do you renounce Satan?

All: I do.

Celebrant:
And all his works?

All: I do.

Celebrant:
And all his empty show?

All: I do.

Profession of Faith

239. Then the celebrant continues: RM
Do you believe in God,
the Father almighty,
Creator of heaven and earth?

All: I do.

Celebrant:
Do you believe in Jesus Christ, his only Son, our Lord,
who was born of the Virgin Mary,
suffered death and was buried,
rose again from the dead
and is seated at the right hand of the Father?

All: I do.

Celebrant:
Do you believe in the Holy Spirit,
the holy catholic Church,
the communion of saints,
the forgiveness of sins,
the resurrection of the body,
and life everlasting?

All: I do.

And the celebrant concludes:
And may almighty God, the Father of our Lord Jesus Christ,
who has given us new birth by water and the Holy Spirit
and bestowed on us forgiveness of our sins,

keep us by his grace,
in Christ Jesus our Lord,
for eternal life.

All: Amen.

Sprinkling with Baptismal Water

240. The celebrant sprinkles the people with the blessed water, while all sing the following or another chant that is baptismal in character: RM

I saw water flowing from the Temple,
from its right-hand side, alleluia;
and all to whom this water came were saved
and shall say: Alleluia, alleluia. *(Cf. Ezekiel 47:1-2, 9)*

CELEBRATION OF THE EUCHARIST

241. The Creed is omitted, and the Universal Prayer (Prayer of the Faithful), which the neophytes take part in for the first time, immediately takes place. When the offerings are carried to the altar, some of the neophytes may bring them forward. 232

242. In Eucharistic Prayer I, mention of the neophytes is made in the proper form of the **Hanc igitur (Therefore, Lord, we pray)**, at the Easter Vigil from *The Roman Missal*, Order of Mass, no. 87, and outside the Easter Vigil from the Ritual Mass for the Conferral of Baptism. At the Easter Vigil and outside the Easter Vigil, in Eucharistic Prayer I, mention of the godparents is made in the section **Memento, Domine (Remember, Lord, your servants)** from the Ritual Mass for the Conferral of Baptism. If Eucharistic Prayer II, III, or IV is used, the proper formula for the neophytes is used from the Ritual Mass for the Conferral of Baptism. 233

243. It is desirable that the neophytes receive Holy Communion 234
under both kinds, together with their godfathers, godmothers, RM
and Catholic parents and spouses, as well as their lay catechists. It is even appropriate that, with the consent of the Diocesan Bishop, where the occasion suggests this, all the faithful be admitted to Holy Communion under both kinds.

Before Communion, that is, before **Ecce Agnus Dei** (**Behold the Lamb of God**), the celebrant may briefly remind the neophytes of the preeminence of so great a Sacrament, which is the climax of their Initiation and the center of the whole Christian life. He may do so in these or other words:

Dear neophytes, USA
(on this most sacred night)
you have been reborn by water and the Holy Spirit,
and will receive, for the first time,
the Bread of life and the Chalice of salvation.

May the Body and Blood of Christ the Lord
help you all to grow deeper in his friendship
and in communion with the entire Church;
may it be your constant food for the journey of life
and a foretaste of the eternal banquet of heaven.

Behold the Lamb of God . . .

PERIOD OF MYSTAGOGY

244. After this last step is complete, the community together with 37
the neophytes, by meditation on the Gospel, by participation in the Eucharist, and by the exercise of charity, makes progress in understanding the Paschal Mystery more deeply and carrying it over more and more into the practice of daily life. This is the final period of Initiation for the neophytes, that is, the Period of "Mystagogy."

245. A genuinely fuller and more fruitful understanding of the 38
"mysteries" is acquired by the newness of the explanation and especially by the experience of the Sacraments they have received. For neophytes have been renewed in mind, have intimately tasted the good word of God, have shared communion in the Holy Spirit, and have come to realize how sweet the Lord is. From this experience, proper to a Christian and enhanced by day-to-day living, they draw forth a new understanding of the faith, the Church, and the world.

246. This new participation in the Sacraments, just as it enlightens 39
understanding of the Sacred Scriptures, at the same time so in- 235
creases a person's knowledge of others and enriches the experience of the community that the relationship between the neophytes and the rest of the faithful becomes easier and more practical. Therefore the Period of Mystagogy is of great importance in enabling the neophytes, assisted by their godparents, to form closer relationships with the faithful and to communicate to them a new view of things as well as new enthusiasm. To strengthen their first steps, it is desirable that, in all circumstances, neophytes receive thoughtful and friendly help from the community of the faithful, their godparents, and their pastors. The greatest care should be taken that they receive a full and joyful inclusion into the community.

247. Since the character and value of this period should arise from 40
this new personal experience both of the Sacraments and of the

community, the principal place for "Mystagogy" is the so-called "Masses for the neophytes" or Masses of the Sundays of Easter Time because at them, in addition to the gathered community and their participation in the mysteries, the neophytes find, especially in Year A of the Lectionary, readings particularly suited to them. For that reason, the entire local community should be invited to those Masses together with the neophytes and their godparents, and the texts they contain can be used also when Initiation is celebrated outside the normal times.

248. Throughout Easter Time at Sunday Masses neophytes should 236
be allowed their own special places among the faithful. All the neophytes should make an effort to participate in these Masses with their godparents. The Homily and, as circumstances suggest, also the Universal Prayer (Prayer of the Faithful) should take account of them.

249. To close the Period of Mystagogy at the end of Easter Time, 237
some sort of celebration should be held near Pentecost Sunday, even with additional festivities according to the customs of the region.

250. On the anniversary of Baptism it is desirable for the neophytes 238
to be gathered again to give thanks to God, to share their spiritual experience, and to renew their fervor.

251. To begin pastoral contact with the new members of his 239
Church, the Bishop, particularly if he was not able to preside at the Sacraments of Initiation, should see to it that at least once a year, insofar as it can be done, he meets the recently baptized neophytes and presides for a celebration of the Eucharist at which they may receive Communion under both kinds.

PART II

RITES FOR PARTICULAR CIRCUMSTANCES

CHAPTER II

ORDER OF INITIATION OF CHILDREN WHO HAVE REACHED CATECHETICAL AGE

252. This rite is intended for children who have not been baptized at the time of infancy and have reached the age of discretion and catechesis. They come to Christian Initiation, brought by either parents or guardians, or moved on their own initiative with the permission of these same people. Those who grasp and nourish their own faith and are moved by their own conscience, are already suitable. Nevertheless, they cannot yet be treated as adults because, as children, they depend on parents or guardians and are extremely susceptible to the influence of companions as well as society. 306

253. Their Initiation requires not only personal conversion of a maturity suitable to their age, but also the help of education necessary at that age. From that point it must be adapted also to the spiritual journey of the children, namely their increase in faith and the catechetical instruction that they receive. As with adults, therefore, their Initiation is also extended over some years, if necessary, before they may approach the Sacraments. Their Initiation is marked by various steps and periods and organized by rites: the Rite for Entrance into the Catechumenate (nos. **260–276**), the optional Rite of Election (nos. **277–290**), the Scrutinies or Penitential Rites (nos. **291–303**) and the Celebration of the Sacraments of Initiation (nos. **304–329**); corresponding to the periods of adult Initiation are the periods of children's catechetical formation that lead up to and follow the steps of their Initiation. 307 USA

254. Since, however, the progress of the children depends on the formation they receive, as much by the help and example of companions as by parents, both should be considered. 308

a) For, since the children being initiated usually belong to some group of already baptized companions who are preparing with catechesis for Confirmation and the Eucharist, the Initiation in progress is shared and supported within this catechetical group as if upon a foundation.

b) Still, it is desired that the same children, insofar as possible, likewise find help and example from their parents, whose permission is required for their Initiation, and also to lead their future Christian life. Therefore the time of Initiation will fittingly offer the family an opportunity to speak with Priests and catechists.

255. According to the circumstances, it is useful for several children in the same situation to join together at the same time in the celebrations of this Order, so that they may help one another by mutual example on the journey of the catechumenate. 309

256. As to the time of the celebrations, it is desired that, insofar as 310
possible, the final period of preparation, begun by the second step, USA
the Penitential Rites (or by the optional Rite of Election), coincide with Lent, and the Sacraments themselves be celebrated at the Easter Vigil (cf. no. **8**). But before children may be admitted to the Sacraments at the Paschal Feasts, it must be discerned not only whether they are now ready, but also whether the period conforms to the order of catechetical instruction that they are taking. Insofar as possible, care should be taken that the children approach the Sacraments of Initiation while their companions who have already been baptized are admitted to Confirmation or the Eucharist.

257. Celebrations should take place with the active participation of some of the congregation, which, comprising a fitting number of the faithful, is made up of parents and family, and also of companions of the catechetical group and some adult relatives. For usually when children of this age are initiated, the presence of the whole parish community is not desirable; it is enough that it be represented. 311

258. The Conferences of Bishops may accept fitting adaptations 312
and amendments to this Order as it has been prepared, by which USA
it may respond more fully to the needs and circumstances of the region, and to pastoral opportunities. The United States Conference of Catholic Bishops has done this by providing an optional "Rite of Election" before "Second Step: Scrutinies or Penitential Rites." The Rites of "Handing On," in use for adults (cf. nos. **157–162, 178–183**), may be added, adapted to the age of the children. So when this Order is translated into vernacular languages, care must be taken that the invitations and intercessions and prayers be accommodated to the understanding of children. If appropriate, e.g., when some prayer of the Roman Ritual is translated into the local language, another prayer that offers the same thoughts more suitable for children may also be approved by the Conference of Bishops (cf. *Christian Initiation*, General Introduction, no. 32).

259. Ministers employing this rite should freely and wisely use 313
the options that are given to them in *Christian Initiation*, General Introduction (nos. 34–35) and in the special Introductions to the *Order of Baptism of Children* (no. 31) and of the *Order of Christian Initiation of Adults* (no. **35**).

FIRST STEP: RITE FOR ENTRANCE INTO THE CATECHUMENATE

260. First of all, this rite should be celebrated in the presence of a 314
small though active congregation, lest the children be distracted by USA
a large assembly (cf. no. **257**). Parents or guardians of the children, as far as possible, should be present. But if they are unable to come, they indicate the assent they have given to the children; and in their place "sponsors" may be present (cf. no. **10**), namely suitable faithful who, in this case, take the place of parents and present the children. The presiding celebrant is a Priest or Deacon.

261. The celebration takes place in church or in a place favorable 315
to the experience of a warm welcome, according to the age and 329
understanding of the children. The first part, or the introductory rite, may take place, depending on circumstances, at the entrance to the church or another place; the second part, or the Liturgy of the Word, in the church itself or in a place chosen for it.

The celebration is not normally combined with celebration of the Eucharist.

RITE OF RECEPTION

262. The celebrant, wearing liturgical vestments, comes to the 316
place where the children, their parents or guardians or, even, as the circumstances warrant, their sponsors are gathered.

PRELIMINARY INSTRUCTION

263. Then, together with the congregation of those present he greets them simply and warmly. The celebrant then speaks to the children and their parents, expressing the joy and happiness of the Church. Next he invites the children and their parents or sponsors, if they are present, to come forward and stand before him. 316 317

DIALOGUE

264. The celebrant then questions each child using the questions and answers given below. It is permissible for the celebrant to use other words that will allow the children to give such answers as: 318

I want to do the will of God;
I want to follow the word of God;
I want to be baptized;
I want faith;
I want to be (become) a friend of Jesus;
I want to enter (join) the Christian family.

If, however, the number of children is too numerous, the celebrant may question all of them together, draw out answers from some of them, and then ask the others if they agree.

Celebrant:
N., what do you want to become?

Child:
A Christian.

Celebrant:
Why do you want to become a Christian?

Child:
Because I believe in Christ.

Celebrant:
What does faith in Christ offer you?

Child:
Eternal life.

The celebrant concludes the dialogue with a brief instruction, adapted to the circumstances and age of the children, and may use these or similar words. As circumstances suggest, the children may repeat these last words of Christ, to show their consent. 319

Since you already believe in Christ
and want to be prepared for Baptism,
we welcome you with great joy into the Christian family,
where you will come to know Christ better day by day.
With us you will try to live as children of God,
for Christ has taught us:
You shall love God with all your heart;
love one another as I have loved you.

Dialogue with the Parents and the Congregation

265. Then the celebrant, addressing the children again, asks them if they have asked for the consent of their parents or sponsors who presented them. He may do so in this or a similar way: 320

N. and N.,
go and ask your parents (sponsors)
to come here and stand with you
to give their consent.

The children go to their parents or sponsors and they bring them before the celebrant, who continues:

Dear parents (sponsors),
your children, N. and N., have asked to be prepared for
Baptism.
Do you consent to their request?

Parents or sponsors:
We do.

Celebrant:
Are you willing to play your part
in their preparation for Baptism?

Parents or sponsors:
We are.

Then the celebrant questions all present in these or similar words: 321

These children are setting out today on a journey.
They will need the support of our faith and love.
Are you, their friends and companions,
ready to help them along the road to Baptism?

All:
We are.

Signing

266. Next the Cross is traced on the forehead of each child or, at 322
the discretion of the Diocesan Bishop, in front of the forehead (cf. 323
nos. **33.3**, **54**); the signing of the other parts of the body may be USA
added. The celebrant alone says the words and does the signing.

Signing of the Forehead

267. Then the celebrant turns toward the children and says: 322

N. and N., Christ has called you to be his friends.
Always remember him and be faithful to him.

That is why I sign you with the sign of Christ's Cross.
It is the sign of Christians.

From now on, let this sign remind you of Christ and his love.

The celebrant passes along in front of them, and in silence makes the Sign of the Cross on the forehead of each child.

As circumstances suggest, he invites the parents and godparents to make the Sign of the Cross on the forehead of the children in silence:

Parents and catechists (N. and N.),
since you belong to Christ,
I ask you also to sign the children with the sign of Christ.

As circumstances suggest, the signing may be concluded with the singing of an acclamation praising Christ, for example: USA

Glory and praise to you, Lord Jesus Christ!

Signing of the Other Senses

268. If it seems appropriate, especially if the children are a little older, the signing of the other parts of the body may be added. The celebrant alone says the words and does the signing. As circumstances suggest, however, the same signing of the senses may also be done by their parents (or even their sponsors) or by their catechists, as the celebrant alone says the formula in the plural over all the children at once. As circumstances suggest, the signings each time they are made may be concluded with the singing of an acclamation praising Christ, for example: **Glory and praise to you, Lord Jesus Christ!** 323

The celebrant says, while he signs the ears:

I (we) sign your ears with the sign of the Cross:
that you may hear the words of Christ.

While he signs the eyes:

I (we) sign your eyes with the sign of the Cross:
that you may see the works of Christ.

While he signs the mouth:

I (we) sign your lips with the sign of the Cross:
that you may speak as Christ speaks.

While he signs the chest:

I (we) sign your chest with the sign of the Cross:
that you may receive Christ into your heart by faith.

While he signs the shoulders:

I (we) sign your shoulders with the sign of the Cross:
that you may have the strength of Christ.

[While he signs the hands: USA

I (we) mark your hands with the sign of the cross,
that you may touch others with the gentleness of Christ.

While he signs the feet:

I (we) mark your feet with the sign of the cross,
that you may walk in the way of Christ.]

While he signs the entire body:

I (we) sign you totally with the sign of Christ's Cross
in the name of the Father, and of the Son, ✠ and of the
Holy Spirit:
that you may live with Jesus now and for ever.

Child:

Amen.

Introduction into the Church

269. After the signing, the celebrant invites the catechumens to enter the church in these or similar words: 324

Now you can take your place in the Christian assembly.
Come and listen to the Lord, who speaks to us,
and join us in praying to him.

Once these words of invitation have been heard, the children enter and take places either with their parents (their sponsors) or with the baptized companions of their catechetical group (cf. no. **254.1**), so that it is clear that they now are a part of the congregation.

Meanwhile, during the entrance, Psalm 95 (94) or Psalm 122 (121) or another suitable chant is sung.

Psalm 95 (94)

1 Come, let us ring out our joy to the Lord;
hail the rock who saves us.
2 Let us come into his presence, giving thanks;
let us hail him with a song of praise.

3 A mighty God is the Lord,
a great king above all gods.
4 In his hand are the depths of the earth;
the heights of the mountains are his.
5 To him belongs the sea, for he made it,
and the dry land that he shaped by his hand.

6 O come; let us bow and bend low.
Let us kneel before the Lord who made us,
7 for he is our God, and we the people,
the people of his pasture, the flock of his hand.

O that today you would listen to his voice!
8 "Harden not your hearts as at Meribah,
as on that day at Massah in the desert
9 when your forebears put me to the test;
when they tried me, though they saw my work.

10 For forty years I abhorred that generation,
and I said, 'Their heart goes astray;
this people does not know my ways.'
11 Then I took an oath in my anger,
'Never shall they enter my rest.' "

Psalm 122 (121)

1 I rejoiced when they said to me,
"Let us go to the house of the LORD."
2 And now our feet are standing
within your gates, O Jerusalem.

3 Jerusalem is built as a city
bonded as one together.
4 It is there that the tribes go up,
the tribes of the LORD,
as it is decreed for Israel,
to give thanks to the name of the LORD.

5 There were set the thrones for judgment,
the thrones of the house of David.
6 For the peace of Jerusalem pray,
"May they prosper, those who love you."
7 May peace abide in your walls,
and security be in your towers.

8 For the sake of my family and friends,
let me say, "Peace upon you."
9 For the sake of the house of the LORD, our God,
I will seek good things for you.

LITURGY OF THE WORD

Instruction

270. After the children have reached their places, a book of the Sacred Scriptures is carried in procession and set in a place of honor. The celebrant may explain briefly the dignity of God's word, which is proclaimed and heard in the Christian congregation. 325

A brief Liturgy of the Word immediately follows.

Readings

271. Scripture readings are chosen that can be adapted to the 326
understanding of the children and to their progress in the cate- USA
chetical formation they and their companions have received. Such readings may be chosen from those given below or those given in the *Lectionary for Mass*, nos. 751–755 (Ritual Masses: Christian Initiation Apart from the Easter Vigil), or elsewhere in the Lectionary; the following texts may also be used:

First Reading

Gen 12:1-4a: *Go forth from the land of your kinsfolk to a land that I will show you.*

Responsorial Psalm

Ps 33 (32):4-5, 12-13, 18-19, 20 and 22

℟. (12b) Blessed the people the Lord has chosen as his heritage.

Or:

℟. (22) May your merciful love be upon us, as we hope in you, O Lord.

Verse before the Gospel

Jn 1:41, 17b
We have found the Messiah: Jesus Christ,
through whom came truth and grace.

Gospel

Jn 1:35-42: *Behold, the Lamb of God. We have found the Messiah.*

Or also:

Other Readings

Ez 36:25-28: *A new heart and a return to the land given to your fathers.*
Eph 4:1-6a: *The calling to be followed: one faith, one Baptism.*
Gal 5:13-17, 22-23a, 24-25: *One commandment and one Spirit.*

Mk 12:28c-31: *The first commandment.*
Lk 8:4-9, 11-15: *The parable of the sower.*
Lk 19:1-10: *Zacchaeus.*
Jn 6:44-47: *No one can come to me unless the Father draw him.*
Jn 13:34-35: *A new commandment.*
Jn 15:9-11 or: 12-17: *Love one another.*

Homily

272. The celebrant then gives a brief Homily in explanation of the readings. 326

A period of silence is recommended, in which all the children are invited to pray in their hearts. 327

A suitable chant follows.

Presentation of the Gospels

273. As circumstances suggest, during or immediately after the singing, a book containing the Gospels may be presented to the children. They should be prepared for this presentation either beforehand in the Homily or by a brief explanation at this moment. 328

INTERCESSIONS

274. Then, the following Intercessions are offered, in these or similar words. 329

Celebrant:

Let us pray for these beloved children,
who are your sons and daughters,
your companions and friends,
and who are now making their way to God.

Lector:

That day by day
you may increase their desire to live with Jesus:

℟. Lord, hear our prayer.

Lector:

That by their life in the Church
they may find happiness:

℟. Lord, hear our prayer.

Lector:

That you may give them strength and perseverance
in preparing for Baptism:

℟. Lord, hear our prayer.

Lector:

That you may lovingly keep from them
the temptations of fear and discouragement:

℟. Lord, hear our prayer.

Lector:

That you may grant them the happiness
of receiving Baptism, Confirmation, and the Eucharist:

℟. Lord, hear our prayer.

Prayer over the Children

275. The celebrant concludes with the following prayer: 329

O Lord, who have inspired in these children
the desire to become fully Christian,
grant that they may persevere on their journey to you
and know that their prayers and our petitions are heard.
Through Christ our Lord.

All:
Amen.

Dismissal

276. The celebration concludes with a liturgical song. 329

But, if the Eucharist is to be celebrated (cf. no. **261**), the catechumens are dismissed beforehand. USA

Celebrant:
Go in peace,
and may the Lord remain with you.

All:
Thanks be to God.

RITE OF ELECTION OR ENROLLMENT OF NAMES (Optional)

USA

277. The optional liturgical rite called both "Election" and "Enrollment of Names" may be celebrated with children of catechetical age, especially those whose catechumenate has extended over a long period of time. This celebration, which usually coincides with the beginning of Lent, marks the beginning of the period of final preparation for the Sacraments of Initiation, during which the children will be encouraged to follow Christ with greater generosity.

278. In the Rite of Election, on the basis of the testimony of parents, godparents and catechists, and of the children's reaffirmation of their intention, the Church judges their state of readiness and decides on their advancement toward the Sacraments of Initiation. Thus the Church makes her "Election," that is, the choice and admission of those children who have the dispositions that make them fit to take part, at the next major celebration, in the Sacraments of Initiation.

279. The Rite should take place in the cathedral church, in a parish church or, if necessary, in some other suitable and fitting place. If the Election of children of catechetical age is to take place within a celebration in which older catechumens are also to receive the Church's Election, the rite for adults (nos. **129–137**) should be used, with appropriate adaptation of the texts to be made by the celebrant.

280. It should be celebrated within the Mass of the First Sunday of Lent, after the Homily. If the Rite happens to be celebrated on another day, it begins with the Liturgy of the Word. In this case, if the readings for the day are not suitable, they should be chosen from those assigned to the First Sunday of Lent (cf. *Lectionary for Mass*, nos. 22–24), or other suitable texts. The proper Ritual Mass for the Election or Enrollment of Names may be celebrated with the color violet on any day except those listed in nos. 1–4 of the

Table of Liturgical Days. The Mass of the Friday of the Fourth Week of Lent may also be used. If, however, the Eucharist is not celebrated, the Rite is concluded with the Dismissal of both the elect and the faithful.

LITURGY OF THE WORD

Homily

281. The Bishop, or the celebrant who acts as a delegate of the Bishop, gives the Homily. This should be brief and suitable to the understanding of the children. The entire community should be encouraged to give good example to the children and to show their support and interest in them as they prepare to celebrate the Paschal Sacraments.

Presentation of the Children

282. After the Homily, the Priest responsible for the Initiation of the children, or a Deacon, a catechist, or a representative of the community, presents the catechumens for Election, in these or similar words:

(Most) Reverend Father,
these children, whom I now present to you,
are completing their preparation for Christian Initiation.
God's love has strengthened them,
and our community has supported them with prayer and good
example.

As Easter approaches, they ask to be admitted
to the Sacraments of Baptism, Confirmation, and the Eucharist.

The celebrant replies:
My dear children who are to be chosen in Christ,
come forward now with your parents and godparents.

One by one, the children are called by name. Each catechumen, accompanied by some or all of his (her) parents and godparents, comes forward and stands before the celebrant.

If there are a large number of children, all are presented together, for example, each group by its own catechist. But in this case, the catechists should be advised to call each child forward by name in a special celebration held before they come to the common rite.

Affirmation by the Parents and Godparents (and the Assembly)

283. Then the celebrant addresses the assembly in these or similar words:

Dear parents and godparents (and members of this assembly),
these children have asked to be initiated
into the sacramental life of the Church this Easter.
In the name of God's holy Church,
I invite you to give your recommendation on their behalf.

He addresses the parents, godparents (and assembly):
Have these children shown themselves to be sincere
in their desire for Baptism, Confirmation, and the Eucharist?

Parents, godparents (and assembly):
They have.

Celebrant:
Have they listened to the word of God?

Parents, godparents (and assembly):
They have.

Celebrant:

Have they tried to live as his faithful followers?

Parents, godparents (and assembly):

They have.

Celebrant:

Have they taken part in this community's life of prayer and service?

Parents, godparents (and assembly):

They have.

Questioning and Petitioning of the Catechumens

284. Next, the celebrant, looking at the catechumens, addresses and questions them in these or similar words:

My dear children, your parents and godparents (and this entire community)
have spoken in your favor.
The Church in the name of Christ accepts their word
and calls you to the Paschal Sacraments.

Now you must let the whole Church know
that you have heard Christ calling you
and that you want to follow him.

Therefore, do you wish to enter fully into the life of the Church
through the Sacraments of Baptism, Confirmation, and the Eucharist?

Children:

We do.

Celebrant:

Then offer your names for enrollment.

The children give their names, either going with their godparents to the celebrant or while remaining in place, and the actual inscription of the names may be carried out in various ways. The children may inscribe their names themselves or they may call out their names, which are inscribed by the godparents or by the one who presented the children (cf. no. **282**). As the Enrollment is taking place, a suitable chant, for example, Psalm 16 (15) may be sung.

If, however, there are a large number of catechumens a list of names may be given to the celebrant, with these or similar words: **These are the names of those seeking Initiation**, or, when the Bishop is celebrant and catechumens from several parishes have been presented to him: **These are the names of the catechumens from the parish of** N. **seeking Initiation**.

Psalm 16 (15)

1 Preserve me, O God, for in you I take refuge.
2 I say to the LORD, "You are my Lord.
You, you alone are my good."

3 As for the holy ones who dwell in the land,
they are noble, and in them is all my delight.
4 Those who choose other gods increase their sorrows.
I will not take part in their offerings of blood.
Nor will I take their names upon my lips.

5 O LORD, it is you who are my portion and cup;
you yourself who secure my lot.
6 Pleasant places are marked out for me:
a pleasing heritage indeed is mine!

7 I will bless the LORD who gives me counsel,
who even at night directs my heart.
8 I keep the LORD before me always;
with him at my right hand, I shall not be moved.

9 And so, my heart rejoices, my soul is glad;
even my flesh shall rest in hope.
10 For you will not abandon my soul to Sheol,
nor let your holy one see corruption.

11 You will show me the path of life,
the fullness of joy in your presence,
at your right hand, bliss forever.

Reception or Election

285. At the conclusion of the Enrollment of Names, the celebrant, after he has briefly explained the meaning of the rite that has taken place, turns toward the catechumens, addressing them in these or similar words:

My dear children, I am happy to declare you among the elect of God.
You have been chosen to be initiated at Easter
through the Sacraments of Baptism, Confirmation, and the Eucharist.

Children:
Thanks be to God.

The celebrant continues:
God is always faithful to those he calls.
On your part, you must strive to know, love and serve the Lord more and more with each passing day.
Continue to rely upon your godparents, parents and catechists for the help you will need to be faithful to the way of Jesus.

Then, turning toward the parents, godparents, and the entire assembly, the celebrant addresses them in these or similar words:

Dear friends, you have spoken in favor of these young people.
Accept them as chosen in the Lord.

Encourage them to live the way of the Gospel.
Offer them the support of your love and concern.
Above all, be a good model to them of Christian living
so that by your example they may grow deeper in the faith of the Church.

And he invites the parents and godparents to place their hand on the shoulder of the elect whom they are receiving into their care, or to make some other gesture to indicate the same intent.

Recognition of the Godparent(s)

286. The celebrant may speak briefly of the new relationship which will exist between the parents and godparents of the elect. He may conclude by extending his hands over the parents and godparents while praying in these or similar words:

May the Lord God Almighty bring joy to your hearts
as the hope of eternal life shines forth upon these elect.
By word and example, prove to be steadfast witnesses of the faith.
May these children grow as active members of God's people.
And may you be a constant support to each other in Christ Jesus our Lord.

Parent(s) and godparent(s):
Amen.

Intercessions for the Elect

287. Then, the community prays for the elect. The celebrant may adapt the introduction and the intentions to fit various circumstances. Moreover, the usual intentions for the Church and the whole world should be added if the elect are to be dismissed after the Intercessions and the Universal Prayer (Prayer of the Faithful) is omitted during Mass (cf. no. **290**).

Celebrant:

My brothers and sisters,
as we begin this Lenten season,
we look forward to the Initiation of these children at Easter
into the mystery of Christ's Passion, Death, and Resurrection.
Let us pray that this Lent will be for them, and for all of us,
a time of genuine Christian renewal.

Lector:

That together we may grow this Lent
in our love for God and neighbor,
let us pray to the Lord:

℟. Lord, hear our prayer.

Lector:

That these elect may be freed from selfishness
and learn to put others first,
let us pray to the Lord:

℟. Lord, hear our prayer.

Lector:

That their parents, godparents, and catechists
may be living examples of the Gospel to inspire these children,
let us pray to the Lord:

℟. Lord, hear our prayer.

Lector:

That their teachers may always convey to them
the beauty of God's word,
let us pray to the Lord:

℟. Lord, hear our prayer.

Lector:

That these children may share with others
the joy they have found in their friendship with Jesus,
let us pray to the Lord:

℟. Lord, hear our prayer.

Lector:
That together with the adults who have been elected,
these children may learn to love the Church
and proudly profess what they believe,
let us pray to the Lord:

℟. Lord, hear our prayer.

Lector:
That our community, during this Lenten period,
may grow in charity and be constant in prayer,
let us pray to the Lord:

℟. Lord, hear our prayer.

Prayer over the Elect

288. The celebrant, extending his hands over the elect, concludes the Intercessions with one of the following prayers:

A

Lord God,
you created us
and you give us life.
Bless these children
and add them to your family.
May they be joyful in the life you won for us.
Through Christ our Lord.

℟. Amen.

B

Father of love and power,
it is your will to establish everything in Christ
and to draw us into his all-embracing love.
Guide the elect of your Church:

strengthen them in their vocation,
build them into the kingdom of your Son,
and seal them with the Spirit of your promise.
Through Christ our Lord.

℟. Amen.

Dismissal of the Elect

289. If the Eucharist is to be celebrated, the elect are normally dismissed at this point by use of option A or B; if the elect are to stay for the celebration of the Eucharist, option C is used; if the Eucharist is not to be celebrated, the entire assembly is dismissed by use of option D.

A

The Deacon or the celebrant dismisses the elect with this or a similar instruction:

My dear children, elect of God,
you have entered with us on the Lenten journey.
Christ will be for you the way, the truth, and the life.
Until we gather again, go in peace.

Elect:

Amen.

The elect go out.

B

As an optional formula for dismissing the elect, the Deacon or the celebrant may use these or similar words:

My dear children, go now. Think about God's word and know that we are with you and will pray for you. We look forward to the day when you will join us at the Lord's table.

C

If, however, for serious reasons the elect do not leave (cf. no. **75.3**) and must remain with the faithful, they are to be instructed that though they are present at the celebration of Eucharist, they cannot take part as the baptized do. They may be reminded of this by the Deacon or the celebrant in these or similar words:

Although you cannot join us at the Lord's table, stay with us as a sign of our hope that all God's children will eat and drink with the Lord and work with his Holy Spirit to make a new earth.

D

If, however, the Eucharist is not celebrated, a suitable chant, as circumstances suggest, may be added, and the faithful and the elect may be dismissed together using these or similar words:

Go in peace,
and may the Lord remain with you.

All:
Thanks be to God.

CELEBRATION OF THE EUCHARIST

290. After the dismissal, the Eucharist is celebrated. The Universal Prayer (Prayer of the Faithful) for the needs of the Church and the whole world begins immediately. Then, if required, the Creed is said, and the Preparation of the Gifts follows. But for pastoral reasons the Universal Prayer (Prayer of the Faithful) and the Creed may be omitted.

SECOND STEP: SCRUTINIES OR PENITENTIAL RITES

291. These Penitential Rites, which are among the distinctive moments of the catechumenate for children, belong to the category of Scrutinies, which occur in the Order of Initiation of adults (nos. **138–177**). Therefore, since they aim for the same goal, it is permitted to apply and adapt the norms that are set forth for the Scrutinies (nos. **141–146**). 330

292. Since the Scrutinies normally belong to the final period of preparation for Baptism, the Penitential Rites require that the children's faith and spiritual understanding already approach what is needed for Baptism. 331

293. These Rites, in which their godparents and companions of the catechetical group participate together with the catechumens, are adapted to all those present, so that the penitential celebrations may also assist those who are not catechumens. Indeed during this celebration some children who are already baptized and enrolled in the catechetical group may be admitted to the Sacrament of Penance for the first time. In this case, care should be taken that timely introductions, prayer intentions, and actions that pertain to such children be inserted into the celebration. 332

294. Penitential Rites are celebrated during Lent if catechumens are to be initiated at the Paschal Solemnities; if not, then at a more appropriate time. At least one rite is to be held. If it can be done conveniently, however, a second may be added. Its formulas will be composed in a similar way to the first; for the Intercessions and Prayer of Exorcism, however, the texts shown in nos. **153–154**, **167–168**, **174–175** are used, appropriately adapted. 333

INTRODUCTION OF THE RITE

295. The celebrant welcomes those who have gathered and in a few words explains the meaning of the Rite for each group taking part in it, namely: the children who are catechumens, the children who are already baptized, particularly those who will celebrate the Sacrament of Penance for the first time, the parents and friends, catechists and Priests, etc. All these participants will hear for themselves the blessed message of the forgiveness of sins and will praise the mercy of God the Father. 334

A suitable song expressing joy and faith in the mercy of God the Father may be sung.

296. The celebrant concludes with this prayer: 335

A

Let us pray.

Gentle and merciful God,
who are revealed in pardoning
and who delight in making holy,
graciously wipe away the stain of sin
from us who are penitent
and restore our hearts to life.
Through Christ our Lord.

℟. Amen.

B

Let us pray.

Grant to us, O Lord, the gifts of pardon and peace,
that we may be cleansed from our sins
and serve you with untroubled hearts.
Through Christ our Lord.

℟. Amen.

LITURGY OF THE WORD

Readings and Homily

297. One or several readings may be read from those in the following list. If there are two or several readings, Responsorial Psalms from the Ritual Mass for Christian Initiation Apart from the Easter Vigil (*Lectionary for Mass*, no. 753) or other chants are used between them. 336

Readings

Ez 36:25-28: *A new heart and a new spirit.*
Is 1:16-18: *The cleansing of sins.*
Mk 1:1-5, 14-15: *Repent and believe the Gospel.*
Mk 2:1-12: *The healing of the paralytic.*
Lk 15:1-7: *The Parable of the lost sheep.*
1 Jn 1:8–2:2: *Jesus Christ our Savior.*

The readings ordinarily assigned to the Scrutinies for adults may also be used:

Jn 4:1-14: *The Samaritan woman.*
Jn 9:1, 6-9, 13-17, 34-39: *The man born blind.*
Jn 11:3-7, 17, 20-27, 33b-45: *The raising of Lazarus.*

Responsorial Psalms

Ps 23 (22):1b-3a, 4, 5, 6
℟. (1) The Lord is my shepherd; there is nothing I shall want.

Ps 27 (26):1bcde, 4, 8b-9, 13-14
℟. (1a) The Lord is my light and my salvation.

Ps 32 (31):1bc-2, 5, 11
℟. (1a) Blessed are those whose transgression is forgiven.

Ps 89 (88):3-4, 16-17, 21-22, 25, 27
℟. (2a) I will sing forever of your mercies, O Lord.

Homily

298. After the readings the celebrant explains the sacred texts in a short Homily. 336

During the Homily or immediately after it, the celebrant, by words of encouragement and by pausing for periods of silent reflection, prepares the entire congregation for repentance and conversion of heart. 337

If, however, there are baptized children, enrolled in the catechetical class, the celebrant turns to them and invites them to show by some external sign their faith in Christ the Savior and sorrow for their sins.

Intercessions

299. After a brief period of silence, so that all may be led to heartfelt contrition, the celebrant invites the congregation to pray. According to the circumstances, it is permissible to adapt the celebrant's instruction and the intentions by using the formulas in nos. **153, 167, 174**, with the necessary changes. 338

Celebrant:

Let us pray for N. and N.,
who are preparing for the Sacraments of Christian Initiation,
for N. and N.,
who are to receive God's forgiveness
in the Sacrament of Penance for the first time,
and for ourselves, who await the mercy of Christ.

Lector:

That we may open our hearts to the Lord Jesus
with gratitude and faith,
let us pray to the Lord:

℟. Lord, hear our prayer.

Lector:
That we may sincerely seek
to be aware of our weaknesses and sins,
let us pray to the Lord:

℟. Lord, hear our prayer.

Lector:
That, in the spirit of God's children,
we may openly admit our frailty and faults,
let us pray to the Lord:

℟. Lord, hear our prayer.

Lector:
That in the presence of Christ Jesus
we may pour out our sorrow for our sins,
let us pray to the Lord:

℟. Lord, hear our prayer.

Lector:
That we may be delivered from present evils
and mercifully protected from evils to come,
let us pray to the Lord:

℟. Lord, hear our prayer.

Lector:
That we may learn from our heavenly Father
through his divine love
to triumph over all human sins,
let us pray to the Lord:

℟. Lord, hear our prayer.

Exorcism

300. Then the celebrant, with hands extended over the children, prays one of the following: 339

A

Let us pray.

Father of mercies,
who handed over your beloved Son
to confer the freedom of sons and daughters
on humanity held captive by sin,
look with mercy on these your servants,
who have already known temptation
and recognized their faults,
and be mindful of their hope.
Grant that they may be led from darkness into your
unfailing light,
be cleansed of their sins
and, rejoicing in peace,
be kept unharmed on their journey through life.
Through Christ our Lord.

All:

Amen.

B 392

The celebrant, inviting the children to pray to God with him, says:

Most merciful Father,
look upon N. and N.,
who are soon to be baptized.

Children:

We have heard the words of Jesus
and we love them.

Celebrant:

They are really trying to live as your children,
but they find it difficult.

Children:

Yes, heavenly Father,
we want always to do what pleases you,
but sometimes we find it hard.

Celebrant:

Most merciful Father,
free these young people
from the spirit of laziness and wrongdoing
and help them always walk in your light.

Children:

We want to walk with Jesus,
who gave his life for us.
Help us, heavenly Father.

Celebrant:

If they stumble on the way
by doing what does not please you,
take care of them and give them your strength,
so that they can get up
and once again continue their journey to you
with our Lord Jesus Christ.

Children:

Heavenly Father, give us your strength.

Anointing with the Oil of Catechumens or Laying On of the Hand

301. The rite continues with the Anointing with the Oil of Catechumens (option A). But for pastoral reasons, for example if the children have been anointed already, a laying on of the hand may be used (option B). 340 USA

A
Anointing with the Oil of Catechumens

If the oil is to be blessed by the Priest, the Priest blesses it, saying this prayer (for the chant, cf. no. **102**): USA

O God, strength and protection of your people, 131
who have made the oil you created a sign of strength,
graciously bless ✠ this oil,
and grant courage to the catechumens
who will be anointed with it,
so that, receiving divine wisdom and power,
they may understand more deeply
the Gospel of your Christ,
they may undertake with a generous heart
the labors of the Christian life,
and, made worthy of adoption
as your sons and daughters,
they may rejoice to be born anew and to live in your Church.
Through Christ our Lord.

℟. Amen.

The celebrant continues saying: 340

132

May the strength of Christ the Savior protect you.
As a sign of this we anoint you with the oil of salvation
in the same Christ our Lord,
who lives and reigns for ever and ever.

Children:

Amen.

Each child is anointed with the Oil of Catechumens on the breast or on both hands or even on other parts of the body, if this seems desirable.

If there are a large number of catechumens, it is permissible to use several ministers.

The anointing may be followed by a Blessing of the catechumens (no. **97**).

B 340

Laying On of the Hand

The celebrant faces the children and says:

May the strength of Christ the Savior protect you;
who lives and reigns for ever and ever.

Children:

Amen.

Then, in silence, the celebrant immediately places his hand on each catechumen.

Dismissal of the Catechumens

302. The Deacon or the celebrant immediately dismisses the catechumens using option A or similar words, or else sends them back to their places, if they are not to leave the church, using option B: 341

A

N. and N., in our presence
the Lord Jesus has extended his mercy to you.
Go now in peace.

Children:
Thanks be to God.

B

N. and N., in our presence
the Lord Jesus has extended his mercy to you.
Return to your places now and continue with us in prayer.

Children:
Thanks be to God.

LITURGY OF PENANCE

303. Next, the liturgy of the Sacrament of Penance begins for baptized children. After the celebrant's instruction, individual confession, first of those who will celebrate the Sacrament of Penance for the first time, then of the others in the assembly, follows. 342

After a suitable chant or a prayer of thanksgiving all then leave.

THIRD STEP: CELEBRATION OF THE SACRAMENTS OF INITIATION

304. To show the paschal character of Baptism, it is suggested that 343
this Sacrament be celebrated at the Easter Vigil or on a Sunday, when the Church commemorates the Resurrection of the Lord (cf. *Order of Baptism of Children*, Introduction, no. 9), taking into account the points set forth in no. **256**.

305. Baptism is celebrated during the Mass in which the neophytes 344
first take part in the Eucharist. Confirmation is conferred at the same time either by the Bishop or by the Priest who administers Baptism.

306. If Baptism is celebrated apart from the Easter Vigil or Easter 345
Sunday, either the Mass of the day or the Ritual Mass for the Conferral of Baptism is used. Readings are chosen among those given in the *Lectionary for Mass*, "Christian Initiation Apart from the Easter Vigil" (nos. 751–755); it is also permitted to use readings of the Sunday or feast.

307. A godparent accompanies each catechumen, chosen by the 346
child and approved by the Priest (cf. no. **11**; *Christian Initiation*, General Introduction, no. 10).

308. Baptized Catholic children of the catechetical group may be USA
completing their Christian Initiation in the Sacraments of Confirmation and the Eucharist at this same celebration. When the Bishop himself will not be the celebrant, he should grant the faculty to confirm such children to the Priest who will be the celebrant.[1] For their Confirmation, previously baptized children of the catechetical group are to have their own sponsors. If possible,

[1] Cf. *Order of Confirmation*, Introduction, no. 7b.

these should be the persons who were godparents for their Baptism, but other qualified persons may be chosen.[2]

LITURGY OF THE WORD

309. When the children who are catechumens, their parents 347
(guardians), godparents, companions in the catechetical group and friends, and members of the parish are gathered, Mass begins, and the Liturgy of the Word takes place with the readings indicated in no. **306**.

The Homily then follows the readings.

CELEBRATION OF BAPTISM

Celebrant's Instruction

310. After the Homily, the catechumens, with the parents and 348
godparents, go to the font, if this is in view of the faithful. Other- USA
wise they gather in the sanctuary where a vessel of water should be prepared beforehand. The celebrant addresses the family, companions, and all the faithful, using this or a similar instruction:

Dear brothers and sisters,
let us humbly call upon the grace of almighty God,
that N. and N.,
who with the approval of their parents
are asking to be baptized,
may be numbered among the children of adoption in Christ.

[2] Cf. *ibidem*, nos. 5 and 6.

Blessing of Water

311. Next, the celebrant turns toward the font and says the Blessing given in option A with hands extended. 349 USA

When Baptism is celebrated outside the Easter Vigil (cf. no. **26**), the celebrant may use option A or the other blessing formulas given in no. **222** as options B and C.

During Easter Time (cf. no. **26**), however, if baptismal water 350
blessed at the Easter Vigil is available, so that the Baptism may not lack an element of thanksgiving and petition, the Blessing and Invocation of God over the Water takes place in accordance with option B below; he may also use the second Easter Time thanksgiving formula given in no. **222** as option E.

A 349

Blessing of Water: The celebrant turns toward the font and says the following Blessing with hands extended (for the chant, cf. no. **222**):

O God, who by invisible power
accomplish a wondrous effect
through sacramental signs
and who in many ways have prepared water, your creation,
to show forth the grace of Baptism;

O God, whose Spirit
in the first moments of the world's creation
hovered over the waters,
so that the very substance of water
would even then take to itself the power to sanctify;

O God, who by the outpouring of the flood
foreshadowed regeneration,
so that from the mystery of one and the same element of water
would come an end to vice and a beginning of virtue;

O God, who caused the children of Abraham
to pass dry-shod through the Red Sea,
so that the chosen people,
set free from slavery to Pharaoh,
would prefigure the people of the baptized;

O God, whose Son,
baptized by John in the waters of the Jordan,
was anointed with the Holy Spirit,
and, as he hung upon the Cross,
gave forth water from his side along with blood,
and after his Resurrection, commanded his disciples:
"Go forth, teach all nations, baptizing them
in the name of the Father and of the Son and of the Holy Spirit,"
look now, we pray, upon the face of your Church
and graciously unseal for her the fountain of Baptism.

May this water receive by the Holy Spirit
the grace of your Only Begotten Son,
so that human nature, created in your image
and washed clean through the Sacrament of Baptism
from all the squalor of the life of old,
may be found worthy to rise to the life of newborn children
through water and the Holy Spirit.

The celebrant touches the water with his right hand and continues:

May the power of the Holy Spirit,
O Lord, we pray,
come down through your Son
into the fullness of this font,
so that all who have been buried with Christ
by Baptism into death
may rise again to life with him.
Who lives and reigns with you in the unity of the Holy Spirit,
God, for ever and ever.

℟. Amen.

The people sing the following or some other suitable acclamation (for the chant, cf. no. **222**): RM

Springs of water, bless the Lord;
praise and exalt him above all for ever.

B

389.2

Easter Time Thanksgiving over Water Already Blessed: The celebrant turns toward the font containing the blessed water and says the following:

Blessed are you, God the almighty Father,
for you have created water to cleanse and give life.

All:

Blessed be God (or another suitable acclamation of the people).

Celebrant:

Blessed are you, God the Only Begotten Son, Jesus Christ,
for you poured forth water with blood from your side,
so that from your Death and Resurrection the Church might be born.

All:

Blessed be God.

Celebrant:

Blessed are you, God the Holy Spirit,
for you anointed Christ at his baptism in the waters of the Jordan,
that we might all be baptized into you.

All:

Blessed be God.

Celebrant:
By the mystery of this blessed water,
graciously lead to spiritual rebirth your servants (N. and N.),
whom you have called to this cleansing water,
that they may have eternal life.
Through Christ our Lord.

All:
Amen.

Profession of Faith

Profession of Faith of the Community

312. Then, before the children's Renunciation of Sin and Profession of Faith, the celebrant may, according to the circumstances, invite the parents, godparents, and all present to profess their faith: 351

After long preparation,
N. and N. are now to be baptized,
and, with new life received from God in his goodness,
they will become Christians.

From now on, we will need to help them more than ever.
This is especially true of you, their parents,
who have given permission for them to be baptized
and who have the primary responsibility for their upbringing.
We, who have prepared them to meet Christ
as he comes to them today,
will also offer them our help.

And so,
before these children make the profession of faith in our presence,
let us in their presence
and in accordance with our conscience
renew the profession of our faith,
which is the faith of the Church.

Then together with the celebrant all recite the Profession of Faith, using either the Apostle's Creed (option A) or the Niceno-Constantinopolitan Creed (option B).

A 351

Apostles' Creed

Then all together with the celebrant say:

I believe in God,
the Father almighty,
Creator of heaven and earth,
and in Jesus Christ, his only Son, our Lord,

At the words that follow, up to and including **the Virgin Mary,** all bow.

who was conceived by the Holy Spirit,
born of the Virgin Mary,
suffered under Pontius Pilate,
was crucified, died and was buried;
he descended into hell;
on the third day he rose again from the dead;
he ascended into heaven,
and is seated at the right hand of God the Father almighty;
from there he will come to judge the living and the dead.

I believe in the Holy Spirit,
the holy catholic Church,
the communion of saints,
the forgiveness of sins,
the resurrection of the body,
and life everlasting. Amen.

B 351

Niceno-Constantinopolitan Creed 186

Then all together with the celebrant say:

I believe in one God,
the Father almighty,
maker of heaven and earth,
of all things visible and invisible.

I believe in one Lord Jesus Christ,
the Only Begotten Son of God,
born of the Father before all ages.
God from God, Light from Light,
true God from true God,
begotten, not made, consubstantial with the Father;
through him all things were made.
For us men and for our salvation
he came down from heaven,

At the words that follow, up to and including **and became man**, all bow.

and by the Holy Spirit was incarnate of the Virgin Mary,
and became man.

For our sake he was crucified under Pontius Pilate,
he suffered death and was buried,
and rose again on the third day
in accordance with the Scriptures.
He ascended into heaven
and is seated at the right hand of the Father.
He will come again in glory
to judge the living and the dead
and his kingdom will have no end.

I believe in the Holy Spirit, the Lord, the giver of life,
who proceeds from the Father and the Son,
who with the Father and the Son is adored and glorified,
who has spoken through the prophets.

I believe in one, holy, catholic and apostolic Church.
I confess one Baptism for the forgiveness of sins
and I look forward to the resurrection of the dead
and the life of the world to come. Amen.

Profession of Faith of the Children Who Are Catechumens

313. The celebrant turns toward the children who are catechumens 352
and briefly addresses them, in these or similar words: USA

Children (N. and N.), you have asked to be baptized
and you have spent a long time in preparation.

Your parents have agreed to your wish;
your catechists, companions, and friends have helped you;
and today they all promise you
the example of their faith and their devoted support.

Before you may be baptized, reject Satan
and in the presence of the Church profess your faith.

Renunciation of Sin

314. The celebrant questions all the catechumens together using 353
one of the following formulas.

A

Celebrant:
Do you renounce Satan,
and all his works and empty promises?

Children:
I do.

B

Celebrant:
Do you renounce sin,
so as to live in the freedom of the children of God?

Children:
I do.

Celebrant:
Do you renounce the lure of evil,
so that sin may have no mastery over you?

Children:
I do.

Celebrant:
Do you renounce Satan,
the author and prince of sin?

Children:
I do.

315. The Anointing with the Oil of Catechumens is to be omitted, 354
as decreed by the United States Conference of Catholic Bishops USA
(cf. no. **33.7**).

Profession of Faith

316. The celebrant, informed by the godparents of the name of each child, asks each child individually to make the Profession of Faith, then immediately baptizes the child by immersion or by pouring of water. 355

Celebrant:

N., do you believe in God,
the Father almighty,
Creator of heaven and earth?

Child:

I do.

Celebrant:

Do you believe in Jesus Christ, his only Son, our Lord,
who was born of the Virgin Mary,
suffered death and was buried,
rose again from the dead
and is seated at the right hand of the Father?

Child:

I do.

Celebrant:

Do you believe in the Holy Spirit,
the holy catholic Church,
the communion of saints,
the forgiveness of sins,
the resurrection of the body,
and life everlasting?

Child:

I do.

If there are a great many children to be baptized, the Profession of Faith may be made simultaneously either by all together or group by group. The Baptism of each child follows. USA

Rite of Baptism

317. The celebrant baptizes each child either by immersion (option A) or by the pouring of water (option B). Each Baptism may be followed by a short acclamation (cf. Appendix II, nos. **595–597**), sung or said by the people. 356

When there are a great number of children to be baptized, if there are several Priests or Deacons present, those to be baptized may be divided into groups among the individual ministers. In baptizing, either by immersion (option A) or by the pouring of water (option B), these ministers say the sacramental formula for each child. While the rite is taking place, singing by the people is desirable; it is also permitted to have readings or to observe sacred silence. 222

A 356

If Baptism is by immersion of the whole body or of the head only, decency and decorum should be observed. Either or both godparents touch the one to be baptized. Touching the child, the celebrant immerses him (her) or his (her) head three times, raising him (her) out of the water each time and baptizing him (her) by calling upon the Most Holy Trinity only once: 220

N., I BAPTIZE YOU IN THE NAME OF THE FATHER,

He immerses the child the first time.

AND OF THE SON,

He immerses the child the second time.

AND OF THE HOLY SPIRIT.

He immerses the child the third time.

B 356

The celebrant, taking baptismal water from the font and pouring it three times on the child's bowed head, baptizes the child in the name of the Most Holy Trinity. The godfather or godmother places his (her) right hand on the right shoulder of the child being baptized:

N., I BAPTIZE YOU IN THE NAME OF THE FATHER,

He pours water the first time.

AND OF THE SON,

He pours water the second time.

AND OF THE HOLY SPIRIT.

He pours water the third time.

EXPLANATORY RITES

318. If the neophytes are to be confirmed, the Anointing with Chrism after Baptism is omitted (no. **319**), and the Explanatory Rites (nos. **320–321**) are carried out immediately. 357

ANOINTING AFTER BAPTISM

319. If for some special reason, the celebration of Confirmation is separated from the Baptism (cf. no. **215**), then, after the immersion or the pouring of water, the celebrant administers the Anointing with Chrism. If, however, there are a large number of newly baptized and several Priests or Deacons are present, each of them may anoint some of the newly baptized with Chrism. 358

The celebrant says the following over all the newly baptized before the anointing:

Almighty God, the Father of our Lord Jesus Christ,
has given you new birth by water and the Holy Spirit,
granted you the remission of all sins,
and joined you to his people.
He now anoints you with the Chrism of salvation,
so that you may remain members of Christ,
Priest, Prophet and King,
unto eternal life.

Children:
Amen.

Then, in silence, the celebrant anoints each of the newly baptized with sacred Chrism on the crown of the head.

Clothing with a White Garment

320. The celebrant says the following formula. At the words **Receive, therefore, the white garment** the godparents place the white garment on the newly baptized children, unless another color more suited to local custom should be required. If circumstances suggest, this rite can be omitted. 359

Celebrant:
N. and N., you have become a new creation
and have clothed yourselves in Christ.
Receive, therefore, the white garment
and bring it unstained
before the judgment seat of our Lord Jesus Christ,
that you may have eternal life.

Children:
Amen.

Handing On of a Lighted Candle

321. The celebrant, then, takes the paschal candle in his hands or touches it, saying: 360

Come forward, godfathers and godmothers,
that you may hand on the light to the newly baptized.

A godparent of each of the neophytes goes to the celebrant, lights a candle from the paschal candle, and then presents it to the neophyte. Then the celebrant says:

You have been made light in Christ.
Walk always as children of light,
that persevering in faith
you may run to meet the Lord when he comes
with all the Saints in the heavenly court.

Children:
Amen.

CELEBRATION OF CONFIRMATION

322. Between the celebration of Baptism and Confirmation, the congregation may, as circumstances suggest, sing a suitable chant. 361

The celebration of Confirmation may take place either in the sanctuary or in the baptistery, as the circumstances of the place dictate. 362

If previously baptized children of the catechetical group are to be confirmed, they with their sponsors join the newly baptized children to receive the Sacrament. USA

323. If the Bishop has conferred Baptism, he should now also administer Confirmation. If the Bishop is not present, Confirmation is to be given by the Priest who conferred Baptism (cf. *Code of Canon Law*, can. 866; no. **308**). 362

When those to be confirmed are too numerous, Priests who may be designated for this role can be associated to the minister of Confirmation to administer the Sacrament (cf. no. **14**).

Invitation

324. Then the celebrant, addressing the children to be confirmed, briefly instructs them in these or similar words: 363

Dear children, you have been born again in Christ,
and have become members of Christ and of his priestly people.
It now remains for you to share
in the outpouring among us of the Holy Spirit,
who was sent by the Lord upon the Apostles at Pentecost
to be given by them and their successors to the baptized.

Therefore, you also are to receive the promised power of the Holy Spirit,
so that, being more perfectly conformed to Christ,
you may bear witness to the Lord's Passion and Resurrection
and become active members of the Church
for the building up of the Body of Christ in faith and charity.

Then the celebrant (while the Priests associated with him remain by his side) standing, facing the people, with hands joined, says:

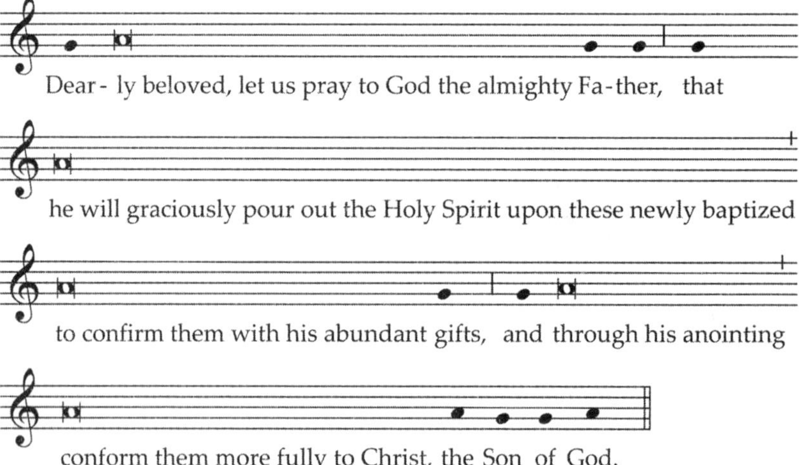
Dear- ly beloved, let us pray to God the almighty Fa-ther, that
he will graciously pour out the Holy Spirit upon these newly baptized
to confirm them with his abundant gifts, and through his anointing
conform them more fully to Christ, the Son of God.

Dearly beloved,
let us pray to God the almighty Father,
that he will graciously pour out the Holy Spirit
upon these newly baptized
to confirm them with his abundant gifts,
and through his anointing
conform them more fully to Christ, the Son of God.

And all pray in silence for a while.

The Laying On of Hands

325. Then the celebrant lays hands over all those to be confirmed 364
(as do the Priests who are associated with him). But the celebrant
alone says (for the chant, cf. no. **234**):

Almighty God, Father of our Lord Jesus Christ,
who brought these your servants to new birth
by water and the Holy Spirit,
freeing them from sin:
send upon them, O Lord, the Holy Spirit, the Paraclete;
give them the spirit of wisdom and understanding,
the spirit of counsel and fortitude,
the spirit of knowledge and piety;
fill them with the spirit of the fear of the Lord.
Through Christ our Lord.

All:

Amen.

The Anointing with Chrism

326. The sacred Chrism is brought by a minister to the celebrant. 365

If other Priests are associated with the celebrant in conferring the Sacrament, the vessels of sacred Chrism are given to them by the Bishop, if he is present.

Each of those to be confirmed goes to the celebrant (or to the Priests); or, if appropriate, the celebrant (and the Priests) goes to each of those to be confirmed. In addition, the godparent places his (her) right hand on the shoulder of the one to be confirmed and says his (her) name to the celebrant; or the one to be confirmed alone says his (her) own name. During the anointing a suitable chant may be sung.

The minister of the Sacrament dips the tip of the thumb of his right hand in the Chrism and, with the thumb, makes the Sign of the Cross on the forehead of the one to be confirmed, as he says:

N., BE SEALED WITH THE GIFT OF THE HOLY SPIRIT.

The newly confirmed:

Amen.

The celebrant adds:

Peace be with you.

The newly confirmed:

And with your spirit.

CELEBRATION OF THE EUCHARIST

327. The Creed is omitted, and the Universal Prayer (Prayer of the Faithful), which the neophytes take part in for the first time, immediately takes place. 366

When the offerings are carried to the altar, some of the neophytes may bring them forward.

328. In Eucharistic Prayer I, mention of the neophytes is made in the proper form of the **Hanc igitur (Therefore, Lord, we pray)**, at the Easter Vigil from *The Roman Missal*, Order of Mass, no. 87, and outside the Easter Vigil from the Ritual Mass for the Conferral of Baptism. At the Easter Vigil and outside the Easter Vigil, in Eucharistic Prayer I, mention of the godparents is made in the section **Memento, Domine (Remember, Lord, your servants)** from the Ritual Mass for the Conferral of Baptism. If Eucharistic Prayer II, III, or IV is used, the proper formula for the neophytes is used from the Ritual Mass for the Conferral of Baptism. 367

329. The newly baptized children may receive Holy Communion under both kinds, together with their godparents, and Catholic parents, as well as their lay catechists. 368

Before Communion, that is, before **Ecce Agnus Dei (Behold the Lamb of God)**, the celebrant may briefly remind the neophytes of the preeminence of so great a Sacrament, which is the climax of their Initiation and the center of the whole Christian life. He may do so in these or other words:

Dear children, USA
(on this most sacred night)
you have been reborn by water and the Holy Spirit,
and will receive, for the first time,
the Bread of life and the Chalice of salvation.

May the Body and Blood of Christ the Lord
help you all to grow deeper in his friendship
and in communion with the entire Church;
may it be your constant food for the journey of life
and a foretaste of the eternal banquet of heaven.

Behold the Lamb of God . . .

The celebrant should also pay special attention to any previously baptized children who for the first time are to receive Communion at the divine table. These children, together with their parents, godparents, sponsors for Confirmation, and catechists, may also receive Communion under both kinds.

PERIOD OF MYSTAGOGY

330. A suitable period of postbaptismal catechesis or Mystagogy 369
should be provided to assist the young neophytes. For this period it will be desirable to adapt the norms that pertain to adults (nos. **244–251**).

CHAPTER III

SIMPLER ORDER OF ADULT INITIATION

331. In extraordinary circumstances when an individual has been unable to go through all the steps of Initiation or when the local Ordinary, judging the sincerity of the individual's Christian conversion and religious maturity, decides that he or she may receive Baptism without delay, he may permit the use of this simpler rite in individual cases (cf. no. **34.4**), in which either everything is completed on one occasion (nos. **340–369**), or the option is also given to have, in addition to the celebration of the Sacraments, one or other of the rites of the catechumenate or of the Period of Purification and Enlightenment (nos. **332–335**). 240

Expanded Form

332. In extraordinary circumstances, such as sickness, advanced age, change of residence, long journeys, etc.: 274

a) when the individual was not able to begin the catechumenate with the proper rite, or, having begun, to complete all the rites;

b) or when it would be harmful to his or her spiritual welfare if through the use of the rite given in nos. **340–369** he or she were deprived of the benefits of a longer preparation,

then it would be important, with the Bishop's permission, to expand the abbreviated form with one or more elements of the complete Order.

333. This expanded rite offers the option of allowing either for an individual to accompany others who are more advanced by adding appropriate initial rites of the complete Order (e.g., Entrance 275 into the Catechumenate [nos. **48–74**], Minor Exorcisms [no. **94**], Blessings [no. **97**], etc.); or for an individual to join who began the rite with others but did not complete it (e.g., Election [cf. nos. **118–128**], Rites of Purification and Enlightenment [cf. nos. **141–149**], and the Sacraments themselves [cf. nos. **206–217**]).

334. Adaptations, which must be made with pastoral prudence, 276
comparing the abbreviated form with the expanded rite, may be provided in the following way:

1) simply by adding; for example, rites of the Period of the Catechumenate (nos. **81–103**), the Rites of Handing On (nos. **157–162, 178–182**);
2) by dividing and enlarging the Rite of Reception (nos. **340–345**) or the Liturgy of the Word (nos. **346–352**). In the Rite of Reception, no. **342** can be expanded to resemble the Rite for Entrance into the Catechumenate (nos. **48–74**), by removing nos. **343–344**, if appropriate. The subsequent nos. **343–344** may take the place of the Rite of Election. In the Liturgy of the Word, nos. **349–351** may be adapted to one or other of the Scrutinies (nos. **152–154, 166–168, 173–175**), etc.;
3) by using part of this simpler rite in place of some or all of the rites of the normal Order; or, when inquirers (known as the "well-disposed") are received (cf. no. **39.3**), by joining the Rite for Entrance into the Catechumenate (nos. **48–74**) with the Election (nos. **129–137**).

335. In using this augmented rite, care should be taken: 277

1) that the catechesis of the individual be complete;
2) that the rite be celebrated with the active participation of some of the congregation;
3) that, after the Sacraments have been received, a Period of Mystagogy be offered to the neophyte, insofar as this is possible.

Abbreviated Form

336. Before an individual may be baptized, having chosen a godfather (or godmother) (cf. no. **11**) and having come to know the local community (cf. nos. **39**, **75.2**), the individual must be instructed and prepared for an adequate period. During it, the reasons he or she has requested Baptism may be purified, and conversion and faith may mature. 241

337. Besides the presentation and reception of the one to be initiated, the rite expresses the person's public and firm resolve to request Christian Initiation, as well as the approval of the Church; then, after a suitable Liturgy of the Word, the celebration of all the Sacraments of Initiation takes place. 242

338. The rite is usually celebrated within Mass, for which appropriate readings are to be chosen from those indicated in the *Lectionary for Mass* (nos. 751–755), or they may also be taken from those readings designated for the current Sunday or Feast of the day. The presidential prayers are to be taken from the Ritual Mass for the Conferral of Baptism, or from some other Mass; after Baptism and Confirmation, the neophyte participates in the celebration of the Eucharist for the first time. 243 253

339. As far as possible, the celebration should take place on a Sunday (cf. no. **27**), with the active participation of the local community. 244

RITE OF RECEPTION

340. Before the Liturgy of the Word, while the faithful, if circumstances suggest, sing a psalm or suitable hymn, the Priest, wearing sacred vestments, goes to the outside of the church or to the vestibule or entrance, or even to some other suitable place in the church, where the one to be initiated is standing with his (her) godparent. 245

Greeting

341. The celebrant warmly greets the individual. He speaks to him (her), his (her) godparent, and those present, pointing out the joy and happiness of the Church. It is appropriate for him to recall for the godparent and friends the particular experience and religious response by which the one to be initiated, following his (her) own spiritual path, has come to this celebration on this day. 246

The celebrant then invites the person and his (her) godparent to come forward. As they are taking their place before him, a suitable chant may be sung, for example, Psalm 63 (62):2-9:

Psalm 63 (62):2-9

2 O God, you are my God; at dawn I seek you;
for you my soul is thirsting.
For you my flesh is pining,
like a dry, weary land without water.
3 I have come before you in the sanctuary,
to behold your strength and your glory.

4 Your loving mercy is better than life;
my lips will speak your praise.
5 I will bless you all my life;
in your name I will lift up my hands.
6 My soul shall be filled as with a banquet;
with joyful lips, my mouth shall praise you.

7 When I remember you upon my bed,
I muse on you through the watches of the night.
8 For you have been my strength;
in the shadow of your wings I rejoice.
9 My soul clings fast to you;
your right hand upholds me.

Dialogue

342. Facing the individual, the celebrant then questions him (her). The celebrant may use other words in asking the individual about his (her) intentions and may permit replies in his (her) own words; for example, after the first question: **What do you ask of God's Church?** or **What do you desire?** or **For what reason have you come?**, he may receive such answers as: **The grace of Christ** or **Entry into the Church** or **Eternal life** or other suitable replies. The celebrant may then adapt his questions to his (her) replies. 247

Celebrant:
N., what do you ask of God's Church?

The one being initiated:
Faith.

Celebrant:
What does faith offer you?

The one being initiated:
Eternal life.

Initial Commitment

343. Then the celebrant, adapting his words, as required, to the replies he received, addresses the individual in these or similar words: 248

This is eternal life:
to know the true God
and Jesus Christ, whom he has sent.
For Christ has been raised from the dead
and established by God
as Prince of life and Lord of all things,
visible and invisible.

You would not ask for this life and for Baptism today,
unless you had already come to know Christ
and wanted to become his disciple.
And so, have you listened to Christ's word
and sought to keep his commandments?
Have you shared in fraternal communion and prayer?
Have you done all these things
in order to become a Christian?

The one being initiated:
I have.

Affirmation by the Godparent

344. The celebrant turns toward the godparent and asks: 249
Do you, coming here as godfather (godmother) of N.,
judge him (her) before God
to be worthy of admission today
to the Sacraments of Christian Initiation?

Godparent:
I do.

Celebrant:
You have testified on behalf of N.
Are you prepared to continue helping him (her),
by your words and example, to serve Christ?

Godparent:
I am.

Then the celebrant, with hands joined, says: 250
Let us pray.

We give you thanks, most merciful Father,
for this your servant,
because he (she) has already sought you,
who have gone before him (her) in many ways
and because today in the presence of the Church
he (she) has responded to your call.
Now therefore grant in your kindness
that he (she) may joyfully attain
the fulfillment of your loving plan.
Through Christ our Lord.

All:
Amen.

Introduction into the Church

345. The celebrant then invites the individual and his (her) god- 251
parent to enter the church, while saying these or similar words: USA

N., come into the church,
to partake with us at the table of God's word.

Then with a gesture, he invites them to enter.

Meanwhile, the following antiphon is sung with Psalm 34 (33):2-3, 6 and 9, 10-11 and 16 or another suitable chant:

Come, children, and hear me;
I will teach you the fear of the Lord.

Psalm 34 (33):2-3, 6 and 9, 10-11 and 16

[2] I will bless the LORD at all times,
praise of him is always in my mouth.
[3] In the LORD my soul shall make its boast;
the humble shall hear and be glad. ℟.

6 Look toward him and be radiant;
let your faces not be abashed.
9 Taste and see that the LORD is good.
Blessed the man who seeks refuge in him. ℟.

10 Fear the LORD, you his holy ones.
They lack nothing, those who fear him.
11 The rich suffer want and go hungry,
but those who seek the LORD lack no blessing.
16 The LORD turns his eyes to the just one,
and his ears are open to his cry. ℟.

LITURGY OF THE WORD

346. When the one to be initiated and his (her) godparent have 252
arrived at their seats and the celebrant has reached the sanctuary,
the Introductory Rites of the Mass are omitted, and the Liturgy of
the Word begins.

READINGS

347. The readings are those already indicated in no. **338.** 253

HOMILY

348. Then the Homily takes place. 253

INTERCESSIONS AND PENITENTIAL RITE

349. After the Homily, the one to be initiated and the godparent 254
come before the celebrant. Then the entire congregation offers the
following or similar Intercessions.

Celebrant:

Let us pray for our dear brother (sister)
who asks for Christ's Sacraments,
praying also for ourselves, sinners that we are,
that we may all draw nearer to Christ by faith and repentance
and walk without faltering in newness of life.

Lector:

That the Lord will renew and kindle in all of us
a spirit of true repentance,
let us pray to the Lord:

℟. Lord, hear our prayer.

Lector:

That we, who have died to sin
and been saved by Christ through Baptism,
may be living signs of his grace,
let us pray to the Lord:

℟. Lord, hear our prayer.

Lector:

That with trust in God's mercy and with contrite heart
this his servant may prepare to meet Christ the Savior,
let us pray to the Lord:

℟. Lord, hear our prayer.

Lector:

That by following Christ,
who takes away the sin of the world,
our brother (sister) may be healed of the contagion of that sin
and freed from its affliction,
let us pray to the Lord:

℟. Lord, hear our prayer.

Lector:
That he (she) may be cleansed by the Holy Spirit
and directed by his guidance into all holiness,
let us pray to the Lord:

℟. Lord, hear our prayer.

Lector:
That, buried with Christ through the Sacrament of Baptism,
he (she) may die to sin and live always for God,
let us pray to the Lord:

℟. Lord, hear our prayer.

Lector:
That he (she) may come before the Father
bearing fruits of holiness and love,
let us pray to the Lord:

℟. Lord, hear our prayer.

Lector:
That the entire world,
for which the Father gave his beloved Son,
may believe in his love and turn to him,
let us pray to the Lord:

℟. Lord, hear our prayer.

350. After the Intercessions the one to be initiated bows his (her) head or kneels and joins the congregation in making a general confession, which may be omitted, as circumstances suggest: 254 USA RM

I confess to almighty God
and to you, my brothers and sisters,
that I have greatly sinned,
in my thoughts and in my words,
in what I have done and in what I have failed to do,

And, striking their breast, they say:

through my fault, through my fault,
through my most grievous fault;

Then they continue:

therefore I ask blessed Mary ever-Virgin,
all the Angels and Saints,
and you, my brothers and sisters,
to pray for me to the Lord our God.

Prayer of Exorcism

351. Omitting **May almighty God**, the celebrant concludes the Intercessions, by saying this prayer: 255

Lord God almighty,
who sent your Only Begotten Son
when the human race was held captive by slavery to sin
that you might endow it with the freedom of your children,
we pray to you most humbly for this your servant,
who has known the snares of this world
and been tempted by the wiles of the devil.
Now that he (she) has acknowledged in your presence
that he (she) is a sinner,
deliver him (her) from the power of darkness
by the Passion and Resurrection of your Son,
and unfailingly watch over him (her),
fortified on his (her) journey through life
by the grace of Christ.
Who lives and reigns for ever and ever.

All:

Amen.

The Laying On of Hands

352. The celebrant faces the one to be initiated and says: 256

May the strength of Christ the Savior protect you; USA
who lives and reigns for ever and ever.

All:

Amen.

Then, in silence, the celebrant immediately lays hands on the individual.

CELEBRATION OF BAPTISM

Celebrant's Instruction

353. Then the individual with his (her) godparent goes to the font. 257
The celebrant stands and gives the following or similar Instruction:

Dear brothers and sisters,
let us beg the mercy of God the almighty Father
for this servant of God N.,
who is seeking holy Baptism.
May God bestow light and strength
on the one he has called and led to this hour,
that he (she) may hold fast to Christ with resolute spirit
and profess the faith of the Church.
May God also give him (her) renewal by the Holy Spirit,
whom we will fervently invoke upon this water.

Blessing of Water

354. Next, the celebrant turns toward the font and says the Blessing given in option A with hands extended, or the other blessing formulas given in no. **222** as options B and C. 258

During Easter Time (cf. no. **26**), however, if baptismal water blessed at the Easter Vigil is available, so that the Baptism may not lack an element of thanksgiving and petition, the Blessing and Invocation of God over the Water takes place in accordance with option B below; he may also use the second Easter Time thanksgiving formula given in no. **222** as option E.

A

Blessing of Water: The celebrant turns toward the font and says the following Blessing with hands extended (for the chant, cf. no. **222**):

O God, who by invisible power
accomplish a wondrous effect
through sacramental signs
and who in many ways have prepared water, your creation,
to show forth the grace of Baptism;

O God, whose Spirit
in the first moments of the world's creation
hovered over the waters,
so that the very substance of water
would even then take to itself the power to sanctify;

O God, who by the outpouring of the flood
foreshadowed regeneration,
so that from the mystery of one and the same element of water
would come an end to vice and a beginning of virtue;

O God, who caused the children of Abraham
to pass dry-shod through the Red Sea,
so that the chosen people,
set free from slavery to Pharaoh,
would prefigure the people of the baptized;

O God, whose Son,
baptized by John in the waters of the Jordan,
was anointed with the Holy Spirit,
and, as he hung upon the Cross,
gave forth water from his side along with blood,
and after his Resurrection, commanded his disciples:
"Go forth, teach all nations, baptizing them
in the name of the Father and of the Son and of the Holy Spirit,"
look now, we pray, upon the face of your Church
and graciously unseal for her the fountain of Baptism.

May this water receive by the Holy Spirit
the grace of your Only Begotten Son,
so that human nature, created in your image
and washed clean through the Sacrament of Baptism
from all the squalor of the life of old,
may be found worthy to rise to the life of newborn children
through water and the Holy Spirit.

The celebrant touches the water with his right hand and continues:

May the power of the Holy Spirit,
O Lord, we pray,
come down through your Son
into the fullness of this font,
so that all who have been buried with Christ
by Baptism into death
may rise again to life with him.
Who lives and reigns with you in the unity of the Holy Spirit,
God, for ever and ever.

All:

Amen.

B 389.2

Easter Time Thanksgiving over Water Already Blessed: The celebrant turns toward the font containing the blessed water and says the following:

Blessed are you, God the almighty Father,
for you have created water to cleanse and give life.

All:

Blessed be God (or another suitable acclamation of the people).

Celebrant:

Blessed are you, God the Only Begotten Son, Jesus Christ,
for you poured forth water with blood from your side,
so that from your Death and Resurrection the Church might be born.

All:

Blessed be God.

Celebrant:

Blessed are you, God the Holy Spirit,
for you anointed Christ at his baptism in the waters of the Jordan,
that we might all be baptized into you.

All:

Blessed be God.

Celebrant:

By the mystery of this blessed water,
graciously lead to spiritual rebirth your servant N.,
whom you have called to this cleansing water,
that he (she) may have eternal life.
Through Christ our Lord.

All:

Amen.

Profession of Faith

355. After the consecration of the font (or prayer of thanksgiving), 259
the celebrant continues with the Profession of Faith, which in- USA
cludes the Renunciation of Sin and the Profession itself.

Renunciation of Sin

356. Using one of the following formulas, the celebrant questions 259
the one to be initiated. USA

At the discretion of the Diocesan Bishop, the formulas for the Renunciation of Sin may be made more specific and detailed as circumstances might require (cf. no. **33.8**).

A

Celebrant:
Do you renounce sin,
so as to live in the freedom of the children of God?

The one being initiated:
I do.

Celebrant:
Do you renounce the lure of evil,
so that sin may have no mastery over you?

The one being initiated:
I do.

Celebrant:
Do you renounce Satan,
the author and prince of sin?

The one being initiated:
I do.

B

Celebrant:

Do you renounce Satan,
and all his works and empty promises?

The one being initiated:

I do.

C

Celebrant:

Do you renounce Satan?

The one being initiated:

I do.

Celebrant:

And all his works?

The one being initiated:

I do.

Celebrant:

And all his empty show?

The one being initiated:

I do.

Profession of Faith

357. Then the celebrant asks the individual: 260

N., do you believe in God,
the Father almighty,
Creator of heaven and earth?

The one being initiated:

I do.

Celebrant:

Do you believe in Jesus Christ, his only Son, our Lord,
who was born of the Virgin Mary,
suffered death and was buried,
rose again from the dead
and is seated at the right hand of the Father?

The one being initiated:

I do.

Celebrant:

Do you believe in the Holy Spirit,
the holy catholic Church,
the communion of saints,
the forgiveness of sins,
the resurrection of the body,
and life everlasting?

The one being initiated:

I do.

Rite of Baptism

358. After the Profession of Faith, the individual is immediately 260
baptized by immersion (option A) or by pouring of water (option 261
B). After the Baptism, a brief acclamation (cf. Appendix II, nos. **595–597**) may be sung by the people.

A 261

If Baptism is by immersion of the whole body or of the head only, decency and decorum should be observed. Either or both godparents touch the one to be baptized. Touching the individual, the celebrant immerses him (her) or his (her) head three times, raising the individual out of the water each time and baptizing him (her) by calling upon the Most Holy Trinity only once:

N., I baptize you in the name of the Father,

He immerses the individual the first time.

and of the Son,

He immerses the individual the second time.

and of the Holy Spirit.

He immerses the individual the third time.

B 262

If, however, Baptism is by the pouring of water, either or both godparents place the right hand on the right shoulder of the one to be baptized, and the celebrant, taking baptismal water and pouring it three times on the person's bowed head, baptizes him (her) in the name of the Most Holy Trinity:

N., I BAPTIZE YOU IN THE NAME OF THE FATHER,

He pours water the first time.

AND OF THE SON,

He pours water the second time.

AND OF THE HOLY SPIRIT.

He pours water the third time.

EXPLANATORY RITES

359. The Explanatory Rites (nos. **360–361**) are carried out immediately after Baptism. After these rites, Confirmation is celebrated, as described below (nos. **362–366**). 263 USA

CLOTHING WITH A WHITE GARMENT

360. The celebrant says the following formula. At the words **Receive, therefore, the white garment** the godparent places the white garment on the newly baptized, unless another color more suited to local custom should be required. If circumstances suggest, this rite can be omitted. 264

Celebrant:

N., you have become a new creation
and have clothed yourself in Christ.
Receive, therefore, the white garment
and bring it unstained
before the judgment seat of our Lord Jesus Christ,
that you may have eternal life.

The newly baptized:

Amen.

Handing On of a Lighted Candle

361. The celebrant then takes the paschal candle in his hands or touches it, saying: 265

Come forward, godfather (godmother),
that you may hand on the light to the newly baptized.

The godparent goes to the celebrant, lights a candle from the paschal candle, and presents it to the neophyte.

Then the celebrant says to the newly baptized:

You have been made light in Christ.
Walk always as a child of light,
that persevering in faith
you may run to meet the Lord when he comes
with all the Saints in the heavenly court.

The newly baptized:

Amen.

CELEBRATION OF CONFIRMATION

362. Between the celebration of Baptism and Confirmation, the congregation may, as circumstances suggest, sing a suitable chant. 266

363. If the Bishop has conferred Baptism, he should now also administer Confirmation. If the Bishop is not present, Confirmation is to be given by the Priest who conferred Baptism (cf. *Code of Canon Law*, can. 866). 267

INVITATION

364. The celebrant briefly addresses the neophyte standing before him, in these or similar words: 268

N., you have been born again in Christ,
and have become a member of Christ and of his priestly people.
Now you are to share
in the outpouring among us of the Holy Spirit,
who was sent by the Lord upon the Apostles at Pentecost
to be given by them and their successors to the baptized.

Therefore, you also are to receive the promised power of the
Holy Spirit,
so that, being more perfectly conformed to Christ,
you may bear witness to the Lord's Passion and Resurrection
and become an active member of the Church
for the building up of the Body of Christ in faith and charity.

Then the celebrant standing, facing the people, with hands joined, says:

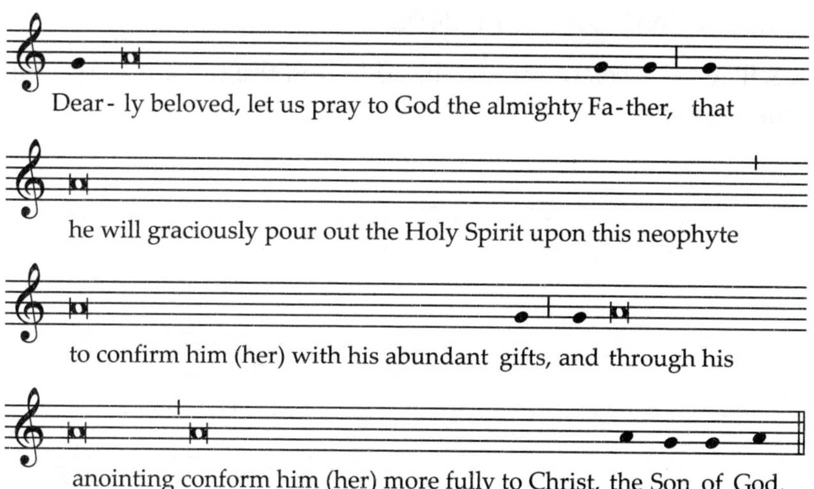
Dear - ly beloved, let us pray to God the almighty Fa-ther, that
he will graciously pour out the Holy Spirit upon this neophyte
to confirm him (her) with his abundant gifts, and through his
anointing conform him (her) more fully to Christ, the Son of God.

Dearly beloved,
let us pray to God the almighty Father,
that he will graciously pour out the Holy Spirit
upon this neophyte
to confirm him (her) with his abundant gifts,
and through his anointing
conform him (her) more fully to Christ, the Son of God.

And all pray in silence for a while.

The Laying On of Hands

365. Then the celebrant lays hands upon the person to be confirmed as he says: 269

Al - mighty God, Father of our Lord Je - sus Christ, who brought this
your servant to new birth by water and the Holy Spirit, freeing
him (her) from sin: send upon him (her), O Lord, the Holy Spir-it, the
Par - a - clete; give him (her) the spirit of wisdom and understanding,
the spirit of coun-sel and for - ti - tude, the spirit of knowl-edge and
pi - e - ty; fill him (her) with the spirit of the fear of the Lord.
Through Christ our Lord. R. A - men.

Almighty God, Father of our Lord Jesus Christ,
who brought this your servant to new birth
by water and the Holy Spirit,
freeing him (her) from sin:
send upon him (her), O Lord, the Holy Spirit, the Paraclete;
give him (her) the spirit of wisdom and understanding,
the spirit of counsel and fortitude,
the spirit of knowledge and piety;
fill him (her) with the spirit of the fear of the Lord.
Through Christ our Lord.

All:
Amen.

The Anointing with Chrism

366. The sacred Chrism is brought by a minister to the celebrant. 270

The one to be confirmed goes to the celebrant. In addition, the godparent places his (her) right hand on the shoulder of the one to be confirmed and says his (her) name to the celebrant; or the one to be confirmed alone says his (her) own name.

The celebrant dips the tip of the thumb of his right hand in the Chrism and, with the thumb, makes the Sign of the Cross on the forehead of the one to be confirmed, as he says:

N., BE SEALED WITH THE GIFT OF THE HOLY SPIRIT.

The newly confirmed:
Amen.

The celebrant adds:
Peace be with you.

The newly confirmed:
And with your spirit.

CELEBRATION OF THE EUCHARIST

367. The Creed is omitted, and the Universal Prayer (Prayer of the Faithful), which the neophyte takes part in for the first time, immediately takes place. 271

The neophyte brings the offerings forward to the altar.

368. In Eucharistic Prayer I, mention of the neophyte is made in the proper form of the **Hanc igitur** (**Therefore, Lord, we pray**), and of the godparent in the section **Memento, Domine** (**Remember, Lord, your servants**) from the Ritual Mass for the Conferral of Baptism. If Eucharistic Prayer II, III, or IV is used, the proper formula for the neophyte is used from the Ritual Mass for the Conferral of Baptism. 272

369. It is desirable that the neophyte receive Holy Communion under both kinds, together with his (her) godfather, godmother, and Catholic parents and spouse, as well as his (her) lay catechists. 273

Before Communion, that is, before **Ecce Agnus Dei** (**Behold the Lamb of God**), the celebrant may briefly remind the neophyte of the preeminence of so great a Sacrament, which is the climax of his (her) Initiation and the center of the whole Christian life. He may do so in these or other words:

N., (on this most sacred night) USA
you have been reborn by water and the Holy Spirit,
and will receive, for the first time,
the Bread of life and the Chalice of salvation.

May the Body and Blood of Christ the Lord
help you to grow deeper in his friendship
and in communion with the entire Church;
may it be your constant food for the journey of life
and a foretaste of the eternal banquet of heaven.

Behold the Lamb of God . . .

CHAPTER IV

SHORTER ORDER OF ADULT INITIATION TO BE USED IN NEAR DANGER OF DEATH OR AT THE POINT OF DEATH

370. Anyone in near danger of death, whether or not a catechu- 278
men, may be baptized with the shorter rite appearing below (nos. **375–399**), as long as he or she is not yet at the very point of death and is able to hear questions and respond to them.

371. If the person has already been received as a catechumen, he 279
or she should promise to complete the usual catechesis after recovering strength. If the person is not a catechumen, he or she must show serious signs of conversion to Christ and Renunciation of False Worship, and should not appear tied by obstacles to a moral life (e.g., "simultaneous" polygamy, etc.); additionally, he or she should promise to follow an appropriate complete course of Initiation after health has been restored.

372. This rite is particularly suited for catechists and laypersons. 280

Nevertheless, a Priest or a Deacon, in the case of a very urgent need, may use this rite. Normally, however, a Priest or Deacon ought to use the Simpler Order (nos. **340–369**), having introduced adaptations required by the place and time.

However, a Priest who baptizes and has sacred Chrism and time available should not neglect to confer Confirmation after Baptism, omitting in this case the Anointing with Chrism after Baptism (no. **228**).

Also, if it can be done, the Priest or Deacon, or if appropriate a catechist or layperson possessing the faculty to distribute Holy Communion, should administer the Eucharist to the neophyte. In this case, the Sacrament may be brought before the celebration of the rite, and, at the time of this celebration, be placed with honor on a table covered with a white cloth.

373. However, at the point of death, or if death is threatening, 281
when time is pressing, the minister, omitting everything else, pours water, even if it has not been blessed, but is natural, onto the head of the sick person, saying the usual formula (cf. *Christian Initiation*, General Introduction, no. 23).

374. For those who were baptized in near danger of death or at 282
the point of death, if they return to health, provision should be 294
made for their instruction with suitable catechesis, and, having been received at the church at a fitting time, they should be given the other Sacraments of Initiation. In such a case the principles that are established in nos. **400–410** are kept, with due adaptations. A sick person in danger of death, who has received all or some of the Sacraments of Initiation, if he or she has recovered, must complete the usual catechesis and the Sacraments or rites, which could not be celebrated (cf. nos. **371, 400–410**).

BEGINNING OF THE RITE

375. The catechist or layperson, after he (she) has greeted the fam- 283
ily briefly in a friendly manner, immediately speaks with the sick person about his (her) request for Baptism and, if the sick person is not a catechumen, about his (her) reasons for conversion. After deciding to baptize him (her), he (she) should, if necessary, instruct the person briefly.

376. Then he (she) invites the family, the person designated as 284
godparent, and the friends and neighbors present to gather around the sick person and selects one or two of those present as witnesses. Water, even if it is not blessed, is prepared.

Dialogue

377. The minister, turning toward the sick person, questions him (her) in these or similar words: 285

Dear brother (sister), you have asked to be baptized
because you wish, as Christians do, to have eternal life.
Eternal life is this:
to know the true God and Jesus Christ, whom he has sent.
This is the faith of Christians.
Do you know this?

Sick person:
I do.

Minister:
Along with faith in Jesus Christ,
you will need to strive, as Christians do,
to follow his commandments.
Do you know this?

Sick person:
I do.

Minister:
Are you therefore willing to lead a Christian way of life?

Sick person:
I am.

Minister:
Promise, therefore,
that once you have recovered your strength,
you will spend time getting to know Christ better
and follow a course of Christian instruction.
Do you so promise?

Sick person:
I do.

Affirmation by the Godparent and Witnesses

378. The minister, turning toward the godparent and the witnesses, questions them in these or similar words: 286

You have heard what N. has promised.
As his (her) godparent, do you promise to remind him (her) of it
and to help him (her) to learn the teaching of Christ,
to take part in the life of the community,
and to become a good Christian?

Godparent:
I do.

Minister:
And will you who have witnessed this promise
assist in its fulfillment?

Witnesses:
We will.

The minister turns toward the sick person and says: 287
Therefore, in keeping with the command of the Lord Jesus,
you will be baptized into eternal life.

LITURGY OF THE WORD

Gospel

379. According to time and circumstances, the minister reads some words from a Gospel and, if possible, explains them, for example: 287

Mt 22:35-40: *This is the greatest and the first commandment.*
Mt 28:18-20: *Go, therefore, and make disciples of all nations, baptizing them in the name of the Father, and of the Son, and of the Holy Spirit.*

Mk 1:9-11: *Jesus was baptized in the Jordan by John.*
Jn 3:1-6: *No one can see the Kingdom of God without being born from above.*
Jn 6:44-47: *Whoever believes has eternal life.*

INTERCESSIONS FOR THE ONE TO BE INITIATED

380. The minister, then, invites those present to offer the Intercessions with him (her). The minister may adapt or shorten the intentions according to the condition of the sick person. The Intercessions may be omitted if it is foreseen that the sick person may become greatly fatigued. 288 ASPC 109, 123

Minister:
Let us call upon the mercy of almighty God
for our sick brother (sister),
who is asking for the grace of Baptism,
and for his (her) godparent
and for all his (her) family and friends.

Lector:
Increase his (her) faith in Christ,
your Son and our Savior:
℟. Lord, we ask you, hear our prayer.

Lector:
Grant his (her) desire to have eternal life
and to enter the Kingdom of Heaven:
℟. Lord, we ask you, hear our prayer.

Lector:
Fulfill his (her) hope of knowing you,
the Creator of the world and our Father:
℟. Lord, we ask you, hear our prayer.

Lector:
Forgive his (her) sins through Baptism
and make him (her) holy:

℟. Lord, we ask you, hear our prayer.

Lector:
Grant him (her) the salvation that Christ won
by his Passion and Resurrection:

℟. Lord, we ask you, hear our prayer.

Lector:
Adopt him (her) into your family by your love:

℟. Lord, we ask you, hear our prayer.

[Lector:
Restore him (her) to health
and give him (her) time to know Christ more deeply and to imitate him:

℟. Lord, we ask you, hear our prayer.]

Lector:
Keep all of us, who have been baptized into the one Body,
always united in faith and love as Christ's disciples:

℟. Lord, we ask you, hear our prayer.

Prayer over the One to Be Initiated

381. The minister concludes the Intercessions with this prayer: 289

Hear our prayer, O Lord,
and as you look with favor
on the faith and desire of your beloved servant N.,
grant that, by this water,
through which you have chosen to give men and women heavenly birth,

he (she) may be conformed to the Passion and Resurrection
of Christ,
obtain forgiveness of all his (her) sins,
be established as a child of your adoption,
and be numbered among your holy people.
[Grant also that, being restored to health,
he (she) may give you thanks in the Church,
and, holding fast to the commandments of Christ,
become more fully his disciple.]
Through Christ our Lord.

All:
Amen.

CELEBRATION OF BAPTISM

RENUNCIATION OF SIN

382. The minister, looking at the sick person, first asks for his (her) Renunciation of Sin. As circumstances suggest, the minister may use the longer formula in no. **356** and may make pertinent adaptations (cf. no. **72**). 290

Minister:
Do you renounce Satan,
and all his works and empty promises?

Sick person:
I do.

Profession of Faith

383. A Profession of Faith is then made. One of the following formulas may be used. 290

A

Minister:
N., do you believe in God,
the Father almighty,
Creator of heaven and earth?

Sick person:
I do.

Minister:
Do you believe in Jesus Christ, his only Son, our Lord,
who was born of the Virgin Mary,
suffered death and was buried,
rose again from the dead
and is seated at the right hand of the Father?

Sick person:
I do.

Minister:
Do you believe in the Holy Spirit,
the holy catholic Church,
the communion of saints,
the forgiveness of sins,
the resurrection of the body,
and life everlasting?

Sick person:
I do.

B USA

Sick person: 199

I believe in God,
the Father almighty,
Creator of heaven and earth,
and in Jesus Christ, his only Son, our Lord,

At the words that follow, up to and including **the Virgin Mary**, all bow.

who was conceived by the Holy Spirit,
born of the Virgin Mary,
suffered under Pontius Pilate,
was crucified, died and was buried;
he descended into hell;
on the third day he rose again from the dead;
he ascended into heaven,
and is seated at the right hand of God the Father almighty;
from there he will come to judge the living and the dead.

I believe in the Holy Spirit,
the holy catholic Church,
the communion of saints,
the forgiveness of sins,
the resurrection of the body,
and life everlasting. Amen.

Rite of Baptism

384. The minister, using the name chosen by the sick person, baptizes him (her), saying: 291

N., I BAPTIZE YOU IN THE NAME OF THE FATHER,

The minister pours water the first time.

AND OF THE SON,

The minister pours water the second time.

AND OF THE HOLY SPIRIT.

The minister pours water the third time.

ANOINTING AFTER BAPTISM

385. If the minister of Baptism is a Deacon, after the pouring of 291
water, he can administer the Anointing with Chrism after Baptism 263
in the usual way:

Almighty God, the Father of our Lord Jesus Christ,
has given you new birth by water and the Holy Spirit,
granted you the remission of all sins,
and joined you to his people.
He now anoints you with the Chrism of salvation,
so that you may remain as a member of Christ,
Priest, Prophet and King,
unto eternal life.

The newly baptized:
Amen.

Then, in silence, the minister anoints the newly baptized with sacred Chrism on the crown of the head.

386. If the minister is not a Priest, the rite continues with the celebration of Viaticum (no. **393**). USA

387. If neither Confirmation nor Holy Communion can be given, USA
one of the alternative concluding rites (no. **399**, option B) follows 292
Baptism.

CELEBRATION OF CONFIRMATION

388. If Baptism has been conferred by a Priest, he may also confer Confirmation (cf. above, no. **372**). 293

In case of urgent necessity, the invitation (no. **389**) may be omitted; it is sufficient that the anointing with Chrism be done while he says the words, N., BE SEALED WITH THE GIFT OF THE HOLY SPIRIT, preceded, if possible, by the Laying On of Hands with the prayer **Almighty God**.

INVITATION

389. He may begin with an instruction in these or similar words: 293

N., you have been born again in Christ,
and have become a member of Christ and of his priestly people.
It now remains for you to share
in the outpouring among us of the Holy Spirit,
who was sent by the Lord upon the Apostles at Pentecost
to be given by them and their successors to the baptized.

Then, as circumstances suggest, the Priest invites those present to pray in silence for a while.

THE LAYING ON OF HANDS

390. As he lays his hands over the sick person to be confirmed, he says (for the chant, cf. no. **365**): 293

Almighty God, Father of our Lord Jesus Christ,
who brought this your servant to new birth
by water and the Holy Spirit,
freeing him (her) from sin:

send upon him (her), O Lord, the Holy Spirit, the Paraclete;
give him (her) the spirit of wisdom and understanding,
the spirit of counsel and fortitude,
the spirit of knowledge and piety;
fill him (her) with the spirit of the fear of the Lord.
Through Christ our Lord.

All:
Amen.

The Anointing with Chrism

391. Then the Priest dips the tip of the thumb of his right hand in the Chrism and, with the thumb, makes the Sign of the Cross on the forehead of the one to be confirmed, as he says: 293

N., BE SEALED WITH THE GIFT OF THE HOLY SPIRIT.

The newly confirmed:
Amen.

The Priest adds:
Peace be with you.

The newly confirmed:
And with your spirit.

392. If Viaticum will not be celebrated, one of the alternative concluding rites (no. **399**, option A) follows Confirmation. USA

CELEBRATION OF VIATICUM

393. Holy Communion as Viaticum is administered immediately USA
after Confirmation, or after Baptism, when Confirmation is not 294
conferred.

Invitation to Prayer

394. The minister may give the following or similar instruction: if 294
Viaticum follows the celebration of Confirmation, the minister uses option A or similar words; if Confirmation is not celebrated and Viaticum follows Baptism, the minister uses option B or similar words.

A

Minister:

N., God the Father has freed you from your sins,
given you a new birth
and made you his son (daughter) in Christ.
But now, before you receive the Body of Christ,
and in the spirit of filial adoption which you have received
today,
join us in praying as our Lord himself taught us.

And the neophyte and all present together with the minister say:

Our Father . . .

B

Minister:

N., God the Father has freed you from your sins,
given you a new birth
and made you his son (daughter) in Christ.
God willing,
you will soon receive the fullness of the Holy Spirit through
Confirmation.

But now, before you receive the Body of Christ,
and in the spirit of filial adoption which you have received today,
join us in praying as our Lord himself taught us.

And the neophyte and all present together with the minister say:

Our Father . . .

Holy Communion as Viaticum

395. The minister, facing the neophyte, takes the Sacrament and, holding it slightly raised, says: 294 ASPC 130, 131

Behold the Lamb of God,
behold him who takes away the sins of the world.
Blessed are those called to the supper of the Lamb.

The neophyte and those who are present together say:

Lord, I am not worthy
that you should enter under my roof,
but only say the word
and my soul shall be healed.

The minister gives Communion to the neophyte, saying:

The Body of Christ (or: **The Blood of Christ**).

The neophyte replies:

Amen.

And immediately, or after giving Communion, the minister adds:

May he protect you and lead you to eternal life.

The neophyte replies:

Amen.

Others present who wish to receive Communion may receive the Sacrament.

A short period of silent prayer may follow.

Prayer after Communion

396. After Communion, the minister says the concluding prayer: 294

Let us pray.

O Lord, holy Father, almighty and eternal God,
with faith we entreat you
that the most holy Body (most holy Blood)
of our Lord Jesus Christ your Son
may benefit our brother (sister) who receives it
as an everlasting remedy
for both body and soul.
Through Christ our Lord.

All:

Amen.

CONCLUDING RITES

Blessing

397. The minister blesses the sick person and the others present, ASPC
using one of the following Blessings. 133

A

A minister who is a Priest or Deacon says:

May the Lord Jesus Christ be with you to defend you.
℟. Amen.

May he go before you to lead you and behind you to guard you.
℟. Amen.

May he look upon you, keep you safe and bless you.

℟. Amen.

(And may almighty God bless all of you,
who are gathered here,
the Father, and the Son, ✠ and the Holy Spirit.

℟. Amen.)

B

A lay minister invokes God's blessing and signs himself (herself) with the Sign of the Cross, saying:

May the Lord bless us,
protect us from all evil
and lead us to everlasting life.

℟. Amen.

Sign of Peace

398. Then both the minister and those present may offer a Sign of Peace to the sick person. ASPC 133

ALTERNATIVE CONCLUDING RITES

399. When the celebration is concluded after Confirmation and Viaticum is not given, the rite is concluded by use of option A. If neither Confirmation nor Viaticum can be given, immediately after Baptism, the rite is concluded by use of option B. 292 USA

A

The minister addresses the sick person in the following words:

N., God the Father has freed you from your sins,
given you a new birth
and made you his son (daughter) in Christ.
Soon, God willing,
you will approach the altar of God
and will become a partaker at the table of his sacrifice.
In the spirit of filial adoption which you have received today,
join us now in praying as our Lord himself taught us.

And the neophyte and all present together with the minister say the Lord's Prayer:

Our Father . . .

The Blessing (no. **397**) and Sign of Peace (no. **398**) may then be given.

B

The minister addresses the sick person in the following words:

N., God the Father has freed you from your sins,
given you a new birth
and made you his son (daughter) in Christ.
God willing,
you will soon receive the fullness of the Holy Spirit through Confirmation
and, approaching the altar of God,
will become a partaker at the table of his sacrifice.
In the spirit of filial adoption which you have received today,
join us now in praying as our Lord himself taught us.

And the neophyte and all present together with the minister say the Lord's Prayer:

Our Father . . .

The Blessing (no. **397**) and Sign of Peace (no. **398**) may then be given.

CHAPTER V

PREPARING ADULTS FOR CONFIRMATION AND THE EUCHARIST WHO WERE BAPTIZED AS INFANTS AND DID NOT RECEIVE CATECHESIS

400. The following pastoral advice pertains to those adult Catho- 295
lics who, having been baptized as infants, did not afterwards re- USA
ceive catechesis, and therefore have not received Confirmation and the Eucharist. It may, however, be adapted to similar cases, especially that of an adult who was baptized in danger of or at the point of death (cf. no. **374**), or who was validly baptized in another Christian community.

Even if adults in this situation have not yet heard the proclamation of the mystery of Christ, their circumstance nonetheless differs from the circumstance of catechumens because they have already been brought into the Church and become children of God by Baptism. Hence their conversion is based on Baptism already received, the strength of which they should further develop.

401. With the same reasoning that applies to catechumens, the 296
preparation of uncatechized adults demands a lengthy period (cf. no. **76**) in which the faith poured into them at Baptism ought to grow, in order to attain maturity and be fully formed through the pastoral instruction that is handed on to them; their own Christian life must be strengthened by an appropriate formation offered to them, by catechesis adapted for them, contact with the community of the faithful, and participation in certain liturgical rites.

402. The plan of catechesis corresponds for the most part to the 297
one set forth for catechumens (cf. no. **75.1**); nevertheless, in educating them, the Priest, Deacon, or catechist should take account of the special condition of these adults who have already been enriched by Baptism.

403. As in the case of catechumens, the community of the faithful 298
should also offer these adults its help through mutual charity and prayer (cf. nos. **4**, **75.2**), and by testifying to their suitability when they are to be admitted to the Sacraments (cf. nos. **120**, **121**).

404. Adults should be presented to the community by a sponsor 299
(cf. no. **10**). But at the time of their formation, each of them, with the approval of the Priest, chooses a godparent, who acts with the person as the delegate of the community, and who will have the same responsibilities for the person as the godparent for a catechumen (cf. no. **11**). The godparent chosen at this time, however, may also be the baptismal godparent, as long as he or she is indeed capable of fulfilling this office.

405. The period of preparation is sanctified by liturgical actions, 300
of which the first is a rite by which adults are received into the USA
community and acknowledge that they have a share in it because they have already been signed with Baptism. The Rite of Welcoming the Candidates, which follows in section A, is provided for this purpose.

406. From this time on they participate in celebrations of the Lit- 301
urgy of the Word, both those at which the group of the faithful is gathered and those that are designed in a similar way for catechumens (cf. nos. **81–84**).

407. Nonetheless, to signify God's action in this task of prepara- 302
tion, there may fittingly be used certain rites of the catechumenate USA
proper that respond to the circumstance and spiritual benefit of these adults, such as the Rites of Handing On of the Creed (nos. **157–162**), or of the Lord's Prayer (nos. **178–182**), or even of the Presentation of the Gospels (no. **64**). The additional rites in sections B, C, and D may also be used in accordance with the individual needs and circumstances of the candidates.

408. The period of catechesis for uncatechized Catholics is fittingly 303
inserted into the liturgical year, but especially what pertains to the final preparation, which for the most part is scheduled within Lent. Indeed, throughout this period they gather for appropriately planned sacred penitential activities, which will lead to the celebration of the Sacrament of Penance.

409. The climax of the entire formation, moreover, will normally 304
be the Easter Vigil, in which the adult Catholics will profess baptismal faith, receive the Sacrament of Confirmation, and participate in the Eucharist. The faculty to confirm a Catholic previously baptized as an infant must be received from the Diocesan Bishop. If Confirmation cannot be given during the Easter Vigil itself because the Bishop or an extraordinary minister of Confirmation is not present, it is to be conferred as soon as possible, and indeed, insofar as it is possible, during Easter Time.

410. Finally the Catholic adults will bring to completion their 305
Christian formation and incorporation into the community, experiencing the Period of Mystagogy together with the neophytes.

OPTIONAL RITES FOR BAPTIZED BUT UNCATECHIZED ADULTS

A. RITE OF WELCOMING THE CANDIDATES USA

411. This optional rite welcomes baptized but uncatechized adults who are seeking to complete their Christian Initiation through the Sacraments of Confirmation and the Eucharist or to be received into the full communion of the Catholic Church.

412. The prayers and ritual gestures acknowledge that such candidates are already part of the community because they have been marked by Baptism. Now the Church surrounds them with special care and support as they prepare to be sealed with the gift of the Holy Spirit in Confirmation and take their place at the banquet table of Christ's sacrifice.

413. Once formally welcomed into the life of the community, these adults, besides regularly attending Sunday Mass, take part in Celebrations of the Word of God in the full Christian assembly and in celebrations arranged especially for the benefit of the candidates.

414. The rite will take place on specified days throughout the year (cf. no. **18**) that are suited to local conditions.

415. When the Rite of Welcoming the Candidates for the Sacraments of Confirmation and the Eucharist is to be combined with the Rite for Entrance into the Catechumenate, the alternate rite given in Appendix I, 1 is used (nos. **505–529**).

RECEIVING THE CANDIDATES

416. When this rite is celebrated within Mass, the Entrance Chant is sung as usual. Because they are already numbered among the baptized, the candidates are seated in a prominent place among the faithful.

Greeting

417. The celebrant warmly greets the candidates. He speaks to them, their sponsors, and all present, pointing out the joy and happiness of the Church. He reminds the assembly that these candidates have already been baptized. If it seems opportune, he may also indicate briefly the particular path which has led the candidates to seek the completion of their Christian Initiation.

Then he invites the sponsors and candidates to come forward. As they are taking their places before the celebrant, a suitable chant may be sung, for example, Psalm 63 (62):2-9:

Psalm 63 (62):2-9

2 O God, you are my God; at dawn I seek you;
for you my soul is thirsting.
For you my flesh is pining,
like a dry, weary land without water.
3 I have come before you in the sanctuary,
to behold your strength and your glory.

4 Your loving mercy is better than life;
my lips will speak your praise.
5 I will bless you all my life;
in your name I will lift up my hands.
6 My soul shall be filled as with a banquet;
with joyful lips, my mouth shall praise you.

7 When I remember you upon my bed,
I muse on you through the watches of the night.
8 For you have been my strength;
in the shadow of your wings I rejoice.
9 My soul clings fast to you;
your right hand upholds me.

Dialogue

418. Then the celebrant first asks or calls out the civil or family name of the individual candidates, if necessary, unless their names are already known because of the small number of candidates. They should always reply individually, even if the celebrant asks the question only once because of their number. This is done in the following or similar way.

A

Celebrant:
What is your name?

Candidate:
N.

B

The celebrant, if he wishes, calls out the name of each candidate, who answers:

Present.

The celebrant continues with the following questions. When there is a large number of candidates, the remaining questions may be answered by all the candidates as a group. The celebrant may use other words in asking the candidates about their intentions and may permit them to reply in their own words.

Celebrant:
What do you ask of God's Church?

Candidate:
To be accepted as a candidate for catechetical instruction
leading to Confirmation and the Eucharist
(or: **leading to Reception into the full communion of the Catholic Church**).

Candidates' Declaration of Intent

419. Then the celebrant, adapting his words, as required, to the replies received, addresses the candidates again in these or similar words:

A

Blessed be the God and Father of our Lord Jesus Christ,
who, in his great mercy has given us a new birth unto a living hope,
a hope which draws its life from Christ's Resurrection from the dead.
By Baptism into Christ Jesus, this hope of glory became your own.
Christ opened for you the way of the Gospel that leads to eternal life.
Now, under the guidance of the Holy Spirit,
you desire to continue that journey of faith.

Are you prepared to reflect more deeply on the mystery of your Baptism,
to listen with us to the Apostles' instruction,
and to join with us in a life of prayer and service?

Candidates:

I am.

B

Celebrant:

Please declare before this community
the reasons why you desire to enter more fully into the life of the Church.

The candidates respond with a brief personal witness.

Affirmation by the Sponsors and the Assembly

420. Then the celebrant turns to the sponsors and all the faithful and questions them in these or similar words:

Sponsors, you now present these candidates to us.
Are you, and all who are gathered with us,
ready to help these candidates
complete their Christian Initiation
(or: **prepare for Reception into the full communion of the Catholic Church**)?

All:
We are.

The celebrant, with hands joined, says:

Father of mercy,
we thank you for these servants.
You have already consecrated them in Baptism
and now you call them to the fullness of the Church's sacramental life:
we praise and bless you, Lord.

All:
We praise and bless you, Lord.

Signing of the Candidates with the Cross

421. Next the Cross is traced on the forehead of the candidates; at the discretion of the celebrant the signing of one, several, or all of the senses may follow. The celebrant alone says the formulas accompanying each signing.

Signing of the Forehead

422. The celebrant speaks to the candidates in these or similar words:

Dear candidates, you have expressed your desire
to share fully in the life of the Catholic Church.
I now mark you with the sign of Christ's Cross
and call upon your catechists and sponsors to do the same.

Then the celebrant makes the Sign of the Cross over them all together, while the catechists or sponsors make it over the individual candidates, as he says:

Receive the Cross on your forehead
as a reminder of your Baptism
into Christ's saving Death and Resurrection.

As circumstances suggest, the signing may be concluded with the singing of an acclamation praising Christ, for example:

Glory and praise to you, Lord Jesus Christ!

Signing of the Other Senses

423. The signings are carried out by the catechists or sponsors (and, if required in special circumstances, these may be done by several Priests or Deacons).

As circumstances suggest, the signings each time they are made may be concluded with the singing of an acclamation praising Christ, for example: **Glory and praise to you, Lord Jesus Christ!** The formula, however, is always spoken by the celebrant, who says:

While the ears are being signed:

Receive the sign of the Cross on your ears,
that you may hear the voice of the Lord.

While the eyes are being signed:

Receive the sign of the Cross on your eyes,
that you may see the glory of God.

While the lips are being signed:

Receive the sign of the Cross on your lips,
that you may respond to the word of God.

While the chest is being signed:

Receive the sign of the Cross on your chest,
that Christ may dwell in your heart by faith.

While the shoulders are being signed:

Receive the sign of the Cross on your shoulders,
that you may bear the gentle yoke of Christ.

[While the hands are being signed:

Receive the sign of the Cross on your hands,
that Christ may be known in the work which you do.

While the feet are being signed:

Receive the sign of the Cross on your feet,
that you may walk in the way of Christ.]

Then, without touching them, the celebrant alone makes the Sign of the Cross over all the candidates, while he says:

I sign all of you
in the name of the Father, and of the Son, ✠ and of the
Holy Spirit,
that you may live for ever and ever.

Candidates:

Amen.

424. The celebrant concludes the signing of the forehead (and senses) with the Collect for the Mass of the day or with the following prayer:

Let us pray.

Almighty God,
who through the Cross and Resurrection of your Son
have given life to your people,
grant, we pray,
that, following in the footsteps of Christ,
your servants, who in Baptism accepted
the sign of the Cross,
may possess its saving power in their lives
and show it forth in their deeds.
Through Christ our Lord.

℟. Amen.

LITURGY OF THE WORD

Instruction

425. The celebrant next speaks briefly to the candidates and their sponsors, helping them to understand the dignity of God's word, which is proclaimed and heard in the church.

Readings

426. The readings are those assigned for the day. According to the norms of the Lectionary, other appropriate readings may be substituted.

Homily

427. A Homily follows that explains the readings.

Presentation of the Gospels

428. Then, if the celebrant so wishes, books containing the Gospels are distributed with dignity and reverence to the candidates. The celebrant uses a suitable formula, such as:

Receive the Gospel of Jesus Christ, the Son of God.

It is fitting for the candidate to respond with appropriate words to the celebrant's gift and words.

Profession of Faith

429. The Creed, when required, is said.

Universal Prayer (Prayer of the Faithful)

430. The Universal Prayer (Prayer of the Faithful) follows. One or more of the following intentions for the candidates are added to the intentions for the Church and the whole world.

Lector:

That God our Father reveal his Christ to these candidates more each day,
let us pray to the Lord:

℟. Lord, hear our prayer.

Lector:

That these candidates come to a deeper appreciation of the gift of their Baptism,
which joined them to Christ,
let us pray to the Lord:

℟. Lord, hear our prayer.

Lector:

That they find in our community visible signs of unity and generous love,
let us pray to the Lord:

℟. Lord, hear our prayer.

Lector:

That their hearts and ours become more responsive to the needs of others,
let us pray to the Lord:

℟. Lord, hear our prayer.

Lector:

That in due time these candidates be
(embraced by the Father's merciful forgiveness,)
sealed with the gift of the Holy Spirit
and know the joy of being one with us
at the table of Christ's sacrifice,
let us pray to the Lord:

℟. Lord, hear our prayer.

Concluding Prayer

431. After the Universal Prayer (Prayer of the Faithful), the celebrant, extending his hands toward the candidates, says the following prayer:

Almighty and eternal God,
whose love gathers us together as one,
receive the prayers of your people.

Look kindly on these your servants,
already consecrated to you in Baptism,
and draw them into the fullness of faith.

Keep your family one in the bonds of love.
Through Christ our Lord.

℟. Amen.

Dismissal of the Assembly

432. If the Eucharist is not celebrated, a suitable chant, as circumstances suggest, may be added, and the entire assembly may be dismissed, using these or similar words:

Go in peace,
and may the Lord remain with you.

All:
Thanks be to God.

CELEBRATION OF THE EUCHARIST

433. When the Eucharist is celebrated, the Preparation of the Gifts follows.

B. RITE OF SENDING THE CANDIDATES FOR THE CALLING TO CONTINUING CONVERSION

USA

434. This optional rite is provided for parishes whose candidates seeking to complete their Christian Initiation or to be received into the full communion of the Catholic Church will be called by the Bishop to continuing conversion.

435. Because he is the sign of unity within the particular Church, it is fitting for the Bishop to recognize these candidates. It is the responsibility of the parish community, however, to prepare the candidates for their fuller life in the Church. Through the experience of worship, daily life, and service in the parish community the candidates deepen their appreciation of the Church's tradition and universal character. This rite offers that local community the opportunity to express its joy in the candidates' decision and to send them forth to the celebration of recognition assured of the parish's care and support.

436. The rite is celebrated in the parish church at a suitable time prior to the Rite of Calling the Candidates to Continuing Conversion.

437. When the Rite of Sending the Candidates for the Calling to Continuing Conversion is to be combined with the Rite of Sending Catechumens for Election, the alternate rite given in Appendix I, 2 is used (nos. **530–546**).

LITURGY OF THE WORD

Homily

438. After the readings, the celebrant gives the Homily. This should be suited to the actual situation and should address not just the candidates but the entire community of the faithful, so that all will be encouraged to give good example and to accompany the candidates along the path leading to their complete Initiation.

Presentation of the Candidates

439. The Priest in charge of the candidates' formation, or a Deacon, a catechist, or a representative of the community, presents the candidates, using the following or similar words:

Reverend Father, these candidates, whom I now present to you,
are beginning their final period of preparation
for the Sacraments of Confirmation and the Eucharist
(or: **for Reception into the full communion of the Catholic Church**).

They have found strength in God's grace
and support in our community's prayers and example.
Now they ask that they be recognized
for the progress they have made in their spiritual formation
and that they receive the assurance of our blessings and prayers
as they go forth for the Calling to Continuing Conversion this afternoon (or: **next Sunday** [or specify the day]).

The celebrant replies:

Candidates, come forward, together with your sponsors.

One by one, the candidates are called by name. Each candidate, accompanied by a sponsor, comes forward and stands before the celebrant.

Affirmation by the Sponsors (and the Assembly)

440. Then the celebrant addresses the assembly in these or similar words:

My dear friends, these candidates,
already one with us by reason of their Baptism in Christ,
have asked to complete their Initiation
(or: **have asked to be received into the full communion of the Catholic Church**).
Those who know them have judged them to be sincere in their desire.
During the period of their catechetical formation
they have listened to the word of Christ
and endeavored to follow his commands more perfectly;
they have shared the company of their Christian brothers and sisters in this community
and joined with them in prayer.

And so I announce to all of you here
that our community ratifies their desire
to complete their Initiation
(or: **to be received into full communion**).

Therefore, I ask their sponsors to state their opinion once again,
so that all of you may hear.

He addresses the sponsors:

As God is our witness, do you consider these candidates
ready to receive the Sacraments of Confirmation and the Eucharist
(or: **ready to be received into the full communion of the Catholic Church**)?

Sponsors:

We do.

When appropriate in the circumstances, the celebrant may also ask the entire assembly to express its approval of the candidates.

441. The celebrant concludes the affirmation by the following:

And now, my dear friends, I address you.
Your own sponsors (and this entire community) have spoken in your favor.
The Church, in the name of Christ, accepts their testimony
and sends you to the Calling to Continuing Conversion,
where Bishop N. will exhort you to live in deeper conformity
to the life of Christ.

Universal Prayer (Prayer of the Faithful)

442. The Universal Prayer (Prayer of the Faithful) follows. One or more of the following intentions for the candidates are added to the intentions for the Church and the whole world.

Lector:

That these candidates may renounce self-centeredness
and think of others rather than themselves,
let us pray to the Lord:

℟. Lord, hear our prayer.

Lector:

For their godparents and sponsors, that they may show to the candidates
a constant application of the Gospel
both in their private and in their public lives,
let us pray to the Lord:

℟. Lord, hear our prayer.

Lector:

For their catechists, that they may convey the sweetness of God's word
to those who search for it,
let us pray to the Lord:

℟. Lord, hear our prayer.

Lector:

That they may share with others
the happiness they have found in their faith,
let us pray to the Lord:

℟. Lord, hear our prayer.

Lector:

For our community, that during this (or: **the coming**) Lenten season,
it may be radiant with the fullness of charity and with constancy in prayer,
let us pray to the Lord:

℟. Lord, hear our prayer.

Prayer over the Candidates

443. The celebrant, extending his hands over the candidates, concludes the Universal Prayer (Prayer of the Faithful) with this prayer:

Almighty, most beloved Father,
whose will it is to renew all things in Christ
and who draw all people to him,
graciously guide these candidates of the Church
and grant that, faithful to the calling they have received,
they may be built up into the kingdom of your Son
and be sealed with the promised Holy Spirit.
Through Christ our Lord.

℟. Amen.

Dismissal of the Assembly

444. If the Eucharist is not celebrated, a suitable chant, as circumstances suggest, may be added, and the entire assembly may be dismissed, using these or similar words:

Go in peace,
and may the Lord remain with you.

All:
Thanks be to God.

CELEBRATION OF THE EUCHARIST

445. When the Eucharist is celebrated, the Creed, if required, is said, and the Preparation of the Gifts follows. But for pastoral reasons the Creed may be omitted.

C. RITE OF CALLING THE CANDIDATES TO CONTINUING CONVERSION USA

446. This rite may be celebrated with baptized but uncatechized adults who wish to complete their Christian Initiation through the Sacraments of Confirmation and the Eucharist or who wish to be received into the full communion of the Catholic Church.

447. The rite is intended for celebrations in communities where there are no catechumens.

448. The rite may be celebrated at the beginning of Lent, especially for adult Catholics (cf. no. **409**). The presiding celebrant is the Bishop or the pastor of the parish.

449. If the Calling of Candidates to Continuing Conversion is to be combined with the Rite of Election of catechumens (either in a parish celebration or at one in which the Bishop is celebrant) the alternate rite given in Appendix I, 3 is used (nos. **547–561**).

LITURGY OF THE WORD

Homily

450. After the readings, the celebrant gives the Homily. The Homily, suited to the actual situation, should address not only the candidates but the entire community of the faithful, so that, striving to give good example, they may accompany the candidates in their final preparation leading to the celebration of Confirmation and the Eucharist.

Presentation of the Candidates for Confirmation and the Eucharist

451. After the Homily, the Priest in charge of the candidates' formation, or a Deacon, a catechist, or a representative of the community, presents the candidates, using the following or similar words:

(Most) Reverend Father,
(as the solemn paschal celebrations approach once more,)
the candidates present here,
relying on divine grace
and supported by the prayers and example of the community,
humbly request that, after due preparation,
they be admitted to participate
in the Sacraments of Confirmation and the Eucharist
(or: **to full Eucharistic Communion**).

The celebrant replies:

Let those who desire
to participate fully in the sacramental life of the Church
come forward with their sponsors.

One by one, they are called by name. Each candidate, accompanied by a sponsor, comes forward and stands before the celebrant.

Affirmation by the Sponsors (and the Assembly)

452. Then the celebrant addresses the assembly. If he took part in the previous deliberation about the candidates' suitableness (cf. no. **122**), he may use either option A or option B or similar words; if he has not taken part in the earlier deliberation, he uses option B or similar words.

A

Celebrant:

My dear brothers and sisters,
these candidates have asked to participate fully
in the sacramental life of the Catholic Church.

Those who know them have judged
that they are sincere in their desire.
During the period of their preparation
they have reflected on the mystery of their Baptism
and have come to appreciate more deeply the presence of Christ in their lives.
They have shared in fraternal communion and in the prayers.

And so I am pleased to recognize their desire
to participate fully in the sacramental life of the Church.
As I inform you of this judgment and speak to the sponsors,
I ask them to give their recommendation again, in your presence.

He, then, turns toward the sponsors:

With God as your witness,
do you judge these candidates to be worthy of admission
to the Sacraments of Confirmation and the Eucharist
(or: **into the full communion of the Catholic Church**)?

Sponsors:

We do.

453. Then if the circumstances warrant, the celebrant may ask the entire congregation for its assent:

Now I ask you, the members of this community:
Are you willing to affirm the testimony expressed about these candidates
and support them in faith, prayer, and example

as they prepare to participate more fully in the Church's Sacraments?

All:

We are.

B

Celebrant:

The Christian life and the demands
that flow from the Sacraments cannot be taken lightly.
Therefore, before granting these candidates their request
to share fully in the Church's Sacraments,
it is important that the Church hear the testimony
of their sponsors about their readiness.

He, then, turns toward the sponsors:

Have they faithfully listened to God's word proclaimed by the Church?

Sponsors:

They have.

Celebrant:

Have they come to a deeper appreciation of their Baptism,
in which they were joined to Christ and his Church?

Sponsors:

They have.

Celebrant:

Have they reflected sufficiently on the tradition of the Church,
which is their heritage, and joined their brothers and sisters in prayer?

Sponsors:

They have.

Celebrant:
Have they advanced in a life of love and service of others?

Sponsors:
They have.

Then if the circumstances warrant, the celebrant may ask the entire congregation for its assent:

Now I ask you, the members of this community:
Are you willing to affirm the testimony expressed about these candidates
and include them in your prayer and affection (as we move toward Easter)?

All:
We are.

Act of Recognition

454. Then the celebrant turns toward the candidates, addressing them in these or similar words:

N. and N., the Church recognizes your desire
(to be sealed with the gift of the Holy Spirit and)
to have a place at Christ's eucharistic table.
Join with us (this Lent) in a spirit of repentance.
Hear the Lord's call to conversion
and be faithful to your baptismal covenant.

Candidates:
Thanks be to God.

Then, turning toward the sponsors, the celebrant addresses them in these or similar words:

Sponsors, continue to support these candidates
with your guidance and concern.
May they see in you a love for the Church
and a sincere desire for doing good.
Lead them (this Lent) to the joys of the Easter mysteries.

He invites them to place their hand on the shoulder of the candidate whom they are receiving into their care, or to make some other gesture to indicate the same intent.

Universal Prayer (Prayer of the Faithful)

455. Then the sponsors and the whole congregation join in the Universal Prayer (Prayer of the Faithful). One or more of the following intentions for the candidates are added to the intentions for the Church and the whole world.

Lector:

That these candidates may come to a deeper appreciation
of their Baptism into Christ's Death and Resurrection,
let us pray to the Lord:

℟. Lord, hear our prayer.

Lector:

That God bless those who have nurtured
these candidates in faith,
let us pray to the Lord:

℟. Lord, hear our prayer.

Lector:

That these candidates may (embrace the discipline of Lent as a means of purification
and) approach the Sacrament of Penance with trust in God's mercy,
let us pray to the Lord:

℟. Lord, hear our prayer.

Lector:

That they may open their hearts
to the promptings of God's Holy Spirit,
let us pray to the Lord:

℟. Lord, hear our prayer.

Lector:

That they may approach the table of Christ's sacrifice
with thanksgiving and praise,
let us pray to the Lord:

℟. Lord, hear our prayer.

Lector:

That our community (during this Lenten season)
may be radiant with the fullness of charity and with constancy
in prayer,
let us pray to the Lord:

℟. Lord, hear our prayer.

456. The celebrant, extending his hands over the candidates, concludes the Universal Prayer (Prayer of the Faithful) with this prayer:

Lord God,
whose love brings us to life
and whose mercy gives us new birth,
look favorably upon these candidates,
and conform their lives
to the pattern of Christ's suffering.
May he become their wealth and wisdom,
and may they know in their lives
the power flowing from his Resurrection.
Who lives and reigns for ever and ever.

℟. Amen.

Dismissal of the Assembly

457. If the Eucharist is not celebrated, a suitable chant, as circumstances suggest, may be added, and the entire assembly may be dismissed, using these or similar words:

Go in peace,
and may the Lord remain with you.

All:
Thanks be to God.

CELEBRATION OF THE EUCHARIST

458. When the Eucharist is celebrated, the Creed, if required, is said, and the Preparation of the Gifts follows. But for pastoral reasons the Creed may be omitted.

D. PENITENTIAL RITE (SCRUTINY) USA

459. This Penitential Rite can serve to mark the Lenten purification of baptized but uncatechized adults who are preparing to receive the Sacraments of Confirmation and the Eucharist or to be received into the full communion of the Catholic Church. It is held within a Celebration of the Word of God as a kind of Scrutiny, similar to the Scrutinies for catechumens.

460. Because the Penitential Rite normally belongs to the period of final preparation for the Sacraments, its celebration presumes that the candidates are approaching the maturity of faith and understanding requisite for fuller life in the community.

461. Along with the candidates, their sponsors and the larger liturgical assembly also participate in the celebration of the Penitential Rite. Therefore the rite is to be adapted in such a way that it benefits all the participants. This Penitential Rite may also help to prepare the candidates to celebrate the Sacrament of Penance.

462. This Penitential Rite may be celebrated on the Second Sunday of Lent or on a weekday of Lent, if the candidates are to receive the Sacraments of Confirmation and the Eucharist or be received into the full communion of the Catholic Church at Easter; if not, at the most suitable time.

463. This Penitential Rite is intended solely for celebrations with baptized adults preparing for Confirmation and the Eucharist or Reception into the full communion of the Catholic Church. Because the Prayer of Exorcism in the three Scrutinies for catechumens who have received the Church's Election properly belongs to the elect and uses numerous images referring to their approaching Baptism, those Scrutinies of the elect and this Penitential Rite for those preparing for Confirmation and the Eucharist have been kept separate and distinct. Thus, no combined rite has been included in Appendix I.

INTRODUCTORY RITES

Greeting and Introduction

464. The Priest welcomes the assembly and in a few words explains that the rite will have different meanings for the different participants: the candidates who are already baptized, particularly those preparing to celebrate the Sacrament of Penance for the first time, the sponsors, catechists, Priests, etc. All these participants in their own different ways are going to hear the comforting message of pardon for sin, for which they will praise the Father's mercy.

A song may be sung that joyfully expresses faith in the mercy of God the Father.

Prayer

465. The celebrant then says the Collect prayer for the Second Sunday of Lent (option A) or, on another day, the following prayer (option B):

A

O God, who have commanded us
to listen to your beloved Son,
be pleased, we pray,
to nourish us inwardly by your word,
that, with spiritual sight made pure,
we may rejoice to behold your glory.
Through our Lord Jesus Christ, your Son,
who lives and reigns with you in the unity of the Holy Spirit,
God, for ever and ever.

All:

Amen.

B

Lord of infinite compassion and steadfast love,
your sons and daughters stand before you
in humility and trust.
Look with compassion on us
as we acknowledge our sinfulness.
Stretch out your hand
to save us and raise us up.
Do not allow the power of darkness
to triumph over us,
but keep us free from sin
as members of Christ's body,
and sheep of your own flock.
Through our Lord Jesus Christ, your Son,
who lives and reigns with you in the unity of the Holy Spirit,
God, for ever and ever.

All:

Amen.

LITURGY OF THE WORD

Readings

466. On the Second Sunday of Lent the readings for Mass are those assigned by the *Lectionary for Mass*, nos. 25–27. On other days, appropriate readings from the Lectionary are used.

Homily

467. After the readings, the celebrant explains the sacred texts in the Homily. He should prepare all those in the assembly for conversion and repentance and give the meaning of the Penitential Rite (Scrutiny) in the light of the Lenten liturgy and of the spiritual journey of the candidates.

Prayer in Silence

468. After the Homily, the candidates with their sponsors come forward and stand before the celebrant.

Looking at the faithful, he invites them to pray in silence for the candidates and ask that they be given a spirit of repentance, a sense of sin, and the true freedom of the children of God.

Then he turns toward the candidates, and, at the same time, invites them to pray in silence and instructs them to show their spirit of repentance by bowing or kneeling. Then he concludes in these or similar words:

Candidates, bow your heads (or: **kneel**) and pray.

Then the candidates bow or kneel and all pray in silence for a while. Then, as circumstances suggest, all stand.

Intercessions for the Candidates

469. Then the sponsors and the whole congregation join in the Intercessions for the candidates. If the Eucharist is to be celebrated, intentions for the Church and for the whole world should be added to the following intentions for the candidates.

Celebrant:

My brothers and sisters, let us pray for these candidates
(N. and N.).
Christ has already ransomed them in Baptism.
Now they seek the forgiveness of their sins and the healing of
their weakness,
so that they may be ready
(to be sealed with the gift of the Father and)
to be fed at the Lord's table.
Let us also pray for ourselves, who seek the mercy of Christ.

Lector:

That these candidates may come to a deeper appreciation
of their Baptism into Christ's Death and Resurrection,
let us pray to the Lord:

℟. Lord, hear our prayer.

Lector:

That these candidates may (embrace the discipline of Lent as a
means of purification
and) approach the Sacrament of Penance with trust in God's
mercy,
let us pray to the Lord:

℟. Lord, hear our prayer.

Lector:

That they will acquire the habit
of cherishing and preserving virtue and holiness of life,
let us pray to the Lord:

℟. Lord, hear our prayer.

Lector:

That they may renounce self-centeredness
and think of others rather than themselves,
let us pray to the Lord:

℟. Lord, hear our prayer.

Lector:

That they may share with others
the happiness they have found in their faith,
let us pray to the Lord:

℟. Lord, hear our prayer.

Lector:

That they may accept the call to conversion with an open heart
and not hesitate to make the personal changes it may require of them,
let us pray to the Lord:

℟. Lord, hear our prayer.

Lector:

That the Holy Spirit, who searches every heart,
may strengthen them in their weakness with his power,
let us pray to the Lord:

℟. Lord, hear our prayer.

Lector:

That their families also may put their hope in Christ
and find peace and holiness in him,
let us pray to the Lord:

℟. Lord, hear our prayer.

Lector:

That we ourselves (in preparation for the Paschal Feasts)
may correct our minds, raise our hearts, and perform works of charity,
let us pray to the Lord:

℟. Lord, hear our prayer.

Concluding Prayer

470. After the Intercessions, the rite continues with the Prayer over the Candidates, option A (particularly when celebrated on the Second Sunday of Lent) or option B.

A

The celebrant faces the candidates and, with hands joined, says:

Let us pray.

Lord God,
in the mystery of the Transfiguration
your Son revealed his glory to the disciples
and prepared them for his Death and Resurrection.
Open the minds and hearts of these candidates
to the presence of Christ in their lives.
May they humbly acknowledge their sins and failings
and be freed of whatever obstacles and falsehoods
keep them from adhering wholeheartedly to your kingdom.
Through Christ our Lord.

℟. Amen.

Then, if this can be done conveniently, the celebrant lays hands in silence on each one of the candidates.

Then, with hands extended over the candidates, the celebrant continues:

Lord Jesus,
you are the Only Begotten Son,
whose kingdom these candidates acknowledge
and whose glory they seek.
Pour out upon them the power of your Spirit,
that they may be fearless witnesses to your Gospel
and one with us in the communion of love.
Who live and reign for ever and ever.

℟. Amen.

B

The celebrant faces the candidates and, with hands joined, says:

Let us pray.

Lord our God,
you created us in love
and redeemed us in mercy
through the Blood of your Son.
Enlighten these men and women by your grace,
that, clearly seeing their sins and failings,
they may place all their trust in your mercy
and resist all that is deceitful and harmful.
Through Christ our Lord.

℟. Amen.

Then, if this can be done conveniently, the celebrant lays hands in silence on each one of the candidates.

Then, with hands extended over the candidates, the celebrant continues:

Lord Jesus,
whose love reaches out in mercy
to embrace and heal the contrite of heart,
lead these candidates along the way of holiness,
and heal the wounds of their sins.
May they ever keep safe in all its fullness
the gift your love once gave them
and your mercy now restores.
Who live and reign for ever and ever.

℟. Amen.

If circumstances suggest, a suitable chant may be sung, for example, Psalms 6, 26 (25), 32 (31), 38 (37), 39 (38), 40 (39), 51 (50), 116:1-9 (114), 130 (129), 139 (138), or 142 (141).

Dismissal of the Assembly

471. If the Eucharist is not celebrated, a suitable chant, as circumstances suggest, may be added, and the entire assembly may be dismissed, using these or similar words:

Go in peace,
and may the Lord remain with you.

All:
Thanks be to God.

CELEBRATION OF THE EUCHARIST

472. When the Eucharist is celebrated, the Creed, if required, is said, and the Preparation of the Gifts follows. But for pastoral reasons the Creed may be omitted.

CHAPTER VI

ORDER OF RECEPTION INTO THE FULL COMMUNION OF THE CATHOLIC CHURCH OF THOSE ALREADY VALIDLY BAPTIZED

473. The rite by which a person born and baptized in a separated R1
ecclesial Community is received into the full communion of the Catholic Church according to the Latin Rite,[1] is so arranged that no further burden is imposed than what is necessary to restore communion and unity[2] (cf. Acts 15:28).

474. Nothing more is required of Eastern Christians coming to the R2
fullness of Catholic communion, however, than what a simple profession of Catholic faith requires, even if, by virtue of recourse to the Apostolic See, a transfer to the Latin Rite is permitted to them.[3]

475. In regard to the manner of celebrating the Rite of Reception: R3

a) The rite of the celebration should appear as a celebration of the Church, and its high point should be realized in Eucharistic Communion. Therefore the admission normally should take place during Mass.

[1] Cf. Second Vatican Council, Constitution on the Sacred Liturgy, *Sacrosanctum Concilium,* no. 69b; Decree on Ecumenism, *Unitatis redintegratio,* no. 3; Secretariat for Christian Unity, Ecumenical Directory I, no. 19: *Acta Apostolicæ Sedis* 59 (1967), p. 581.
[2] Cf. Second Vatican Council, Decree on Ecumenism, *Unitatis redintegratio,* no. 18.
[3] Cf. Second Vatican Council, Decree on Eastern Catholic Churches, *Orientalium Ecclesiarum,* nos. 25 and 4.

b) Nonetheless, those aspects that in any way have an air of triumphalism should be carefully avoided. The way in which this Mass will be celebrated must be precisely defined, attentive to circumstances. Consideration must be given both to the good of ecumenism and to the bond between the candidate and the parish community. More appropriately, often it will be a Mass celebrated with only a few relatives and friends. Nevertheless, if for a serious reason a Mass cannot be celebrated, the Reception may be held within a Liturgy of the Word, whenever at least this is possible. The one being received, however, should also be consulted concerning the form to be chosen.

476. If Reception is celebrated outside Mass, its connection with R4
Eucharistic Communion should be made clear by having it followed as soon as possible by a Eucharistic Celebration, in which the newly received fully participates among Catholic brothers and sisters for the first time.

477. For the Reception of those already baptized into the full com- R5
munion of the Catholic Church, both a doctrinal and a spiritual preparation of the candidate is required, according to pastoral needs accommodated to individual cases. A candidate should learn to adhere more and more lovingly to the Church, in which the candidate will find the fullness of his or her Baptism.

At the time of this preparation some sharing in worship may already be taking place, according to the norms established in the Ecumenical Directory.

Equating candidates with catechumens is to be altogether avoided.

478. During the period of their doctrinal and spiritual preparation USA
individual candidates for Reception into the full communion of the Catholic Church may benefit from the celebration of liturgical rites marking their progress in formation. Thus, for pastoral reasons and in light of the catechesis in the faith which these baptized Christians have received previously, one or several of the rites included in Chapter V, "Preparing Adults for Confirmation and the Eucharist Who Were Baptized as Infants and Did Not Receive

Catechesis," may be celebrated as they are presented or in similar words. In all cases, however, discernment should be made regarding the length of catechetical formation required for each individual candidate for Reception into the full communion of the Catholic Church.

479. An abjuration of heresy is no longer required of a person who R6
was born and baptized outside the visible communion of the Catholic Church, but only a profession of faith.[4]

480. The Sacrament of Baptism cannot be repeated, and therefore R7
conditional Baptism is not permitted to be conferred again unless a prudent doubt is present concerning the fact or the validity of the Baptism already conferred. If after a serious investigation has been undertaken concerning the prudent doubt about the fact or validity of the Baptism already conferred, conditional Baptism seems necessary to confer again, the minister should appropriately explain the reasons why Baptism in this case is being conferred conditionally, and he should administer it in a private form.[5]

The local Ordinary should determine in individual cases of conferring conditional Baptism which rites should be kept and which omitted.

481. It is for the Bishop to receive the candidate. A Priest, however, R8
to whom he entrusts the celebration to be performed, has the faculty of confirming the candidate in the very Rite of Reception,[6] unless the one being received has already validly received Confirmation.

482. If the Profession and Reception take place during Mass, the R9
one being received should confess his or her sins with attention to personal circumstances, having made the confessor aware of the forthcoming Reception. Any duly approved confessor may hear this confession.

[4] Cf. Secretariat for Christian Unity, Ecumenical Directory I, nos. 19 and 20: *Acta Apostolicæ Sedis* 59 (1967), p. 581.

[5] Cf. *ibidem*, nos. 14–15: *Acta Apostolicæ Sedis* 59 (1967), p. 580.

[6] Cf. *Order of Confirmation*, Introduction, no. 7.

483. If the situation warrants, a sponsor, namely a man or a woman who had a greater role than others in leading or preparing the candidate, may accompany the one being admitted in the Reception itself; two sponsors may also be permitted. R10

484. In the Eucharistic Celebration itself during which the Reception takes place, or, if this happens outside the solemnities of the Mass, in the Mass that follows, it is permitted not only for the one admitted to receive Holy Communion under both kinds, but also the sponsors, parents, spouse (if these are Catholic), lay catechists who perhaps instructed the one being received, and indeed all Catholics present, if their number or other circumstances suggest it. R11

485. The Rite of Reception may be adapted to various circumstances by the Conferences of Bishops according to the Constitution on the Sacred Liturgy (no. 63). Above all the local Ordinary, paying attention to special conditions of persons and places, may himself adapt the Rite to them, by expanding or abbreviating it, if it seems appropriate.[7] R12

486. The names of those received should be recorded in a special book, along with the date and place of their Baptism (cf. *National Statutes for the Christian Initiation of Adults*, Norm 16 §§1-3). R13

ORDER OF RECEPTION WITHIN MASS

487. If the Reception takes place on a Solemnity or on a Sunday, the Mass of the day should be celebrated; on other days, however, it is permissible to use the Mass for the Unity of Christians. R14

[7] Cf. Secretariat for Christian Unity, Ecumenical Directory I, no. 19: *Acta Apostolicæ Sedis* 59 (1967), p. 581.

LITURGY OF THE WORD

Readings

488. The biblical readings for Mass may be taken in whole or in R29
part, from those provided in the *Lectionary for Mass* for the Mass of the day, or from the Mass for the Unity of Christians (cf. nos. 867–871) or from the Ritual Mass for Christian Initiation Apart from the Easter Vigil (cf. nos. 751–755).

Homily

489. The Reception is carried out after the Homily, in which the R14
celebrant, with gratitude to God, should speak of Baptism as the basis for the candidate's Reception, of the Sacrament of Confirmation, already received or about to be received by the candidate, and of the Most Holy Eucharist, to be celebrated by the candidate for the first time with the Catholic community.

CELEBRATION OF RECEPTION

Invitation

490. At the end of the Homily, the celebrant, in these or similar R14
words, briefly invites the candidate to come forward with his (her) sponsor to profess his (her) faith with the community:

N., since after mature deliberation in the Holy Spirit
and of your own free will
you have asked to be received
into the full communion of the Catholic Church,
I now invite you to come forward with your sponsor
and in the presence of this community
to profess the Catholic faith.

In this faith, today for the first time
you will partake with us at the eucharistic table of the Lord Jesus,
by which the unity of the Church is signified.

Profession of Faith

491. Then the person to be received, together with the faithful, recites the Niceno-Constantinopolitan Creed, which is always said at this Mass: R15

I believe in one God,
the Father almighty,
maker of heaven and earth,
of all things visible and invisible.

I believe in one Lord Jesus Christ,
the Only Begotten Son of God,
born of the Father before all ages.
God from God, Light from Light,
true God from true God,
begotten, not made, consubstantial with the Father;
through him all things were made.
For us men and for our salvation
he came down from heaven,

At the words that follow, up to and including **and became man,** all bow.

and by the Holy Spirit was incarnate of the Virgin Mary,
and became man.

For our sake he was crucified under Pontius Pilate,
he suffered death and was buried,
and rose again on the third day
in accordance with the Scriptures.
He ascended into heaven
and is seated at the right hand of the Father.

He will come again in glory
to judge the living and the dead
and his kingdom will have no end.

I believe in the Holy Spirit, the Lord, the giver of life,
who proceeds from the Father and the Son,
who with the Father and the Son is adored and glorified,
who has spoken through the prophets.

I believe in one, holy, catholic and apostolic Church.
I confess one Baptism for the forgiveness of sins
and I look forward to the resurrection of the dead
and the life of the world to come. Amen.

After this, at the celebrant's invitation, the one to be received adds:

I believe and profess
all that the holy Catholic Church
believes, teaches, and proclaims as revealed by God.

Formula of Reception

492. The celebrant then lays his right hand upon the head of the person to be received, unless Confirmation immediately follows. In either case, he says: R16 R18

N., the Lord receives you into the Catholic Church.
In his mercy he has led you here,
so that in the Holy Spirit
you may have full communion with us
in the faith you have professed before this his family.

If the person received is not confirmed, the greeting immediately follows the formula of Reception (no. **495**). USA

CELEBRATION OF CONFIRMATION

The Laying On of Hands

493. If the person to be received has not yet been confirmed, the R17
celebrant lays his hands over the candidate's head and begins the 269
Rite of Confirmation with the following prayer (for the chant, cf. no. **365**):

Almighty God, Father of our Lord Jesus Christ,
who brought this your servant to new birth
by water and the Holy Spirit,
freeing him (her) from sin:
send upon him (her), O Lord, the Holy Spirit, the Paraclete;
give him (her) the spirit of wisdom and understanding,
the spirit of counsel and fortitude,
the spirit of knowledge and piety;
fill him (her) with the spirit of the fear of the Lord.
Through Christ our Lord.

All:
Amen.

The Anointing with Chrism

494. The godparent places his (her) right hand on the shoulder of R17
the one to be confirmed and says his (her) name to the celebrant; 270
or the one to be confirmed alone says his (her) own name.

The celebrant dips the tip of the thumb of his right hand in the Chrism and, with the thumb, makes the Sign of the Cross on the forehead of the one to be confirmed, as he says:

N., be sealed with the Gift of the Holy Spirit.

The newly confirmed:
Amen.

The celebrant adds:

Peace be with you.

The newly confirmed:

And with your spirit.

Celebrant's Sign of Welcome

495. After Confirmation the celebrant greets the one newly received, taking his (her) hand between his own hands as a sign of R18
friendship and acceptance. With the permission of the Ordinary,
another suitable gesture may be substituted, depending on local
and other circumstances.

Universal Prayer (Prayer of the Faithful)

496. The Universal Prayer follows the Reception (and Confirmation). In his introduction the celebrant should mention Baptism, R19
(Confirmation,) and the Eucharist, and express gratitude to God. R30
The person received into full communion is mentioned at the
beginning of the intentions. The celebrant may use these or similar
words:

Dear brothers and sisters:
our brother (sister) N. has already been incorporated into Christ
through Baptism (and Confirmation);
now, with thanksgiving to God,
we have received him (her) into the full communion of the
Catholic Church
(and confirmed him [her] with the gifts of the Holy Spirit),
so that he (she) may soon share with us at the table of the Lord.
As we rejoice at a newly received member of the Catholic
Church,
let us join him (her) in asking for the grace and mercy of the
Savior.

Lector:

For our brother (sister)
whom we have welcomed among us today,
that with the help of the Holy Spirit
he (she) may persevere faithfully in his (her) resolve,
let us pray to the Lord:

℟. Lord, hear our prayer.

Lector:

For all who believe in Christ and for their communities,
that they may come to perfect unity,
let us pray to the Lord:

℟. Lord, hear our prayer.

Lector:

For the Church (Community) in which N. was baptized
and formed,
that it may know Christ ever more deeply
and proclaim him more effectively,
let us pray to the Lord:

℟. Lord, hear our prayer.

Lector:

For all in whom the desire for heavenly grace is already
kindled,
that they may be led to the fullness of truth in Christ,
let us pray to the Lord:

℟. Lord, hear our prayer.

Lector:

For those who do not yet believe in Christ the Lord,
that, enlightened by the Holy Spirit,
they may enter the way of salvation,
let us pray to the Lord:

℟. Lord, hear our prayer.

Lector:

For all people,
that they may be freed from hunger and war
and live in constant peace and tranquility,
let us pray to the Lord:

℟. Lord, hear our prayer.

Lector:

For ourselves,
that having received the free gift of faith,
we may persevere in it to the end,
let us pray to the Lord:

℟. Lord, hear our prayer.

Celebrant:

Almighty eternal God,
hear the prayers we pour out to you,
that we may continue to serve you with grateful devotion.
Through Christ our Lord.

℟. Amen.

Sign of Peace

497. After the Universal Prayer (Prayer of the Faithful) the sponsor and, if there are only a few persons, all who are present may, if appropriate, greet the newly-received person in a friendly manner. In this case the Sign of Peace before Communion may be omitted. Finally, the person received returns to his (her) place. R20

CELEBRATION OF THE EUCHARIST

498. Then the Mass continues. It is fitting that the person received R21
and the others mentioned in no. **484** above receive the Most Sacred Eucharist under both kinds.

ORDER OF RECEPTION OUTSIDE MASS

499. If, for a serious reason, the Reception takes place outside R22
Mass, a Liturgy of the Word is celebrated.

If, due to extraordinary circumstances, it appears that the Recep- R28
tion is to be celebrated without the Liturgy of the Word, everything takes place as above in nos. **490–497**, beginning with the celebrant's Instruction (no. **490**). This Instruction should begin with a quotation from Sacred Scripture, for example, a text that praises the mercy of God that has led the candidate to be received into full communion and speaks of the Eucharistic Communion soon to be received at a later time.

500. The celebrant, wearing an alb, or at least a surplice, and a R23
stole of festive color, greets those present.

501. The celebration begins with a suitable chant and a reading of R24
Sacred Scripture, which is explained in the Homily (cf. no. **489**).

The biblical readings may be taken in whole or in part, from those R29
provided in the *Lectionary for Mass* for the Mass of the day, or for the Mass for the Unity of Christians (cf. nos. 867–871) or for the Ritual Mass for Christian Initiation Apart from the Easter Vigil (cf. nos. 751–755).

When the rite, however, is celebrated outside Mass, it is preferable that the texts that follow be used (cf. *Lectionary for Mass*, nos. 761–763).

Readings from the New Testament

1. Rom 8:28-39: *He predestined us to be conformed to the image of his Son.*
2. 1 Cor 12:31–13:13: *Love never fails.*
3. Eph 1:3-14: *He chose us in Christ to be holy and without blemish before him.*
4. Eph 4:1-7, 11-13: *One Lord, one faith, one Baptism, one God, the Father of all.*
5. Phil 4:4-8: *Whatever is pure, think about these things.*
6. 1 Thes 5:16-24: *May you entirely, spirit, soul, and body, be preserved blameless, for the coming of our Lord Jesus Christ.*

Responsorial Psalms

1. Ps 27 (26):1, 4, 8b-9abc, 13-14
℟. (1a) The Lord is my light and my salvation.

2. Ps 42 (41):2-3; Ps 43 (42):3, 4
℟. (Ps 42:3a) My soul is thirsting for the living God.

3. Ps 61 (60):2-3b, 3c-4, 5-6, 9
℟. (4a) You are my refuge, O Lord.

4. Ps 63 (62):2, 3-4, 5-6, 8-9
℟. (2b) For you my soul is thirsting, O Lord my God.

5. Ps 65 (64):2, 3-4, 5, 6
℟. (2a) Praise is due to you in Zion, O God.

6. Ps 121 (120):1bc-2, 3-4, 5-6, 7-8
℟. (2a) My help shall come from the Lord.

Gospel Readings

1. Mt 5:2-12a: *Rejoice and be glad, for your reward will be great in heaven.*
2. Mt 5:13-16: *Let your light shine before others.*
3. Mt 11:25-30: *You have hidden these things from the wise and the learned and revealed them to the childlike.*
4. Jn 3:16-21: *So that everyone who believes in him might not perish.*
5. Jn 14:15-23, 26-27: *We will come to him and make our dwelling with him.*
6. Jn 15:1-6: *I am the vine, you are the branches.*

502. Then follows the Reception, to be carried out in the manner R25
described (nos. **489–495**).

503. The Universal Prayer follows the Reception (and Confirma- R19
tion). In his introduction the celebrant should mention Baptism, (Confirmation,) and the Eucharist, and express gratitude to God. The celebrant may use the formula given in no. **496** or similar words. The person received into full communion is mentioned at the beginning of the intentions.

504. The Universal Prayer is concluded with the Lord's Prayer, R26
sung or recited by all present.

The celebrant introduces the Lord's Prayer, in the following or R31
similar words:

Dear brothers and sisters,
let us unite our prayers and offer them,
praying as our Lord Jesus Christ taught us:

All:
Our Father . . .

If the person received was accustomed in his (her) Community to the final doxology **For the kingdom**, etc., it should be added here to the Lord's Prayer.

The celebrant's blessing follows. Then the sponsor and, if there R26
are only a few persons, all who are present may, if appropriate, R27
greet the newly-received person in a friendly manner. After this, all then depart in peace.

APPENDIX I

COMBINED RITES

1. RITE FOR ENTRANCE INTO THE CATECHUMENATE AND OF WELCOMING THE CANDIDATES

USA

505. This rite is for use in communities where catechumens are preparing for Initiation and where baptized but uncatechized adults are beginning catechetical formation either prior to completing their Christian Initiation in the Sacraments of Confirmation and the Eucharist or prior to being received into the full communion of the Catholic Church. For a theological and liturgical introduction to the Rite for Entrance into the Catechumenate see above, nos. **41–47**.

506. In the catechesis of the community and in the celebration of these rites, care must be taken to maintain the distinction between the catechumens and the baptized candidates.

RECEIVING THE CANDIDATES

507. Those entering the catechumenate, along with those who are candidates for the Sacraments of Confirmation and the Eucharist (or Reception into the full communion of the Catholic Church), together with their sponsors and a group of the faithful gather outside the entrance to the church, or in the vestibule or at the entrance, or even at some other suitable part of the church, or lastly, in another suitable place outside the church. The Priest or Deacon, wearing an alb or a surplice, with a stole, or also a cope of festive color, goes to meet them, while, if circumstances suggest, the faithful sing a psalm or an appropriate hymn.

Preliminary Instruction

508. The celebrant warmly greets those entering the catechumenate and the candidates. He speaks to them, their sponsors, and all present, pointing out the joy and happiness of the Church. He may also recall for the sponsors and friends the particular experience and religious response by which they, following their own spiritual path, have come to this step on this day. He uses these or similar words:

Dear friends, the Church joyfully welcomes today those who are entering the catechumenate. In the months to come they will prepare for their Initiation into the Christian faith by Baptism, Confirmation, and the Eucharist.

We also greet those who, already one with us by Baptism, now wish to complete their Christian Initiation through Confirmation and the Eucharist or to be received into the full communion of the Catholic Church.

For all of these, we give thanks and praise to God who has led them by various paths to oneness in faith. My dear friends, you are welcomed in the name of Christ.

Then he invites the sponsors, those entering the catechumenate, and the candidates to come forward. As they are taking their places before the celebrant, a suitable chant may be sung, for example, Psalm 63 (62):2-9:

Psalm 63 (62):2-9

2 O God, you are my God; at dawn I seek you;
for you my soul is thirsting.
For you my flesh is pining,
like a dry, weary land without water.
3 I have come before you in the sanctuary,
to behold your strength and your glory.

4 Your loving mercy is better than life;
my lips will speak your praise.
5 I will bless you all my life;
in your name I will lift up my hands.
6 My soul shall be filled as with a banquet;
with joyful lips, my mouth shall praise you.

7 When I remember you upon my bed,
I muse on you through the watches of the night.
8 For you have been my strength;
in the shadow of your wings I rejoice.
9 My soul clings fast to you;
your right hand upholds me.

Dialogue with Those Entering the Catechumenate and with Candidates for Post-Baptismal Catechesis

509. Then the celebrant first asks or calls out the civil or family name of the individuals, if necessary, unless their names are already known because of their small number. The names of those entering the catechumenate are given first, followed by the names of the candidates for post-baptismal catechesis. They should always reply individually, even if the celebrant asks the question only once because of their number. This is done in the following or similar way.

A

Celebrant:
What is your name?

Individual:
N.

B

The celebrant, if he wishes, calls out the name of each one, who answers:
Present.

The celebrant continues with the following questions for those entering the catechumenate. When there is a large number, the remaining questions may be answered by all of them as a group. The celebrant may use other words in asking them about their intentions and may permit them to reply in their own words; for example, after the first question: **What do you ask of God's Church?** or **What do you desire?** or **For what reason have you come?**, he may receive such answers as: **The grace of Christ** or **Entry into the Church** or **Eternal life** or other suitable replies. The celebrant may then adapt his questions to their replies.

Celebrant:
What do you ask of God's Church?

The one entering:
Faith.

Celebrant:
What does faith offer you?

The one entering:
Eternal life.

The celebrant then addresses the following question to the individual candidates for post-baptismal catechesis. When there is a large number of candidates, the remaining questions may be answered by all the candidates as a group. The celebrant may use other words in asking the candidates about their intentions and may permit them to reply in their own words.

Celebrant:
What do you ask of God's Church?

Candidate:
To be accepted as a candidate for catechetical instruction
leading to Confirmation and the Eucharist
(or: **leading to Reception into the full communion of the Catholic Church**).

510. At the discretion of the Diocesan Bishop (cf. no. **33.2**), the Initial Commitment of those entering the catechumenate (no. **511**) may be replaced by the Rite of Exorcism and Renunciation of False Worship (nos. **70–72**).

Catechumens' Initial Commitment

511. Then the celebrant, adapting his words, as required, to the replies received in no. **509**, addresses those entering the catechumenate in these or similar words:

God, who made the world and all of us
and in whom all living things have their being,
enlightens our minds,
so that we may come to know and worship him.
He has sent Jesus Christ, his faithful witness,
to announce to us what he has seen in heaven and on earth.

Therefore it is now time for you,
who rejoice at Christ's coming,
to listen to his word,
so that, with us, beginning to know God
and to love your neighbor,
you may possess the life of heaven.
Are you ready to lead this life with the help of God?

Those entering:
I am.

Candidates' Declaration of Intent

512. Then the celebrant, adapting his words, as required, to the replies received in no. **509**, addresses the candidates again in these or similar words:

Those of you who seek to complete your Christian Initiation
(or: **to be received into the full communion of the Catholic Church**),
are you prepared to listen with us to the Apostles' instruction,
and to join with us in a life of prayer and service?

Candidates:
I am.

Affirmation by the Sponsors and the Assembly

513. Then the celebrant turns to the sponsors and all the faithful and questions them in these or similar words:

You, the sponsors who are now presenting these men and women to us,
and all of you brothers and sisters gathered here,
are you prepared to help them find Christ and follow him?

All:
We are.

The celebrant, with hands joined, says:

To you, most merciful Father,
we give thanks for these your servants,
because they have already been searching for you,
who in diverse ways have gone ahead of them and knocked at their door,
and because they have answered your call today in our presence.
Therefore, we all praise and bless you, Lord.

All:

We praise and bless you, Lord.

Signing of Those Entering the Catechumenate and of the Candidates with the Cross

514. Next a Cross is traced on the forehead of each one entering the catechumenate (or, at the discretion of the Diocesan Bishop, in front of the forehead for those in whose culture the act of touching may not seem proper; cf. no. **33.3**); at the discretion of the celebrant the signing of one, several, or all of the senses may follow. The celebrant alone says the formulas accompanying each signing.

Signing of the Forehead of Those Entering the Catechumenate

515. Then the celebrant invites those entering the catechumenate and their sponsors in these or similar words:

Dear friends, come forward now with your sponsors
to receive the sign of your new status as catechumens.

With their sponsors, those entering, one by one, approach the celebrant. With his thumb he makes a Cross on the forehead of each person entering. After the celebrant has signed them, the catechists or sponsors, as circumstances so suggest, do the same, unless they are to sign them later, as in no. **56**. The celebrant says:

N., receive the Cross on your forehead.
Christ himself strengthens you
with the sign of his love
(if the renunciation has preceded: **with the sign of his victory**).
Learn now to know him and follow him.

As circumstances suggest, the signing may be concluded with the singing of an acclamation praising Christ, for example:

Glory and praise to you, Lord Jesus Christ!

Signing of the Other Senses of the Catechumens

516. Then the signing of the senses takes place (according to the judgment of the celebrant, however, it can partially or even totally be omitted).

The signings are carried out by the catechists or sponsors (and, if required in special circumstances, these may be done by several Priests or Deacons).

As circumstances suggest, the signings each time they are made may be concluded with the singing of an acclamation praising Christ, for example: **Glory and praise to you, Lord Jesus Christ!** The formula, however, is always spoken by the celebrant, who says:

While the ears are being signed:
Receive the sign of the Cross on your ears,
that you may hear the voice of the Lord.

While the eyes are being signed:
Receive the sign of the Cross on your eyes,
that you may see the glory of God.

While the lips are being signed:

Receive the sign of the Cross on your lips,
that you may respond to the word of God.

While the chest is being signed:

Receive the sign of the Cross on your chest,
that Christ may dwell in your heart by faith.

While the shoulders are being signed:

Receive the sign of the Cross on your shoulders,
that you may bear the gentle yoke of Christ.

[While the hands are being signed:

Receive the sign of the Cross on your hands,
that Christ may be known in the work which you do.

While the feet are being signed:

Receive the sign of the Cross on your feet,
that you may walk in the way of Christ.]

Then, without touching them, the celebrant alone makes the Sign of the Cross over all the catechumens, while he says:

I sign all of you
in the name of the Father, and of the Son, ✠ and of the
Holy Spirit,
that you may live for ever and ever.

Catechumens:

Amen.

If there are few catechumens, the rite of signing with the Cross may be done over each catechumen by the celebrant, who says the formulas in the singular.

517. Next the Cross is traced on the forehead of the candidates for Confirmation and the Eucharist (or Reception into the full communion of the Catholic Church); at the discretion of the celebrant the signing of one, several, or all of the senses may follow. The celebrant alone says the formulas accompanying each signing.

SIGNING OF THE FOREHEAD OF THE CANDIDATES

518. Then the celebrant invites the candidates for Confirmation and the Eucharist and their sponsors in these or similar words:

Dear candidates for Confirmation and the Eucharist
(or: **Reception into full communion**),
come forward now with your sponsors
to receive the sign of your life in Christ.

With their sponsors, the candidates, one by one, approach the celebrant. With his thumb he makes a Cross on the forehead; then, if there is to be no signing of the senses, the sponsor does the same. The celebrant says:

N., receive the Cross on your forehead
as a reminder of your Baptism
into Christ's saving Death and Resurrection.

As circumstances suggest, the signing may be concluded with the singing of an acclamation praising Christ, for example:

Glory and praise to you, Lord Jesus Christ!

SIGNING OF THE OTHER SENSES OF THE CANDIDATES

519. The signings are carried out by the catechists or sponsors (and, if required in special circumstances, these may be done by several Priests or Deacons).

As circumstances suggest, the signings each time they are made may be concluded with the singing of an acclamation praising Christ, for example: **Glory and praise to you, Lord Jesus Christ!** The formula, however, is always spoken by the celebrant, who says:

While the ears are being signed:

Receive the sign of the Cross on your ears,
that you may hear the voice of the Lord.

While the eyes are being signed:

Receive the sign of the Cross on your eyes,
that you may see the glory of God.

While the lips are being signed:

Receive the sign of the Cross on your lips,
that you may respond to the word of God.

While the chest is being signed:

Receive the sign of the Cross on your chest,
that Christ may dwell in your heart by faith.

While the shoulders are being signed:

Receive the sign of the Cross on your shoulders,
that you may bear the gentle yoke of Christ.

[While the hands are being signed:

Receive the sign of the Cross on your hands,
that Christ may be known in the work which you do.

While the feet are being signed:

Receive the sign of the Cross on your feet,
that you may walk in the way of Christ.]

Then, without touching them, the celebrant alone makes the Sign of the Cross over all the candidates, while he says:

I sign all of you
in the name of the Father, and of the Son, ✠ and of the
Holy Spirit,
that you may live for ever and ever.

Candidates:

Amen.

520. The celebrant concludes the signing of the forehead (and the senses) with the following prayer:

Let us pray.

Almighty God,
who through the Cross and Resurrection of your Son
have given life to your people,
grant, we pray,
that, following in the footsteps of Christ,
your servants, whom we have signed with the Cross,
may possess its saving power in their lives
and show it forth in their deeds.
Through Christ our Lord.

℟. Amen.

Introduction into the Church

521. When this has been completed, the celebrant invites the catechumens and candidates, and their sponsors, to enter the church or another suitable place, while saying these or similar words:

N. and N., come into the church,
to partake with us at the table of God's word.

Then with a gesture, he invites them to enter.

Meanwhile, the following antiphon is sung with Psalm 34 (33):2-3, 6 and 9, 10-11 and 16 or another suitable chant:

Come, children, and hear me;
I will teach you the fear of the Lord.

Psalm 34 (33):2-3, 6 and 9, 10-11 and 16

2 I will bless the LORD at all times,
praise of him is always in my mouth.
3 In the LORD my soul shall make its boast;
the humble shall hear and be glad. ℟.

6 Look toward him and be radiant;
let your faces not be abashed.
9 Taste and see that the LORD is good.
Blessed the man who seeks refuge in him. ℟.

10 Fear the LORD, you his holy ones.
They lack nothing, those who fear him.
11 The rich suffer want and go hungry,
but those who seek the LORD lack no blessing.
16 The LORD turns his eyes to the just one,
and his ears are open to his cry. ℟.

SACRED CELEBRATION OF THE WORD OF GOD

Instruction

522. After the catechumens and candidates have reached their seats, the celebrant speaks to them briefly, helping them to understand the dignity of God's word, which is proclaimed and heard in the church.

A book of the Sacred Scriptures is carried in procession and set in a place of honor and, as circumstances so suggest, may also be incensed.

The Sacred Celebration of the Word of God follows.

Readings

523. The readings are those assigned for the day. According to the norms of the Lectionary, other appropriate readings, such as the following, may be used.

First Reading

Gen 12:1-4a: *Go forth from the land of your kinsfolk to a land that I will show you.*

Responsorial Psalm

Ps 33 (32):4-5, 12-13, 18-19, 20 and 22

℟. (12b) Blessed the people the Lord has chosen as his heritage.

Or:

℟. (22) May your merciful love be upon us, as we hope in you, O Lord.

Verse before the Gospel

Jn 1:41, 17b

We have found the Messiah: Jesus Christ,
through whom came truth and grace.

Gospel

Jn 1:35-42: *Behold, the Lamb of God. We have found the Messiah.*

Homily

524. A Homily follows that explains the readings.

Presentation of the Gospels

525. Then, if the celebrant so wishes, books containing the Gospels are distributed with dignity and reverence to the catechumens and candidates; Crosses may also be given to the catechumens, unless they were already handed on to them as a sign of their reception (cf. no. **74**). The celebrant uses a suitable formula, such as:

Receive the Gospel of Jesus Christ, the Son of God.

It is fitting for the catechumens and candidates to respond with appropriate words to the celebrant's gift and words.

Intercessions for the Catechumens and the Candidates

526. Then the whole congregation of the faithful together with the sponsors prays these Intercessions or other, similar ones for the catechumens and candidates. The usual petition for the needs of the Church and of the whole world should be added if, after the catechumens are dismissed, the Universal Prayer (Prayer of the Faithful) is to be omitted in the Eucharistic Celebration (cf. no. **529**).

Celebrant:

These catechumens and candidates, our brothers and sisters,
have already traveled far.
We rejoice with them in the gentle guidance of God,
which has brought them to this day.

Let us pray for them,
that they may have strength to complete the great journey that lies ahead
toward full participation in our way of life.

Lector:

That the heavenly Father reveal his Christ to them more each day,
let us pray to the Lord:

℟. Lord, hear our prayer.

Lector:

That they embrace with generous heart and willing spirit the entire will of God,
let us pray to the Lord:

℟. Lord, hear our prayer.

Lector:

That they enjoy our sincere and unfailing support every step of their way,
let us pray to the Lord:

℟. Lord, hear our prayer.

Lector:

That they find in our community
visible signs of unity and generous love,
let us pray to the Lord:

℟. Lord, hear our prayer.

Lector:
That their hearts and ours become
ever more responsive to the needs of others,
let us pray to the Lord:
℟. Lord, hear our prayer.

Lector:
That in due time these catechumens may be found worthy
of the cleansing waters of rebirth
and of renewal by the Holy Spirit
and these candidates may be found worthy
to complete their Initiation through the Sacraments of Confirmation and the Eucharist
(or: **to be received into the full communion of the Catholic Church**),
let us pray to the Lord:
℟. Lord, hear our prayer.

Concluding Prayer

527. After the Intercessions, the celebrant, extending his hands toward the catechumens and candidates, says the following prayer:

Let us pray.

Almighty ever-living God,
Father of all creation,
who made man and woman in your own image,
welcome these beloved ones who have taken this step,
and grant that, hearing the word of your Christ among us,
they may be made new by its power,
and by your grace attain at last
complete conformity with him.
Who lives and reigns for ever and ever.
℟. Amen.

Dismissal of the Catechumens

528. If the Eucharist is to be celebrated, the catechumens are normally dismissed at this point by use of option A or B; if the catechumens are to stay for the celebration of the Eucharist, option C is used; if the Eucharist is not to be celebrated, the entire assembly is dismissed by use of option D.

A

The celebrant recalls briefly the great joy with which the catechumens have just been received and urges them to strive to live according to the word they have just heard. The group of catechumens leaves but does not immediately disperse, but with the guidance of some of the faithful they remain together to share their joy and their spiritual experience. The Deacon or the celebrant dismisses them in these or similar words:

Catechumens, go in peace,
and may the Lord remain with you.

Catechumens:

Thanks be to God.

B

As an optional formula for dismissing the catechumens, the Deacon or the celebrant may use these or similar words:

My dear friends, this community now sends you forth to reflect more deeply upon the word of God which you have shared with us today. Be assured of our loving support and prayers for you. We look forward to the day when you will share fully in the Lord's table.

C

If, however, for serious reasons the catechumens do not leave (cf. no. **75.3**) and must remain with the faithful, they are to be instructed that, though they are present at the celebration of the Eucharist, they cannot take part as the baptized do. They may be reminded of this by the Deacon or the celebrant in these or similar words:

Although you cannot yet participate fully in the Lord's Eucharist, stay with us as a sign of our hope that all God's children will eat and drink with the Lord and work with his Holy Spirit to recreate the face of the earth.

D

If, however, the Eucharist is not celebrated, a suitable chant, as circumstances suggest, may be added, and the faithful and the catechumens may be dismissed, using these or similar words:

Go in peace,
and may the Lord remain with you.

All:
Thanks be to God.

CELEBRATION OF THE EUCHARIST

529. If the Eucharist is celebrated after the dismissal, the Universal Prayer (Prayer of the Faithful) for the needs of the Church and the whole world begins at once. Then, if required, the Creed is said and the Preparation of the Gifts follows. But for pastoral reasons it is permissible to omit the Universal Prayer and the Creed.

2. RITE OF SENDING CATECHUMENS FOR ELECTION AND CANDIDATES FOR THE CALLING TO CONTINUING CONVERSION

USA

530. This optional rite is provided for parishes whose catechumens will celebrate their Election and whose adult candidates for Confirmation and the Eucharist or Reception into the full communion of the Catholic Church will celebrate their calling to continuing conversion in a subsequent celebration. For a theological and liturgical introduction to the optional Rite of Sending Catechumens for Election see above, nos. **106–109**.

531. As the focal point of the Church's concern for the catechumens, admission to Election belongs to the Bishop who is usually its presiding celebrant. It is within the parish community, however, that the preliminary judgment is made concerning the catechumens' state of formation and progress.

This rite offers that local community the opportunity to express its approval of the catechumens and to send them forth to the celebration of Election assured of the parish's care and support.

532. In addition, those who either are completing their Initiation through the Sacraments of Confirmation and the Eucharist or are preparing for Reception into the full communion of the Catholic Church are also included in this rite, since they too will be presented to the Bishop at the celebration of the Rite of Election for the catechumens.

533. The rite is celebrated in the parish church at a suitable time prior to the Rite of Election.

534. The rite takes place after the Homily in a Celebration of the Word of God (cf. no. **89**) or at Mass.

535. In the catechesis of the community and in the celebration of these rites, care must be taken to maintain the distinction between the catechumens and the baptized candidates.

LITURGY OF THE WORD

Homily

536. After the readings, the celebrant gives the Homily. This should be suited to the actual situation and should address not just the catechumens and candidates but the entire community of the faithful, so that all will be encouraged to give good example and to accompany the catechumens and candidates along the path of the Paschal Mystery.

Presentation of the Catechumens

537. After the Homily, the Priest in charge of the catechumens' Initiation, or a Deacon, a catechist, or a representative of the community, presents the catechumens using the following or similar words:

Reverend Father, these catechumens, whom I now present
to you,
are beginning their final period of preparation and purification
leading to their Initiation.
They have found strength in God's grace
and support in our community's prayers and example.

Now they ask that they be recognized
for the progress they have made in their spiritual formation
and that they receive the assurance of our blessings and prayers
as they go forth to the Rite of Election
celebrated this afternoon (or: **next Sunday** [or specify the day])
by Bishop N.

The celebrant replies:

Those who are to be sent to the celebration of Election in Christ,
come forward, together with those who will be your
godparents.

One by one, the catechumens are called by name. Each catechumen, accompanied by a godparent (or godparents), comes forward and stands before the celebrant.

Affirmation by the Godparents (and the Assembly)

538. Then the celebrant addresses the assembly in these or similar words:

My dear friends, these catechumens
who have been preparing for the Sacraments of Initiation
hope that they will be found ready to participate in the Rite of
Election
and be chosen in Christ for the Paschal Sacraments.
It is the responsibility of this community to inquire about their
readiness
before they are presented to the Bishop.

He addresses the godparents:

I turn to you, godparents,
for your testimony about these catechumens.
Have they taken their formation in the Gospel
and in the Catholic way of life seriously?

Godparents:

They have.

Celebrant:

Have they given evidence of their conversion by the example of
their lives?

Godparents:
They have.

Celebrant:
Do you judge them to be ready
to be presented to the Bishop for the Rite of Election?

Godparents:
We do.

When appropriate in the circumstances, the celebrant may also ask the entire assembly to express its approval of the catechumens.

The celebrant concludes the affirmation by the following:

My dear catechumens, this community gladly recommends you to the Bishop,
who, in the name of Christ, will call you to the Paschal Sacraments.
May God who has begun the good work in you bring it to fulfillment.

539. If the signing of the Book of the Elect is to take place in the presence of the Bishop, it is omitted here. However, if the signed Book of the Elect is to be presented to the Bishop in the Rite of Election, the catechumens may now come forward to sign it or they should sign it after the celebration or at another time prior to the Rite of Election.

Presentation of the Candidates

540. The Priest in charge of the candidates' formation, or a Deacon, a catechist, or a representative of the community, presents the candidates, using the following or similar words:

Reverend Father, these candidates, whom I now present to you,
are beginning their final preparation
for the Sacraments of Confirmation and the Eucharist
(or: **for Reception into the full communion of the Catholic Church**).
They have found strength in God's grace
and support in our community's prayers and example.

Now they ask that they be recognized
for the progress they have made in their spiritual formation
and that they receive the assurance of our blessings and prayers
as they go forth for the Calling to Continuing Conversion this afternoon (or: **next Sunday** [or specify the day]).

The celebrant replies:
Candidates, come forward, together with your sponsors.

One by one, the candidates are called by name. Each candidate, accompanied by a sponsor, comes forward and stands before the celebrant.

Affirmation by the Sponsors (and the Assembly)

541. Then the celebrant addresses the assembly in these or similar words:

My dear friends, these candidates,
already one with us by reason of their Baptism in Christ,
have asked to complete their Initiation
(or: **have asked to be received into the full communion of the Catholic Church**).
Those who know them have judged them to be sincere in their desire.

During the period of their catechetical formation
they have listened to the word of Christ
and endeavored to follow his commands more perfectly;
they have shared the company of their Christian brothers and sisters in this community
and joined with them in prayer.

And so I announce to all of you here
that our community ratifies their desire
to complete their Initiation
(or: **to be received into full communion**).
Therefore, I ask their sponsors to state their opinion once again,
so that all of you may hear.

He addresses the sponsors:

As God is your witness, do you consider these candidates
ready to receive the Sacraments of Confirmation and the Eucharist
(or: **ready to be received into the full communion of the Catholic Church**)?

Sponsors:

We do.

When appropriate in the circumstances, the celebrant may also ask the entire assembly to express its approval of the candidates.

542. The celebrant concludes the affirmation by the following:

And now, my dear friends, I address you.
Your own sponsors (and this entire community) have spoken in your favor.
The Church, in the name of Christ, accepts their testimony
and sends you to the Calling to Continuing Conversion,
where Bishop N. will exhort you to live in deeper conformity
to the life of Christ.

Intercessions for the Catechumens and the Candidates

543. Then the community prays for the catechumens and candidates by use of the following or a similar formula. The celebrant may adapt the introduction and the intentions to fit various circumstances. Moreover, the usual intentions for the Church and the whole world should be added if the catechumens are to be dismissed after the Intercessions and the Universal Prayer (Prayer of the Faithful) is omitted during Mass (cf. no. **546**).

Celebrant:

Dear brothers and sisters,
today we begin the Lenten journey
looking forward to the saving mysteries of the Passion and Resurrection.
These catechumens and candidates, whom we are bringing to the Paschal Sacraments,
look to us for an example of renewal.

Therefore let us pray to the Lord for them and for ourselves,
that being encouraged by our mutual renewal,
we may be made worthy of the paschal graces.

Lector:

That these catechumens and candidates may renounce self-centeredness
and think of others rather than themselves,
let us pray to the Lord:

℟. Lord, hear our prayer.

Lector:

For their godparents and sponsors, that they may show these catechumens and candidates
a constant application of the Gospel
both in their private and in their public lives,
let us pray to the Lord:

℟. Lord, hear our prayer.

Lector:

For their catechists, that they may convey the sweetness of God's word
to those who search for it,
let us pray to the Lord:

℟. Lord, hear our prayer.

Lector:

That they may share with others
the happiness they have found in their faith,
let us pray to the Lord:

℟. Lord, hear our prayer.

Lector:

For our community, that during this (or: **the coming**) Lenten season,
it may be radiant with the fullness of charity and with constancy in prayer,
let us pray to the Lord:

℟. Lord, hear our prayer.

Prayer over the Catechumens and Candidates

544. The celebrant, extending his hands over the catechumens and candidates, concludes the Intercessions with this prayer:

Almighty, most beloved Father,
whose will it is to renew all things in Christ
and who draw all people to him,
graciously guide these catechumens and candidates of the Church
and grant that, faithful to the calling they have received,
they may be built up into the kingdom of your Son
and be sealed with the promised Holy Spirit.
Through Christ our Lord.

℟. Amen.

Dismissal of the Catechumens

545. If the Eucharist is to be celebrated, the catechumens are normally dismissed at this point by use of option A or B; if the catechumens are to stay for the celebration of the Eucharist, option C is used; if the Eucharist is not to be celebrated, the entire assembly is dismissed by use of option D.

A

The Deacon or the celebrant dismisses the catechumens in these or similar words:

My dear friends, you are about to enter with us on the Lenten journey. Christ will be for you the way, the truth, and the life. In his name we send you forth from this community to celebrate with the Bishop the Lord's choice of you to be numbered among his elect. Until we gather again for the Scrutinies, go in peace.

Catechumens:

Amen.

B

As an optional formula for dismissing the catechumens, the Deacon or the celebrant may use these or similar words:

My dear friends, this community now sends you forth to reflect more deeply upon the word of God which you have shared with us today. Be assured of our loving support and prayers for you. We look forward to the day when you will share fully in the Lord's table.

C

If, however, for serious reasons the catechumens do not leave (cf. no. **75.3**) and must remain with the faithful, they are to be instructed that, though they are present at the celebration of the Eucharist, they cannot take part as the baptized do. They may be reminded of this by the Deacon or the celebrant in these or similar words:

Although you cannot yet participate fully in the Lord's Eucharist, stay with us as a sign of our hope that all God's children will eat and drink with the Lord and work with his Holy Spirit to recreate the face of the earth.

D

If, however, the Eucharist is not celebrated, a suitable chant, as circumstances suggest, may be added, and the faithful and the catechumens may be dismissed, using these or similar words:

Go in peace,
and may the Lord remain with you.

All:
Thanks be to God.

CELEBRATION OF THE EUCHARIST

546. After the dismissal, the Eucharist is celebrated. The Universal Prayer (Prayer of the Faithful) for the needs of the Church and the whole world begins immediately. Then, if required, the Creed is said, and the Preparation of the Gifts follows. But for pastoral reasons the Universal Prayer (Prayer of the Faithful) and the Creed may be omitted.

3. RITE OF ELECTION OF CATECHUMENS AND OF CALLING THE CANDIDATES TO CONTINUING CONVERSION

USA

547. This rite is for use when the Election of catechumens and the Calling to Continuing Conversion of candidates preparing either for Confirmation, Eucharist or Reception into the full communion of the Catholic Church are celebrated together. For a theological and liturgical introduction for the Rite of Election of Catechumens see above, nos. **118–127**, and for the Calling of Candidates to Continuing Conversion see above, nos. **446–449**.

548. The rite should normally take place on the First Sunday of Lent, and the presiding celebrant is the Bishop or his delegate.

549. In the catechesis of the community and in the celebration of these rites, care must be taken to maintain the distinction between the catechumens and the baptized candidates.

LITURGY OF THE WORD

Homily

550. After the readings (cf. no. **128**), the Bishop, or the celebrant who acts as delegate of the Bishop, gives the Homily. The Homily, suited to the actual situation, should address not only the catechumens and the candidates but the entire community of the faithful, so that, striving to give good example, they may accompany the catechumens and candidates during the time of their Lenten preparation for celebrating the Paschal Sacraments.

CELEBRATION OF ELECTION

Presentation of the Catechumens

551. After the Homily, the Priest responsible for the Initiation of the catechumens, or a Deacon, a catechist, or a representative of the community, presents the catechumens for Election, in these or similar words:

(Most) Reverend Father,
(as the solemn paschal celebrations approach once more,)
the catechumens present here,
relying on divine grace
and supported by the prayers and example of the community,
humbly request that, after due preparation and celebration of
 the Scrutinies,
they be admitted to participate
in the Sacraments of Baptism, Confirmation, and the Eucharist.

The celebrant replies:

Let those who are to be chosen as the elect
come forward with their godparents.

One by one, they are called by name. Each catechumen, accompanied by a godparent (or godparents), comes forward and stands before the celebrant.

If there are a large number of catechumens, all are presented together, for example, each group by its own catechist. But in this case, the catechists should be advised to call each catechumen forward by name in a special celebration held before they come to the common rite.

Affirmation by the Godparents (and the Assembly)

552. Then the celebrant addresses the assembly. If, however, he took part in the previous deliberation about the catechumens' suitability (cf. no. **122**), he may use either option A or option B or similar words; if he has not taken part in the earlier deliberation, he uses option B or similar words.

A

Celebrant:
My dear brothers and sisters,
these catechumens have asked to be initiated
into the sacramental life of the Church this Easter.

Those who know them have judged
that they are sincere in their desire.
For some time they have listened to Christ's word
and have tried to live according to his commands;
they have shared in fraternal communion and in the prayers.
Now I make known to the whole congregation
that it is the mind of the community to call them to the
Sacraments.
As I inform you of this judgment and speak to the godparents,
I ask them to give their recommendation again, in your
presence.

He, then, turns toward the godparents:
With God as your witness,
do you judge these catechumens to be worthy of admission
to the Sacraments of Christian Initiation?

Godparents:
We do.

Then if the circumstances warrant, the celebrant may ask the entire congregation for its assent:

Now I ask you, the members of this community:
Are you willing to affirm the testimony expressed about these catechumens
and support them in faith, prayer, and example
as we prepare to celebrate the Paschal Sacraments?

All:
We are.

B

Celebrant:
The holy Church of God now wishes to ascertain
whether these catechumens are sufficiently prepared
to be received into the order of the elect
for the solemn paschal celebrations to come.

He, then, turns toward the godparents:
And so, first I ask you their godparents to testify.
Have they faithfully listened to God's word proclaimed by the Church?

Godparents:
They have.

Celebrant:
Have they begun to walk in God's presence,
treasuring the word they have received?

Godparents:
They have.

Celebrant:
Have they persevered in fraternal communion and in the prayers?

Godparents:
They have.

Then if the circumstances warrant, the celebrant may ask the entire congregation for its assent:

Now I ask you, the members of this community:
Are you willing to affirm the testimony expressed about these catechumens
and include them in your prayer and affection as we move toward Easter?

All:
We are.

Questioning and Petitioning of the Catechumens

553. Next, the celebrant, looking at the catechumens, addresses and questions them in these or similar words:

And now, my dear catechumens, I address you.
Your godparents and catechists (and the entire community)
have testified favorably on your behalf.
Trusting in their judgment,
the Church calls you in the name of Christ to the Paschal Sacraments.

Now it falls to you who have long listened to the voice of Christ
to respond in the presence of the Church by stating your intentions.

Is it your will to be initiated into Christ's Sacraments
of Baptism, Confirmation, and the Eucharist?

Catechumens:
It is.

Celebrant:
Then offer your names for enrollment.

The catechumens give their names, either going with their godparents to the celebrant or while remaining in place, and the actual inscription of the names may be carried out in various ways. The catechumens may inscribe their names themselves or they may call out their names, which are inscribed by the godparents or by the one who presented them (cf. no. **130**). As the Enrollment is taking place, a suitable chant, for example, Psalm 16 (15) may be sung.

If, however, there are a large number of catechumens a list of names may be given to the celebrant, with these or similar words: **These are the names of those seeking Initiation**, or, when the Bishop is celebrant and catechumens from several parishes have been presented to him: **These are the names of the catechumens from the parish of** N. **seeking Initiation.**

Psalm 16 (15)

1 Preserve me, O God, for in you I take refuge.
 2 I say to the LORD, "You are my Lord.
 You, you alone are my good."

3 As for the holy ones who dwell in the land,
 they are noble, and in them is all my delight.
4 Those who choose other gods increase their sorrows.
 I will not take part in their offerings of blood.
 Nor will I take their names upon my lips.

5 O LORD, it is you who are my portion and cup;
you yourself who secure my lot.
6 Pleasant places are marked out for me:
a pleasing heritage indeed is mine!

7 I will bless the LORD who gives me counsel,
who even at night directs my heart.
8 I keep the LORD before me always;
with him at my right hand, I shall not be moved.

9 And so, my heart rejoices, my soul is glad;
even my flesh shall rest in hope.
10 For you will not abandon my soul to Sheol,
nor let your holy one see corruption.

11 You will show me the path of life,
the fullness of joy in your presence,
at your right hand, bliss forever.

Reception or Election

554. At the conclusion of the Enrollment of Names, the celebrant, after he has briefly explained the meaning of the rite that has taken place, turns toward the catechumens, addressing them in these or similar words:

N. and N., you have been chosen for Initiation
into the sacred mysteries at the forthcoming Easter Vigil.

Elect:
Thanks be to God.

The celebrant continues:
Now, with divine help,
your duty, like ours, is to be faithful to God,

who is faithful to his call,
and to strive with generous spirit
to reach the full truth of your Election.

Then, turning toward the godparents, the celebrant addresses them in these or similar words:

Godparents, you have spoken in favor of these elect;
receive them now as chosen in the Lord
and accompany them with your help and example,
until they come to share in the Sacraments of divine life.

And he invites them to place their hand on the shoulder of the elect whom they are receiving into their care, or to make some other gesture to indicate the same intent.

CELEBRATION OF THE CALLING TO CONTINUING CONVERSION

PRESENTATION OF THE CANDIDATES

555. The Priest in charge of the candidates' formation, or a Deacon, a catechist, or a representative of the community, presents the candidates, using the following or similar words:

(Most) Reverend Father,
(as the solemn paschal celebrations approach once more,)
the candidates present here,
relying on divine grace
and supported by the prayers and example of the community,
humbly request that, after due preparation,
they be admitted to participate
in the Sacraments of Confirmation and the Eucharist
(or: **to full Eucharistic Communion**).

The celebrant replies:

Let those who desire
to participate fully in the sacramental life of the Church
come forward with their sponsors.

One by one, the candidates are called by name. Each candidate, accompanied by a sponsor, comes forward and stands before the celebrant.

If there are a great many candidates, all are presented in groups, for example, each group by its own catechist. But in this case, the catechists should be advised to have a special celebration beforehand in which they call each candidate forward by name.

Affirmation by the Sponsors (and the Assembly)

556. Then the celebrant addresses the assembly. If he took part in the previous deliberation about the candidates' suitableness (cf. no. **122**), he may use either option A or option B or similar words; if he has not taken part in the earlier deliberation, he uses option B or similar words.

A

Celebrant:

My dear brothers and sisters,
these candidates have asked to be able to participate fully
in the sacramental life of the Catholic Church.

Those who know them have judged
that they are sincere in their desire.
During the period of their preparation
they have reflected on the mystery of their Baptism
and have come to appreciate more deeply the presence of Christ
in their lives.
They have shared in fraternal communion and in the prayers.

And so I am pleased to recognize their desire
to participate fully in the sacramental life of the Church.
As I inform you of this judgment and speak to the sponsors,
I ask them to give their recommendation again, in your presence.

He addresses the sponsors:

With God as your witness,
do you judge these candidates to be worthy of admission
to the Sacraments of Confirmation and the Eucharist
(or: **into the full communion of the Catholic Church**)?

Sponsors:

We do.

Then if the circumstances warrant, the celebrant may ask the entire congregation for its assent:

Now I ask you, the members of this community:
Are you willing to affirm the testimony expressed about these candidates
and support them in faith, prayer, and example
as they prepare to participate more fully in the Church's Sacraments?

All:

We are.

B

Celebrant:

The Christian life and the demands
that flow from the Sacraments cannot be taken lightly.
Therefore, before granting these candidates their request
to share fully in the Church's Sacraments,
it is important that the Church hear the testimony
of their sponsors about their readiness.

He, then, turns toward the sponsors:

Have they faithfully listened to God's word proclaimed by the Church?

Sponsors:

They have.

Celebrant:

Have they come to a deeper appreciation of their Baptism,
in which they were joined to Christ and his Church?

Sponsors:

They have.

Celebrant:

Have they reflected sufficiently on the tradition of the Church,
which is their heritage, and joined their brothers and sisters in prayer?

Sponsors:

They have.

Celebrant:

Have they advanced in a life of love and service of others?

Sponsors:

They have.

Then if the circumstances warrant, the celebrant may ask the entire congregation for its assent:

Now I ask you, the members of this community:
Are you willing to affirm the testimony expressed about these candidates
and include them in your prayer and affection as we move toward Easter?

All:
We are.

Act of Recognition

557. Then the celebrant, turns toward the candidates, addressing them in these or similar words:

N. and N., the Church recognizes your desire
(to be sealed with the gift of the Holy Spirit and)
to have a place at Christ's eucharistic table.
Join with us this Lent in a spirit of repentance.
Hear the Lord's call to conversion
and be faithful to your baptismal covenant.

Candidates:
Thanks be to God.

Then, turning toward the sponsors, the celebrant addresses them in these or similar words:

Sponsors, continue to support these candidates
with your guidance and concern.
May they see in you a love for the Church
and a sincere desire for doing good.
Lead them this Lent to the joys of the Easter mysteries.

He invites them to place their hand on the shoulder of the candidate whom they are receiving into their care, or to make some other gesture to indicate the same intent.

Intercessions for the Elect and the Candidates

558. Then, the community prays for the elect and the candidates using either of the following formulas, options A or B. The celebrant may adapt the introduction and the intentions to fit various circumstances. Moreover, the usual intentions for the Church and the whole world should be added if the elect are to be dismissed after the Intercessions and the Universal Prayer (Prayer of the Faithful) is omitted during Mass (cf. no. **561**).

Celebrant:

Dear brothers and sisters,
today we begin the Lenten journey
looking forward to the saving mysteries of the Passion and Resurrection.
The elect and candidates, whom we are bringing to the Paschal Sacraments,
look to us for an example of renewal.

Therefore let us pray to the Lord for them and for ourselves,
that being encouraged by our mutual renewal,
we may be made worthy of the paschal graces.

A

Lector:

That they may make good use of this season
by persevering in self-denial and by joining us in works of sanctification,
let us pray to the Lord:

℟. Lord, hear our prayer.

Lector:

For our elect, that, remembering this day,
they may remain ever grateful for heavenly blessings,
let us pray to the Lord:

℟. Lord, hear our prayer.

Lector:

That our candidates preparing for Confirmation and the Eucharist

(or: **for Reception into the full communion of the Catholic Church**)
may grow daily in fidelity to their baptismal covenant,
let us pray to the Lord:

℟. Lord, hear our prayer.

Lector:
For their catechists, that they may convey the sweetness of God's word
to those who search for it,
let us pray to the Lord:

℟. Lord, hear our prayer.

Lector:
For their godparents and sponsors, that they may show these catechumens and candidates
a constant application of the Gospel
both in their private and in their public lives,
let us pray to the Lord:

℟. Lord, hear our prayer.

Lector:
For their families,
that they may help them to follow the promptings of the Spirit
without placing any obstacles in their way,
let us pray to the Lord:

℟. Lord, hear our prayer.

Lector:
For our community, that during this Lenten season,
it may be radiant with the fullness of charity and with constancy in prayer,
let us pray to the Lord:

℟. Lord, hear our prayer.

Lector:

For those who are still held back by doubts,
that they may trust in Christ
and come without hesitation to join us in fraternal communion
let us pray to the Lord:

℟. Lord, hear our prayer.

B

Lector:

That our elect and candidates may draw joy from daily prayer:

℟. Lord, we ask you, hear our prayer.

Lector:

That, by praying to you often,
they may live in ever closer union with you:

℟. Lord, we ask you, hear our prayer.

Lector:

That they may rejoice to read your word
and to ponder it in their hearts:

℟. Lord, we ask you, hear our prayer.

Lector:

That they may humbly acknowledge their faults
and undertake wholeheartedly to correct them:

℟. Lord, we ask you, hear our prayer.

Lector:

That they may transform their daily work
into a pleasing offering to you:

℟. Lord, we ask you, hear our prayer.

Lector:

That each day of Lent
they may undertake something that is consecrated to you:

℟. Lord, we ask you, hear our prayer.

Lector:
That with firm resolve
they may abstain from everything that defiles purity of heart:

℟. Lord, we ask you, hear our prayer.

Lector:
That they will acquire the habit
of cherishing and preserving virtue and holiness of life:

℟. Lord, we ask you, hear our prayer.

Lector:
That they may renounce self-centeredness
and think of others rather than themselves:

℟. Lord, we ask you, hear our prayer.

Lector:
That you will graciously protect and bless their families:

℟. Lord, we ask you, hear our prayer.

Lector:
That they may share with others
the happiness they have found in their faith:

℟. Lord, we ask you, hear our prayer.

559. The celebrant, extending his hands over the elect and the candidates, concludes the Intercessions with this prayer:

Almighty, most beloved Father,
graciously guide these elect of the Church
and grant that, faithful to the calling they have received,
they may be built up into the kingdom of your Son
and be sealed with the promised Holy Spirit.

Look also upon these candidates,
and grant that, faithful to the gifts already received in Baptism,
they may be more fully conformed
to the Death and Resurrection of Christ.
Who lives and reigns for ever and ever.

℟. Amen.

Dismissal of the Elect

560. If the Eucharist is to be celebrated, the elect are normally dismissed at this point by use of option A or B; if the elect are to stay for the celebration of the Eucharist, option C is used; if the Eucharist is not to be celebrated, the entire assembly is dismissed by use of option D.

A

The Deacon or the celebrant dismisses the elect with this or a similar instruction:

My dear elect,
you have entered with us on the Lenten journey.
Christ will be for you the way, the truth, and the life,
especially when you gather with us
at the forthcoming Scrutinies.
Now go in peace.

Elect:
Amen.

The elect go out.

B

As an optional formula for dismissing the elect, the Deacon or the celebrant may use these or similar words:

My dear friends, this community now sends you forth to reflect more deeply upon the word of God which you have shared with us today. Be assured of our loving support and prayers for you. We look forward to the day when you will share fully in the Lord's table.

C

If, however, for serious reasons the elect do not leave (cf. no. **75.3**) and must remain with the faithful, they are to be instructed that, though they are present at the celebration of the Eucharist, they cannot take part as the baptized do. They may be reminded of this by the Deacon or the celebrant in these or similar words:

Although you cannot yet participate fully in the Lord's Eucharist, stay with us as a sign of our hope that all God's children will eat and drink with the Lord and work with his Holy Spirit to recreate the face of the earth.

D

If, however, the Eucharist is not celebrated, a suitable chant, as circumstances suggest, may be added, and the faithful and the elect may be dismissed, using these or similar words:

Go in peace,
and may the Lord remain with you.

All:

Thanks be to God.

CELEBRATION OF THE EUCHARIST

561. After the dismissal, the Eucharist is celebrated. The Universal Prayer (Prayer of the Faithful) for the needs of the Church and the whole world begins immediately. Then, if required, the Creed is said, and the Preparation of the Gifts follows. But for pastoral reasons the Universal Prayer (Prayer of the Faithful) and the Creed may be omitted.

4. CELEBRATION AT THE EASTER VIGIL OF THE SACRAMENTS OF INITIATION AND THE RITE OF RECEPTION

USA

562. Pastoral considerations may suggest that along with the celebration of the Sacraments of Christian Initiation of adults, the Easter Vigil should include the Rite of Reception into the full communion of the Catholic Church of those already validly baptized, and even the Baptism of children. But such a decision must be guided by the theological and pastoral directives proper to each rite.

The model provided here simply arranges the ritual elements belonging to such a combined celebration. But the model can only be used properly in the light of nos. **206–217**, regarding celebration of the Sacraments of Christian Initiation, of nos. **400–410**, regarding the Confirmation of Catholics previously baptized as infants, and of nos. **473–486**, regarding the Rite of Reception into the full communion of the Catholic Church.

If the Baptism of children will take place along with the Initiation of adults, it should do so in light of the Introduction to the *Order of Baptism of Children*, with special attention given to no. 28.1, which describes elements of the ritual that are to be carried out in anticipation of the Easter Vigil.

563. Inclusion at the Easter Vigil of the Rite of Reception into full communion may also be opportune liturgically, especially when the candidates have undergone a lengthy period of spiritual formation coinciding with Lent. In the liturgical year the Easter Vigil, the preeminent commemoration of Christ's Paschal Mystery, is the preferred occasion for the celebration in which the elect will enter the Paschal Mystery through Baptism, Confirmation, and the Eucharist. Candidates for Reception, who in Baptism have already been justified by faith and incorporated into Christ,[1] are

[1] Cf. Secretariat for Christian Unity, Ecumenical Directory I, no. 11: *Acta Apostolicæ Sedis* 59 (1967), pp. 578–579; Second Vatican Council, Decree on Ecumenism, *Unitatis redintegratio*, no. 3.

entering fully into a community that is constituted by its communion both in faith and in the sacramental sharing of the Paschal Mystery. The celebration of their Reception at the Easter Vigil provides the candidates with a privileged opportunity to recall and reaffirm their own Baptism, "the sacramental bond of unity" and "the foundation of communion between all Christians."[2]

At the Easter Vigil these candidates can make their profession of faith by joining the community in the renewal of the baptismal promises, and, if they have not yet been confirmed, they can receive the Sacrament of Confirmation, which is intimately connected with Baptism. Since of its nature Baptism points to complete entrance into Eucharistic Communion,[3] the baptismal themes of the Easter Vigil can serve to emphasize why the high point of the candidates' Reception is their sharing in the Eucharist with the Catholic community for the first time (cf. no. **475.1**).

564. The decision to combine the two celebrations at the Easter Vigil must be guided by the provision in the Introduction of the Rite of Reception (no. **475.2**). The decision should, then, be consistent in the actual situation with respect for ecumenical values and be guided by attentiveness both to local conditions and to personal and family preferences. The person to be received should always be consulted about the form of Reception (cf. no. **475.2**). For a theological and liturgical introduction to the celebration of the Sacraments of Initiation at the Easter Vigil see above, nos. **206–217**.

565. In its actual arrangement the celebration itself must reflect the status of candidates for Reception into the full communion of the Catholic Church: such candidates have already been incorporated into Christ in Baptism and anything that would equate them with catechumens is to be absolutely avoided (cf. no. **477**).

[2] Cf. Ecumenical Directory I, no. 11: *Acta Apostolicæ Sedis* 59 (1967), p. 578; Second Vatican Council, Decree on Ecumenism, *Unitatis redintegratio*, no. 22.
[3] Cf. Second Vatican Council, Decree on Ecumenism, *Unitatis redintegratio*, no. 22.

INTRODUCTORY RITES AND LITURGY OF THE WORD

566. Those who will be received into full communion at the Easter Vigil, along with their sponsors, should take places apart from the elect who will be called forward for the celebration of Baptism.

The Homily should include reference not only to the Sacraments of Initiation but also to Reception into full communion (cf. no. **489**).

CELEBRATION OF BAPTISM

567. After the Homily the Baptismal Liturgy begins. The Priest goes with the ministers to the baptismal font, if this can be seen by the faithful. Otherwise a vessel with water is placed in the sanctuary.

Before the presentation of the elect for Baptism, the celebrant, making necessary adjustments according to the number and categories of those being initiated, may address the congregation in these or similar words:

Dear friends,
this evening the Church welcomes diverse groups of people
to the Sacraments of Initiation.
For each of these, we give thanks and praise to God
who has led them by various paths to unity in faith.
First, we welcome our elect:
they will be initiated into the Christian faith tonight
through the Sacraments of Baptism, Confirmation, and the
 Eucharist.
We will pray for them and they will profess our faith,
and they will receive the gift of new life in Christ.

If children are also to be baptized the celebrant may add, in these or similar words:

And on this day in which the Church commemorates
the Resurrection of the Lord,
we also welcome parents and godparents who have brought
their children here
to give thanks to God for the gift of life
and to celebrate new birth in the waters of Baptism.

Presentation of Those to Be Baptized

568. Accordingly, one of the following procedures, options A, B, or C, is chosen for the presentation of those to be baptized.

A

When Baptism Is Celebrated Immediately at the Baptismal Font

The elect are called forward and presented by their godparents in front of the assembled Church or, if they are small children, are carried by their parents and godparents. Those to be baptized and their godparents go to the font, which they stand around in such a way that they do not block the view of the faithful. The celebrant's Instruction (no. **569**) and the Litany (no. **570**) follow.

If, however there are many to be baptized, they may approach while the Litany is being sung.

B

When Baptism Is Celebrated after a Procession to the Font

The elect are called forward and presented by their godparents in front of the assembled Church or, if they are small children, are carried by their parents and godparents. The procession to the baptistery or to the font forms immediately. A minister with the paschal candle leads off, and those to be baptized follow him with their godparents, then the ministers, the Deacon, and the Priest. During the procession, the Litany (no. **570**) is sung. When the procession has reached the font, those to be baptized and their godparents stand around the font in such a way that they do not block the view of the faithful. When the Litany is completed, the Priest gives the address (no. **569**).

If there are a great many to be baptized, they and their godparents simply take their place in the procession.

C

When Baptism Is Celebrated in the Sanctuary

The elect are called forward and presented by their godparents in front of the assembled Church or, if they are small children, are carried by their parents and godparents. Those to be baptized and their godparents take their place before the celebrant in the sanctuary, in such a way that they do not block the view of the faithful. The celebrant's Instruction (no. **569**) and the Litany (no. **570**) follow.

If, however there are many to be baptized, they may approach while the Litany is being sung.

Celebrant's Instruction

569. The celebrant, addressing those present, makes use of this or a similar instruction:

Dear brothers and sisters,
let us beg the mercy of God the almighty Father,
for these servants of God N. and N.,
who are seeking holy Baptism.
May God bestow light and strength
on those whom he has called and led to this hour,
that they may hold fast to Christ with resolute spirit
and profess the faith of the Church.
May he also give them renewal by the Holy Spirit,
whom we will fervently invoke upon this water.

If there are children to be baptized, he may add, in these or similar words:

And let us also invoke the mercy of God
for these children (N. and N.) about to receive the grace of Baptism,
and for their parents, godparents, and all the baptized.

LITANY

570. The Litany is sung by two cantors, with all standing (because it is Easter Time) and responding (for the chant, cf. no. **221**). In the Litany the names of some Saints may be added, especially the Titular Saint of the church and the Patron Saints of the place and of those to be baptized.

Lord, have mercy. Lord, have mercy.
Christ, have mercy. Christ, have mercy.
Lord, have mercy. Lord, have mercy.

Holy Mary, Mother of God, pray for us.
Saint Michael, pray for us.
Holy Angels of God, pray for us.
Saint John the Baptist, pray for us.
Saint Joseph, pray for us.
Saint Peter and Saint Paul, pray for us.
Saint Andrew, pray for us.
Saint John, pray for us.
Saint Mary Magdalene, pray for us.
Saint Stephen, pray for us.
Saint Ignatius of Antioch, pray for us.
Saint Lawrence, pray for us.
Saint Perpetua and Saint Felicity, pray for us.
Saint Agnes, pray for us.
Saint Gregory, pray for us.
Saint Augustine, pray for us.
Saint Athanasius, pray for us.
Saint Basil, pray for us.

Saint Martin, pray for us.
Saint Benedict, pray for us.
Saint Francis and Saint Dominic, pray for us.
Saint Francis Xavier, pray for us.
Saint John Vianney, pray for us.
Saint Catherine of Siena, pray for us.
Saint Teresa of Jesus, pray for us.
All holy men and women, Saints of God, pray for us.

Lord, be merciful, Lord, deliver us, we pray.
From all evil, Lord, deliver us, we pray.
From every sin, Lord, deliver us, we pray.
From everlasting death, Lord, deliver us, we pray.
By your Incarnation, Lord, deliver us, we pray.
By your Death and Resurrection, Lord, deliver us, we pray.
By the outpouring of the Holy Spirit, Lord, deliver us, we pray.

Be merciful to us sinners, Lord, we ask you, hear our prayer.

Bring these chosen ones to new birth through the grace of Baptism, Lord, we ask you, hear our prayer.

Jesus, Son of the living God, Lord, we ask you, hear our prayer.

Christ, hear us, Christ, hear us.
Christ, graciously hear us. Christ, graciously hear us.

The Priest, with hands extended, says the following prayer:

Almighty ever-living God,
be present by the mysteries of your great love
and send forth the spirit of adoption
to create the new peoples
brought to birth for you in the font of Baptism,
so that what is to be carried out by our humble service
may be brought to fulfillment by your mighty power.
Through Christ our Lord.

℟. Amen.

BLESSING OF WATER

571. Next, the celebrant turns toward the font and says the following Blessing with hands extended (for the chant, cf. no. **222**):

O God, who by invisible power
accomplish a wondrous effect
through sacramental signs
and who in many ways have prepared water, your creation,
to show forth the grace of Baptism;

O God, whose Spirit
in the first moments of the world's creation
hovered over the waters,
so that the very substance of water
would even then take to itself the power to sanctify;

O God, who by the outpouring of the flood
foreshadowed regeneration,
so that from the mystery of one and the same element of water
would come an end to vice and a beginning of virtue;

O God, who caused the children of Abraham
to pass dry-shod through the Red Sea,
so that the chosen people,
set free from slavery to Pharaoh,
would prefigure the people of the baptized;

O God, whose Son,
baptized by John in the waters of the Jordan,
was anointed with the Holy Spirit,
and, as he hung upon the Cross,
gave forth water from his side along with blood,
and after his Resurrection, commanded his disciples:
"Go forth, teach all nations, baptizing them
in the name of the Father and of the Son and of the Holy Spirit,"
look now, we pray, upon the face of your Church
and graciously unseal for her the fountain of Baptism.

May this water receive by the Holy Spirit
the grace of your Only Begotten Son,
so that human nature, created in your image
and washed clean through the Sacrament of Baptism
from all the squalor of the life of old,
may be found worthy to rise to the life of newborn children
through water and the Holy Spirit.

And, if appropriate, lowering the paschal candle into the water either once or three times, he continues:

May the power of the Holy Spirit,
O Lord, we pray,
come down through your Son
into the fullness of this font,

and, holding the candle in the water, he continues:

so that all who have been buried with Christ
by Baptism into death
may rise again to life with him.
Who lives and reigns with you in the unity of the Holy Spirit,
God, for ever and ever.

℟. Amen.

Then the candle is lifted out of the water, as the people acclaim (for the chant, cf. no. **222**):

Springs of water, bless the Lord;
praise and exalt him above all for ever.

Profession of Faith

572. After the consecration of the font, the celebrant continues with the Profession of Faith, which includes the Renunciation of Sin and the Profession itself.

Renunciation of Sin

573. As circumstances suggest, the celebrant, informed by the godparents of the name of each person to be baptized, asks each of them, choosing any one of the three formulas below; or he may use the same formulas to question all of the elect together.

At the discretion of the Diocesan Bishop, the formulas for the Renunciation of Sin may be made more specific and detailed as circumstances might require (cf. no. **33.8**).

A

Celebrant:

Do you renounce sin,
so as to live in the freedom of the children of God?

Elect (or parents and godparents):

I do.

Celebrant:

Do you renounce the lure of evil,
so that sin may have no mastery over you?

Elect (or parents and godparents):

I do.

Celebrant:

Do you renounce Satan,
the author and prince of sin?

Elect (or parents and godparents):

I do.

B

Celebrant:
Do you renounce Satan,
and all his works and empty promises?

Elect (or parents and godparents):
I do.

C

Celebrant:
Do you renounce Satan?

Elect (or parents and godparents):
I do.

Celebrant:
And all his works?

Elect (or parents and godparents):
I do.

Celebrant:
And all his empty show?

Elect (or parents and godparents):
I do.

Profession of Faith

574. Then the celebrant, informed again by the godparents of the name of each to be baptized, questions the elect individually. After the Profession of Faith, each one is immediately baptized by immersion or by pouring of water.

When there are a great many to be baptized, the Profession of Faith may be made simultaneously either by all together or group by group.

Celebrant:
N., do you believe in God,
the Father almighty,
Creator of heaven and earth?

Elect (or parents and godparents):
I do.

Celebrant:
Do you believe in Jesus Christ, his only Son, our Lord,
who was born of the Virgin Mary,
suffered death and was buried,
rose again from the dead
and is seated at the right hand of the Father?

Elect (or parents and godparents):
I do.

Celebrant:
Do you believe in the Holy Spirit,
the holy catholic Church,
the communion of saints,
the forgiveness of sins,
the resurrection of the body,
and life everlasting?

Elect (or parents and godparents):
I do.

Rite of Baptism

575. After the Profession of Faith, each elect is immediately baptized by immersion (option A) or by the pouring of water (option B). After each Baptism, a brief acclamation (cf. Appendix II, nos. **595–597**) may be sung by the people.

When there are a great number of the elect to be baptized, if there are several Priests or Deacons present, those to be baptized may be divided into groups among the individual ministers. In baptizing, either by immersion (option A) or by the pouring of water (option B) these ministers say the sacramental formula for each one. While the rite is taking place, singing by the people is desirable; it is also permitted to have readings or to observe sacred silence.

If children are to be baptized, the celebrant asks the parents and godparents of each child:

Is it your will, therefore, that N. should receive Baptism in the faith of the Church?

Parents and godparents:

It is.

A

If Baptism is by immersion of the whole body or of the head only, decency and decorum should be observed. For the Baptism of an adult, either or both godparents touch the one to be baptized. Touching the elect, the celebrant immerses him (her) or his (her) head three times, raising the elect out of the water each time and baptizing him (her) by calling upon the Most Holy Trinity only once:

N., I BAPTIZE YOU IN THE NAME OF THE FATHER,

He immerses the elect the first time.

AND OF THE SON,

He immerses the elect the second time.

AND OF THE HOLY SPIRIT.

He immerses the elect the third time.

B

If, however, Baptism is by the pouring of water, either or both godparents place the right hand on the right shoulder of an adult who is to be baptized, while an infant who is to be baptized is held by a parent or godparent, according to custom. The celebrant, taking baptismal water and pouring it three times on the person's bowed head, baptizes him (her) in the name of the Most Holy Trinity:

N., I BAPTIZE YOU IN THE NAME OF THE FATHER,

He pours water the first time.

AND OF THE SON,

He pours water the second time.

AND OF THE HOLY SPIRIT.

He pours water the third time.

EXPLANATORY RITES

576. The Explanatory Rites (nos. **577–579**) are carried out immediately after Baptism. After these rites, Confirmation normally is celebrated, as described below (nos. **587–591**), in which case the Anointing after Baptism is omitted.

Anointing after Baptism

577. For children, and if for some special reason the celebration of Confirmation for an adult or a child of catechetical age is separated from the Baptism (cf. no. **215**), then, after the immersion or the pouring of water, the celebrant administers the Anointing with Chrism in the usual way. If, however, there are a large number of newly baptized and several Priests or Deacons are present, each of them may anoint some of the newly baptized with Chrism.

The celebrant says the following over all the newly baptized:

Almighty God, the Father of our Lord Jesus Christ,
has freed you from sin,
given you new birth by water and the Holy Spirit,
and joined you to his people.
He now anoints you with the Chrism of salvation,
so that you may remain members of Christ,
    Priest, Prophet and King,
unto eternal life.

All:

Amen.

Then, in silence, the celebrant anoints each of the newly baptized with sacred Chrism on the crown of the head.

Clothing with a White Garment

578. The celebrant says the following formula. At the words **Receive, therefore, the white garment** the godparents place the white garment on the newly baptized, unless another color more suited to local custom should be required. If circumstances suggest, this rite can be omitted.

Celebrant:

N. and N., you have become a new creation
and have clothed yourselves in Christ.
Receive, therefore, the white garment
and bring it unstained
before the judgment seat of our Lord Jesus Christ,
that you may have eternal life.

All:

Amen.

Handing On of a Lighted Candle

579. The celebrant then takes the paschal candle in his hands or touches it, saying:

Come forward, godfathers and godmothers,
that you may hand on the light to the newly baptized.

A godparent of each of the neophytes goes to the celebrant, lights a candle from the paschal candle, and presents it to the neophyte.

Then the celebrant says:

You have been made light in Christ.
Walk always as children of light,
that persevering in faith
you may run to meet the Lord when he comes
with all the Saints in the heavenly court.

All:

Amen.

RENEWAL OF BAPTISMAL PROMISES

Invitation

580. When the Rite of Baptism has been completed all stand, holding lighted candles in their hands, and renew the promise of baptismal faith, unless this has already been done together with those to be baptized (cf. *The Roman Missal*, The Easter Vigil, no. 49). The candidates for Reception into full communion join the rest of the community in this Renunciation of Sin and Profession of Faith. The Priest addresses the faithful in these or similar words:

Dear brethren (brothers and sisters), through the Paschal Mystery
we have been buried with Christ in Baptism,
so that we may walk with him in newness of life.
And so, now that our Lenten observance is concluded,
let us renew the promises of Holy Baptism,
by which we once renounced Satan and his works
and promised to serve God in the holy catholic Church.
And so I ask you:

Renunciation of Sin

581. The celebrant continues with one of the following formulas of renunciation.

If the situation warrants, formula A may be adapted by Conferences of Bishops according to local needs.

A

Celebrant:
Do you renounce sin,
so as to live in the freedom of the children of God?

All: I do.

Celebrant:

Do you renounce the lure of evil,
so that sin may have no mastery over you?

All: I do.

Celebrant:

Do you renounce Satan,
the author and prince of sin?

All: I do.

B

Celebrant:

Do you renounce Satan?

All: I do.

Celebrant:

And all his works?

All: I do.

Celebrant:

And all his empty show?

All: I do.

Profession of Faith

582. Then the celebrant continues:

Do you believe in God,
the Father almighty,
Creator of heaven and earth?

All: I do.

Celebrant:
Do you believe in Jesus Christ, his only Son, our Lord,
who was born of the Virgin Mary,
suffered death and was buried,
rose again from the dead
and is seated at the right hand of the Father?

All: I do.

Celebrant:
Do you believe in the Holy Spirit,
the holy catholic Church,
the communion of saints,
the forgiveness of sins,
the resurrection of the body,
and life everlasting?

All: I do.

And the celebrant concludes:
And may almighty God, the Father of our Lord Jesus Christ,
who has given us new birth by water and the Holy Spirit
and bestowed on us forgiveness of our sins,
keep us by his grace,
in Christ Jesus our Lord,
for eternal life.

All: Amen.

Sprinkling with Baptismal Water

583. The celebrant sprinkles the people with the blessed water, while all sing the following or another chant that is baptismal in character:

I saw water flowing from the Temple,
from its right-hand side, alleluia;
and all to whom this water came were saved
and shall say: Alleluia, alleluia. *(Cf. Ezekiel 47:1-2, 9)*

CELEBRATION OF RECEPTION

INVITATION

584. Unless the baptismal washing and the other Explanatory Rites have occurred in the sanctuary, a procession returns to the sanctuary, formed as before, with the newly baptized or the godparents or parents carrying lighted candles. During this procession, the baptismal canticle **Vidi aquam (I saw water)** or another appropriate chant is sung (*The Roman Missal*, The Easter Vigil, no. 56).

If children were baptized, they and their parents and godparents return to their places.

Before welcoming the candidates for Reception into the sanctuary, the celebrant may address the congregation in these or similar words:

Dear friends,
this evening we also welcome
into the full communion of the Catholic Church
some brothers and sisters who are already one with us by
Baptism:
they are already Christian, and moments ago joined us
in the renewal of our baptismal promises.
Now they will publicly profess the Catholic faith
and so be united with us in the fullness of communion
and be able to join us in the reception of the Holy Eucharist.

Then in the following or similar words the celebrant invites the candidates for Reception, along with their sponsors, to come into the sanctuary and before the community to make a Profession of Faith:

N. and N., since after mature deliberation in the Holy Spirit
and of your own free will
you have asked to be received
into the full communion of the Catholic Church,

I now invite you to come forward with your sponsor
and in the presence of this community
to profess the Catholic faith.
In this faith, today for the first time
you will partake with us at the eucharistic table of the
Lord Jesus,
by which the unity of the Church is signified.

Profession by the Candidates

585. When the candidates for Reception and their sponsors have taken their places in the sanctuary, the celebrant asks the candidates to make the following Profession of Faith. The candidates say:

I believe and profess
all that the holy Catholic Church
believes, teaches, and proclaims as revealed by God.

Formula of Reception

586. Then the candidates with their sponsors go individually to the celebrant, who says to each candidate (laying his right hand on the head of any candidate who is not to receive Confirmation):

N., the Lord receives you into the Catholic Church.
In his mercy he has led you here,
so that in the Holy Spirit
you may have full communion with us
in the faith you have professed before this his family.

CELEBRATION OF CONFIRMATION

587. Before the celebration of Confirmation, the congregation may, as circumstances suggest, sing a suitable chant.

588. If the Bishop has conferred Baptism, he should now also administer Confirmation. If the Bishop is not present, Confirmation is to be given by the Priest who conferred Baptism (cf. *Code of Canon Law*, can. 866).

When those to be confirmed are too numerous, Priests who may be designated for this role can be associated to the minister of Confirmation to administer the Sacrament (cf. no. **14**).

If Confirmation is also to be conferred on some who were baptized as Catholics but who had not received Confirmation, the celebrant may address the congregation in these or similar words:

Dear friends,
finally, we also celebrate the Sacrament of Confirmation,
not only for the newly baptized
and those who just now professed the Catholic faith,
but also, with the permission of Bishop N.,
for some brothers and sisters who were previously baptized
as Catholics
but who have not yet received Confirmation.

The celebrant or another minister invites the previously baptized Catholics by name to come forward with their sponsors.

Invitation

589. The newly baptized with their godparents and, if they have not received the Sacrament of Confirmation, the newly received with their sponsors, together with those baptized as Catholics and their sponsors, stand before the celebrant. He speaks briefly to them in these or similar words:

Dear candidates for Confirmation,
you have been born again in Christ,
and have become members of Christ and of his priestly people.
Now you are to share
in the outpouring among us of the Holy Spirit,
who was sent by the Lord upon the Apostles at Pentecost
to be given by them and their successors to the baptized.

Therefore, you also are to receive the promised power of the
    Holy Spirit,
so that, being more perfectly conformed to Christ,
you may bear witness to the Lord's Passion and Resurrection
and become an active member of the Church
for the building up of the Body of Christ in faith and charity.

Then the celebrant (while the Priests associated with him remain by his side) standing, facing the people, with hands joined, says:

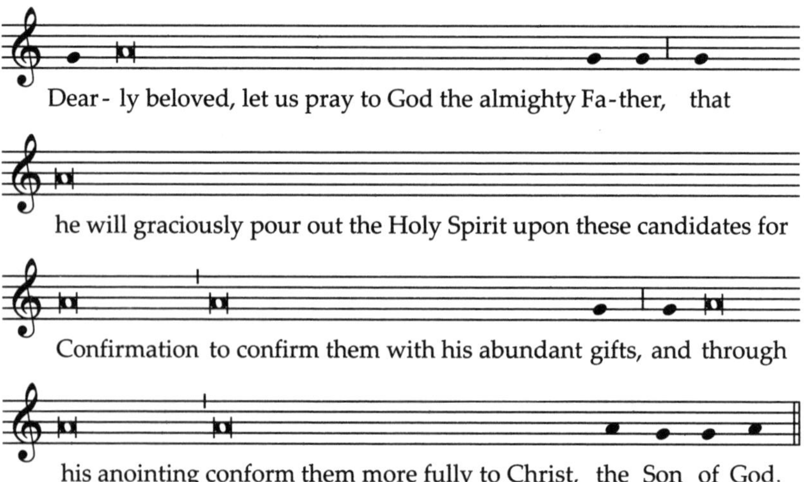
Dear- ly beloved, let us pray to God the almighty Fa-ther, that
he will graciously pour out the Holy Spirit upon these candidates for
Confirmation to confirm them with his abundant gifts, and through
his anointing conform them more fully to Christ, the Son of God.

Dearly beloved,
let us pray to God the almighty Father,
that he will graciously pour out the Holy Spirit
upon these candidates for Confirmation
to confirm them with his abundant gifts,
and through his anointing
conform them more fully to Christ, the Son of God.

And all pray in silence for a while.

The Laying On of Hands

590. Then the celebrant lays hands over all those to be confirmed (as do the Priests who are associated with him). But the celebrant alone says (for the chant, cf. no. **234**):

Almighty God, Father of our Lord Jesus Christ,
who brought these your servants to new birth
by water and the Holy Spirit,
freeing them from sin:
send upon them, O Lord, the Holy Spirit, the Paraclete;
give them the spirit of wisdom and understanding,
the spirit of counsel and fortitude,
the spirit of knowledge and piety;
fill them with the spirit of the fear of the Lord.
Through Christ our Lord.

All:

Amen.

The Anointing with Chrism

591. The sacred Chrism is brought by a minister to the celebrant.

If other Priests are associated with the celebrant in conferring the Sacrament, the vessels of sacred Chrism are given to them by the Bishop, if he is present.

Each of those to be confirmed goes to the celebrant (or to the Priests); or, if appropriate, the celebrant (and the Priests) goes to each of those to be confirmed. In addition, the godparent places his (her) right hand on the shoulder of the one to be confirmed and says his (her) name to the celebrant; or the one to be confirmed alone says his (her) own name. During the anointing a suitable chant may be sung.

The celebrant dips the tip of the thumb of his right hand in the Chrism and, with the thumb, makes the Sign of the Cross on the forehead of the one to be confirmed, as he says:

N., be sealed with the Gift of the Holy Spirit.

The newly confirmed:
Amen.

The celebrant adds:
Peace be with you.

The newly confirmed:
And with your spirit.

After all have received the Sacrament, the newly confirmed as well as the godparents and sponsors are led to their place among the faithful.

CELEBRATION OF THE EUCHARIST

592. The Creed is omitted, and the Universal Prayer (Prayer of the Faithful), which the neophytes take part in for the first time, immediately takes place. When the offerings are carried to the altar, it is desirable that the bread and wine be brought forward by the newly baptized or, if they are children, by their parents or godparents.

593. In Eucharistic Prayer I, mention of the neophytes is made in the proper form of the **Hanc igitur (Therefore, Lord, we pray)** from *The Roman Missal*, Order of Mass, no. 87, and mention of the godparents is made in the section **Memento, Domine** (**Remember, Lord, your servants**) from the Ritual Mass for the Conferral of Baptism. If Eucharistic Prayer II, III, or IV is used, the proper formula for the neophytes is used from the Ritual Mass for the Conferral of Baptism.

594. The neophytes, newly received, and newly confirmed may receive Holy Communion under both kinds, together with their godparents, and Catholic parents and spouses, as well as their lay catechists (cf. nos. **243**, **498**; *Order of Confirmation*, no. 32). It is even appropriate that, with the consent of the Diocesan Bishop, where the occasion suggests this, all the faithful be admitted to Holy Communion under both kinds.

Before Communion, that is, before **Ecce Agnus Dei** (**Behold the Lamb of God**), the celebrant may briefly remind the neophytes of the preeminence of so great a Sacrament, which is the climax of their Initiation and the center of the whole Christian life. He may also mention that for those received into full communion this first full sharing with the Catholic community in Eucharistic Communion is the high point of their Reception. He may do so in these or other words:

Dear neophytes,
on this most sacred night
you have been reborn by water and the Holy Spirit,
and will receive, for the first time,
the Bread of life and the Chalice of salvation.

And you who were previously baptized
and are now completing your Christian Initiation
will also partake in this most blessed Sacrament.

May the Body and Blood of Christ the Lord
help you all to grow deeper in his friendship
and in communion with the entire Church;
may it be your constant food for the journey of life
and a foretaste of the eternal banquet of heaven.

Behold the Lamb of God . . .

APPENDIX II

ACCLAMATIONS, HYMNS, AND CHANTS

595. Acclamations Taken from Sacred Scripture

1. Who is like you, O Lord, among the strong? 390.1
Who is like you, magnificent in holiness,
worthy of awe and praise, worker of wonders! *(Ex 15:11)*

2. God is light and in him there is no darkness at all. *(1 Jn 1:5)* 390.2

3. God is love and whoever abides in love abides in God. 390.3
(1 Jn 4:16)

4. There is one God and Father of all, 390.4
who is over all and through all and in us all. *(Eph 4:6)*

5. Look toward the Lord and be radiant; 390.5
let your faces not be abashed. *(Ps 34 [33]:6)*

6. Blessed be God, who chose you in Christ. *(Cf. Eph 1:3-4)* 390.6

7. You are God's work of art, created in Christ Jesus. *(Eph 2:10)* 390.7

8. You are now God's children, my beloved, 390.8
and what you will be has not yet been revealed. *(1 Jn 3:2)*

9. What great love the Father has given you, 390.9
that you should be called and be children of God. *(1 Jn 3:1)*

10. Blessed are they who wash their robes 390.10
in the blood of the Lamb! *(Rev 22:14)*

11. All of you are one in Christ Jesus. *(Gal 3:28)* 390.11

12. Be imitators of God and walk in love, 390.12
as Christ has loved us. *(Eph 5:1-2)*

596. Hymns in the Style of the New Testament

1. Blessed be the God and Father of our Lord Jesus Christ, 390.13
who in his great mercy has given us new birth into a living hope
through the Resurrection of Jesus Christ from the dead,
into an inheritance that will not perish,
preserved for us in heaven,
for the salvation to be revealed in the last time! *(1 Pt 1:3-5)*

2. Great is the mystery of our religion, 390.14
known before the foundation of the world,
revealed in these last days:
Christ Jesus,
having suffered and been put to death in the flesh,
brought to life in the Spirit,
proclaimed to the nations,
believed in throughout the world:
he entered into heaven,
bestowing gifts on the human race,
and was raised in glory above all the heavens,
so that he might fill all things! *(Cf. 1 Tim 3:16)*

597. Chants Selected from Antiquity and from the Liturgies

1. We believe in you, O Christ: 390.15
pour your light into our hearts
to make us children of light!

2. We come to you, O Lord: 390.16
fill our souls with your life,
that in you we may become
children of adoption.

3. From your side, O Christ, 390.17
bursts forth a spring of water,
by which the squalor of the world is washed away
and life is made new again.

4. The voice of the Father sounds above the waters, 390.18
the glory of the Son shines brightly forth,
and the love of the Holy Spirit gives life.

5. Holy Church, stretch out your hands 390.19
to welcome those brought to new birth from the waters
by the Holy Spirit of God.

6. Rejoice, you newly baptized, 390.20
chosen vessels of the Kingdom,
buried together with Christ in death,
born again of Christ by faith.

7. This is the font of life 390.21
that washes all the world,
flowing from Christ's wounded side.
Hope for the Kingdom of Heaven,
all you reborn in this font.